Best wishes
from

Thanks for the Memories
The Roger Eli Story

Roger Eli with Dave Thomas

Vertical Editions
www.verticaleditions.com

First published in the United Kingdom in 2012 by Vertical Editions, Unit 4a, Snaygill Industrial Estate, Skipton, North Yorkshire BD23 2QR

www.verticaleditions.com

ISBN 978-1-904091-62-2

A CIP catalogue record for this book is available from the British Library

Cover design by HBA, York

Printed and bound by MPG, Bodmin

Contents

This book is dedicated to my wife Andrea and to my mother and father for all the love and support they have given me over the years.

Roger Eli

Foreword by Alastair Campbell

I may have said in one of Dave Thomas' earlier books that the Burnley team of the early 90s played an important part in my elder son Rory's education. When he was learning to read, he used to take a Clarets matchday programme and read the page where the team for every match was listed. Column by column.

His mother, who was hoping he would be more interested in classical music than football, would sit rather forlorn as he recited 'Beresford, Beresford, Beresford, Beresford, Beresford, Measham, Measham, Measham, Measham, Measham, Jakub, Jakub, Jakub, Jakub, Jakub, Deary, Deary, Deary, Deary, Deary all the way to Eli, Eli, Eli, Eli, Eli.' Rory got to Oxford University some years later, so it must have done some good.

Alas, he also defected to Manchester United, but he will always, hopefully, have some great memories of that time and the team that was the first he really followed. Roger Eli will be among those memories. In the days when Rory wanted to get to games early to see the team bus arrive — what is it about football team coaches — the three he looked out for, and who always said hello — were Marlon Beresford, Ian Measham, and Roger Eli. And when he was a Mascot at Brighton on a freezing cold Boxing Day, Roger was as nice as nice could be.

It's one thing to be a lovely bloke. But what fans really want from their footballers is performance, and Roger delivered there too. Of course Clarets always see him as a Burnley man, but earlier in his career he came across some of the really big names of football history; Brian Clough, Eddie Gray and Billy Bremner. Then, with various managers deciding he was either not good enough or too injury prone, he wandered around the lower leagues, and arrived at Burnley when Frank Casper was boss and remembered Roger from his Bury days. Finally, Roger had found his footballing home. Frank converted him to a striker; he was player of the season in 1991/92. He also scored one of the Claret goals of the decade, a header past Peter Shilton in a Cup-tie. Then, more injuries and he missed out on one of the great nights in our history—York away—and after another period on the side-lines left to play in China.

As with many footballers, the closing years of his career saw him scratching a few games here and there with struggling clubs, and this book records the ups and downs of the life of a professional footballer well.

He is now a successful businessman but admits it was not always easy making the transition from football to the rest of his life. This book has some compelling themes that make it tick along—the way in which other peoples' decisions hugely impact our lives (in football the manager above all); the difficult choices that life is always throwing up; the hard and often insensitive world that football can be when players are out of favour or crocked; and in Roger's case the horror of enduring racial abuse at a time when it was tolerated by too many.

So, a good read to remember and celebrate a good career. And as to which of his many clubs means most to him—I could tell that the last time I saw him at a match. Burnley v Sheffield United, Wembley Stadium, Play-off final. Roger was in there in among the rest of us, doing what he had done so many times on the pitch: giving his all for the Clarets.

Alastair Campbell, January, 2012.

Introduction: A Box in the Loft

I'm looking through a box of old mementoes that I've pulled down from the loft. There's lots of the usual stuff in my collection of yesteryear; trophies, awards, certificates, letters, cuttings, newspapers, a few old programmes, pictures, photograph albums, and pennants from games in Russia. This box holds 12 years of my life.

But two things jump out.

The first is a letter dated 1st June 1994. It's short; I'd hesitate to say sweet. It was from Mark Blackbourne the Burnley club secretary:

Dear Roger

Mr Mullen has tried by telephone to contact you in order to discuss the expiration of your contract on the 30th June, 1994. Unfortunately I write to confirm that it has been decided not to offer you further re-engagement when your present contract expires. You have been granted a free transfer and the Football League and the League Clubs have been notified accordingly.

In thanking you most sincerely for your past service, please be assured that we will be pleased to assist you in any possible way, and trust that you will not hesitate to contact us if you feel it necessary.

With kind regards and best wishes for your future.

It came as no surprise all those years ago but it was still hurtful. I thought I'd done enough for Burnley to warrant at least a face to face with manager Jimmy Mullen about the decision to release me. But during the final year I can remember few occasions when he spoke to me.

The memories came back. When I tried to contact him, I managed by phone with little trouble. I was angry but calm. Earlier in the season I'd asked if the chance came, would he release me but he'd said he'd never do that. If I'd been allowed to leave and then gone and scored a hatful of goals for someone else it would have reflected badly on him was all I could think. When we spoke about the termination he made polite noises about helping to fix me up. Sure, I thought. Now that I had heard it from him personally it was the final hurtful confirmation that a period of my life that I had loved, was over. I'd heard that a couple of clubs were interested in signing me earlier, the rumours saying they were Hearts and Sunderland, but nothing had happened. If I'd been released then, when I was fit and desperate to play, I could have made a go of things with enthusiasm and spirit still intact. But when that letter came, in truth, I'd had enough.

But why was I surprised to have received such a curt dismissal? Why should it irritate me still after all this time that Jimmy Mullen couldn't find just five minutes to speak to me face to face before that letter came? Hadn't he treated me like an outcast for the final 12 months?

That termination letter came in June '94. But eventually the remnants of a football career ended in Glasgow in '95, along with the travels, the effort and I suppose the final hopelessness of it all. It was a last attempt to salvage something from a damaged football career that had been hindered by a knee that had been a regular problem and other injuries ranging from a broken leg, broken toes, to broken noses, bruised ribs and Achilles tendons; all of them coming with an almost cruel frequency. When I made the final decision to quit, it was a relief. Without those injuries I might have had more memories, more games played, more goals scored, more rewards, more fame perhaps. But it wasn't to be. There's this expression 'living the dream'. I lived it alright, but not for long enough. I'm thankful for those memories that I do have and the chance I did have to live the dream, but the saddest thing for me was the way it ground to a halt in the final year at Burnley. The best and the worst of times were there at Turf Moor.

The image of the final 12 minutes of my professional football career came back to me. It was in Scotland at Partick Thistle. I'd come on at the end of the game as a sub. The manager wanted one last look at me. It was my last involvement. If it was a film scene it would be one of those classic moments in sepia, in slow motion, with no soundtrack. A close-up of the hero's weary face, lingering shots of a crowd that has no idea what's going on in his head; the silent, impassionate faces of people on the touchline; the joyful, laughing faces of the winning team. And then cut to the sombre, pensive face of the player who has reached the end of the road, wrapped in his thoughts, the eyes vacant, making his final exit.

I looked at that letter again. Its brusqueness still rankles after all these years. Its inadequacy is glaring. You put blood, sweat and tears into a job and that's all you get. There's probably no other job like it where the 'little' man can get something like this and that's it; job over, on yer bike. You can't imagine for one minute Steven Gerrard or Wayne Rooney getting a letter like this. My world was one of constructive dismissal, trying to break a player's spirit so he wants to leave; niggling him, and sometimes humiliating him. I knew it was coming but the brevity, the coldness; the total lack of warmth and the hollowness of the platitudes in those abrupt paragraphs are as blatant now as they were when they were written.

Next, I pulled out the nine pages of notes I made sometime in '93 when my knee was giving me terrible problems until a Blackpool consultant called Steve McLoughlin finally sorted it. The notes run from January to April of that year. It was four months of hell and you could say they were the four months that decided the rest of my career at Burnley Football Club when I simply fell off the radar and out of any of manager Jimmy Mullen's plans. They're handwritten, faded, the paper yellowing and aged, the corners torn and creased. On the day I took them out and read through them again, I could as good as feel the ache and the melancholy all over again. Reading them took me through all that was the downside of being a professional footballer when you can quickly slide from the joy and achievement of being Player of the Year in one season, to despair when things go wrong in the next. It was a difficult exercise writing these notes all those years ago. They make painful reading today. One surgeon in particular fills me with anger even now for the mess he made. He was the person in Manchester I saw. He operated twice, neither of the attempts successful. After the second failed operation I was in more of a mental turmoil than ever.

Slowly I sit there and leaf through the pages. For a while all I do is hold them in my hand. They only partly represent the torment, the stress and the deep anxiety when you wonder if you will actually play again. As I read them I feel the angst and suffering once more. The nine pages are in two bundles. The second, it's clear, was written later, it's a shorter version of the first but with all the significant dates added and, more importantly perhaps, the conclusion that took place.

It doesn't take long to read through those pages. Four months of distress pared down to a few scribbled pages. It was four months that felt like four years as I went through agony until eventually another consultant I saw in Blackpool found the problems and put right what the consultant in Manchester had made such a mess of.

I'd guess any pro footballer who has struggled to come back from injury will identify with what's in those notes. For supporters and fans it's an insight into how things can go wrong in a footballer's life. Hindsight is easy but I sit here now as I did then and think if only I'd let the local man Mr Dennison do the operation immediately rather than choose to go to Manchester. The choices we face, the decisions we make that decide the course of our lives is a recurring theme of this book. That decision was another that altered my career and life. There's no telling if Mr Dennison would have performed a successful operation—but he might have done. He couldn't have done a worse job than the consultant from Manchester.

Again I read through the injury notes I made. It all comes back. What might have been? Decisions I made, crossroads I met, choices I faced. Surgeons, consultants, managers and physios, the hours, days, weeks of blood, sweat and tears.

I was born in Bradford in '65 but my parents came over from the West Indies in the early 1960s. Racism was ever present during my career although I never experienced it as badly as some others. It's a strange feature of football that the uneducated would hero-worship the black players in their own team, but then abuse those who played for other teams. In the eighties and nineties when I played, racism was still a significantly huge part of football. It's so much better now but the undercurrents remain and still rise to the surface.

One of the best football books I have read is Stan Collymore's *Tackling my Demons*. He lays his soul bare as he goes through all the personality problems he had and the regrettable things he did. I never suffered anything as much he did. I guess my story is simply that of someone whose career was cut short before he was even 30. Stan Collymore had fallen out of love with football when he finished but I had not, although I knew it was time to stop. Given the chance, more luck and better understanding I would have carried on far longer. Another fine book *is I'm Not Really Here*, Paul Lake's story of his injury-ravaged years. Even though he never made it back into football as a player, I did. But his is still a book I can identify with.

I made no great fortune from the game, played something over 200 games in total, of which 133 were for Burnley. Injuries, one that dated back to my teenage years, eventually ended my football career. If I have a grumble it's to do with the treatment, or lack of it, and even their mistreatment. I'll never forget the consultant who thought I was Dion Dublin. I'll never forgive his failure to operate successfully on what was a routine problem.

In amongst the years of struggle there were two good seasons, one of them memorable but even then, injured, I missed the one triumphant game that mattered; the game at York that sealed the Fourth Division title and promotion for Burnley in 1992. I'd been Player of the Season, scored the Goal of the Season and had become, in just a handful of games for the club, a hero, a cult figure and supposed legend. There I am, one of the full-length pictures of former players, on the wall running the length of Harry Potts Way, the road that leads to Turf Moor.

It's a funny thing this hero business, the way some players become one and others don't. They'd had years of suffering at Burnley and not a hero to think of. Then along come people like me, John Francis, John Deary, Mike Conroy, Steve Davis all at once and all in the same team. I was someone that fans could identify with; the battler, the goalscorer, the chance discovery, and the player who just got up again whenever he was flattened. Chumbawamba's line 'I get knocked down but I get up again', could have been written for me. But I missed the climax—typical of the cruelty and unfairness of football's Sod's Law. Football is so often heartless and pitiless. If 1992 was the beginning of the Burnley FC comeback, it more or less marked the beginning of the end of my career in league football.

For seven years Burnley had been in the Fourth Division, a once great club that had won countless admirers. Then they had declined and ended up in the bottom end, the dumping ground of league football. Worse than that, in 1987 they had been within an inch of demotion to a life outside the Football League. For seven years the Fourth Division was the background to football poverty, financial problems and supporter despair.

But in 1991–92, manager Jimmy Mullen and a winning team changed all that. Promotion—and Burnley were back. But I have mixed feelings about Jimmy Mullen. For a significant period he was good for me and I was good for him. But there came a point when I might as well have been invisible. Football management is a hard profession. These people are paid to get results but aren't paid to be popular with the players. It's funny how life turns out. Years after I last saw Jimmy Mullen at Burnley he made a beeline for me at a dinner arranged in 2011 to raise funds for the stricken footballer Gary Parkinson. Mullen apologised profusely for the way he had treated me in the final year at Turf Moor when I was a player. I phoned my sister Rhona to tell her. She was as open-mouthed as I was. She was someone I talked to when Mullen had given me the cold shoulder in the final 12 months at Burnley. With her knowledge of employment law, she told me that in her opinion, what was happening was tantamount to constructive dismissal; my life becoming more miserable so that I would want to leave or even end my career. Unfortunately, she didn't know that football is not the real world and back then there was little respect for employment law.

A handful of dates are etched forever into the Burnley history books and club folklore. A Wembley victory in 1914, 1921 and a League title, 1947 a Cup Final and promotion to Division One, 1960 and the League title, 1962 and Wembley, 1973 and promotion back to the First Division, 1981–82 and promotion, 1987 the fateful Orient game. And then in 1992 came the first success for 10 years after so many Fourth Division trials, tribulations and humiliations. Without it there would never have been Stan Ternent's promotion in 2000 or Owen Coyle's Wembley play-off triumph of 2009. The players are the bits of the jigsaw that sometimes fit together successfully. I'm proud to have been one of them at Burnley.

To say that Burnley fans were ecstatic at Bootham Crescent might well be the understatement of the century. The night at York was one of unbridled joy, wild euphoria and disbelieving tears. Had it really happened? Fans pinched themselves; the chairman Frank Teasdale walked around the car park afterwards trying to absorb the impact and clear his head. I'd contributed so much to it and yet had to sit on the sidelines unable to take part in the best night for a decade.

After that there were few appearances for Burnley. The heart was willing. The knee was difficult but I got back to full fitness. Treatment had been largely a shambles. It was all over, other than reserve games or games that were in truth inconsequential, small crowds, one man and his dog, every bit of abuse and criticism crystal clear from the touchline. There was a kind of final attempted swansong in Glasgow but after that it was much a case of what the hell do I do now, a question that nine-tenths of footballers understand so well. Luckily I knew what I would do. Others don't.

Football rejects the broken; there is no place for limbs that do not function. From adulation to fighting for scraps, hanging on, the ache of training on bruised legs; the effort of dragging yourself in for training as youth fades; the feeling that 'it's over, finished,' and then the nostalgic dreams of what might have been. The conveyor belt rejects them, spits them out, damaged goods no longer wanted. Some can handle it, but others can't and their lives spiral downwards. The adrenalin is gone; the life of excitement, successes, the incredible feeling when a goal is scored, the celebrations after a win, the endless laughter, fun and friendships all come to an end. Suddenly there are decisions to be made, paths to choose, transitions, alternatives to find. And it is hard, so terribly hard.

Life for some becomes flat, dull, featureless and lonely. Above all it is empty. Gone for most is the roar of the crowd, the drug-like fix of the ball smashing the back of the net, and the exhilaration of victory. Gone too are the well-wishers, the autograph-hunters, the waves and smiles as you walk down the street, the call of your name and the inevitable 'on the house mate'.

But for just a few, a lucky few, their names and deeds are remembered; some nationally, others like me in East Lancashire, in just that small corner where they made their mark at one small club in one short space of time. I like to think that I belong to the latter group and remain instantly recognisable to Burnley fans of the nineties. My sister had experience of that 'fame'. Having broken down in her car, she contacted the AA to come and sort out the problem. The AA man asked to see her card and seeing the name Eli, asked if she was related to 'the great Roger Eli'. She replied that, yes, she had a brother called Roger, but that he was by no means 'great'. Having a sister like that kept my feet on the ground.

My career began at Leeds United but under other circumstances I could have played at Nottingham Forest with Brian Clough. I was an associate schoolboy there and spent a memorable week with Clough at a youth tournament in Rome. But it was Allan Clarke who signed me for Leeds, and then it was Eddie Gray who took over; then Billy Bremner cleared out many of the young lads that Gray had been nurturing. From then on I wandered round until settling at Burnley. I might only have been at several places for very short spells, the proverbial wanderer, but the football stories accumulated.

For several months Dave Thomas and I met regularly, more often than not in the Potting Shed café in the Woodbank Garden Centre near Bingley. It was midway between my office and where Dave lives. There we'd sit with a breakfast and coffees and the stories spilled out. It was cathartic. Dormant feelings came to the surface. The salmon and scrambled eggs were good too.

We were regular figures there. 'I'm sure that's John Barnes,' someone whispered one day on the next table. Dave was scribbling away taking notes. 'I bet they must be doing a book.' Sometimes I went home thinking what a small world it is; Ces Podd, Wayne Goodison, Alan Cowley who figure in stories that come later, were three people who had crossed both our paths.

It's easy, when you undertake a project like this, to feel reflective and nostalgic. You wonder how things would have turned out if you'd made this decision or that decision instead of the ones you did make. What path would your football career have taken? Was the biggest mistake I ever made leaving Leeds to go to Wolves when there was no-one to give me any sound advice? Agents weren't invented then. Billy Bremner gave me the choice. I could have stuck things out but didn't. I always felt I was good enough to play at Leeds but he preferred the old hands he brought in.

But maybe the biggest influence on everything I ever did was just the way I damaged a knee in a reserve game for Leeds against Blackburn. I stood up badly after I'd hit the floor. That's all I did. It was such a simple, stupid injury. It never left me and it hounded and followed me from that day on. Forever after it was the icepack after every game. The supporters see what they think is the glamour of football but glamour comes in short supply for most footballers. Supporters don't see the treatment table that some players spend so much time on, and they don't feel the pain that follows some players everywhere in their swollen joints. Nor when I played were there the Sky millions and huge wages. We made a living but for many it was only enough to pay the mortgage on a semi, run a little car and provide for a family. There was never that much, if anything, left over in my case. The uncertainty of a footballer's career is horrendous. But what it did provide though was a network of friends and friendships that has lasted for years.

I was never the greatest player in the world and never expected to produce a book. In fact some of the family have made good-natured fun at my expense about it. 'Blimey he must think he's famous.' Far from it; but what happened to me might just happen to other wannabe footballers and they might just learn from this that being a footballer is far from being a bed of roses, money and bling. There's another side to the game, and that's the side that I experienced.

But here it is and I owe various people a vote of thanks. There's my friend Pete Smith, a Sky media man; dedicated Burnley fan Andrew Firmin, and Clarets author Dave Thomas. Dave was a headteacher and has followed Burnley since 1959. His hero was Jimmy McIlroy and way back then he never ever thought that 50 years later he'd produce two marvellous books about him. It was a Burnley fan called Warren Graham who put the idea for this book to Dave. In each chapter if you can't see the joins and the full stops are in the right place, then Dave has done his job. He is the author of nine other Burnley books. I've known Pete for years and he now works in the sports media. Firmo is a prolific 'unpublished' writer and all of his musings are in the magazine of the London Clarets Supporters' Club. The magazine, and his work, goes back many years. What a stroke of luck that some years after the 1991–92 season he wrote a complete account of that memorable season. It was a terrific source of reference. All I had to do was add to it. Firmo is yet another son of Burnley who left many years ago, went to university in Leeds, worked in Nelson local government for a while and then worked his way up to a hugely responsible Civil Service Commonwealth position in London. He was last seen somewhere in South Africa working freelance. The sections on racism include the work of two more Clarets, Lincoln Alison and Tim Quelch. Thanks too to two other people, Dave's friend Winston Sutcliffe and my sister Rhona. They read the chapters over and again until we felt they were right. Then there was the help received from Darren Bentley, Robert Smith, Harry Brooks and Tony Scholes.

It was great fun writing this book and going through the box in the loft, even if some of the items did bring unhappy memories. But so many good ones came back and images in my mind of all the good people I met.

This isn't a book about money. This isn't a book about playing in European Leagues and World Cups, nor is it a sensationalist, tabloid-style, expletive-filled story of recovery from debt, gambling and alcoholism. It's just the story of a player who had his dreams but never made the big-time and met no end of obstacles and crossroads on the way to the brief good times that he did enjoy. And after that, it's about how he experienced the downside of the game when he was just persona non grata to the man who mattered, the man who picked the team, the manager.

For every Terry, Torres or Tevez there are scores of lesser talents that make a living from this great game. Some last for many years in football. For others it's an up and down kind of career and I was one of them. They say everyone has one book in them. Thanks to Dave, Andrew, Pete, publisher Karl at Vertical, Winston and Rhona, and the Potting Shed café people at the Woodbank Garden Centre near Bingley where we had so many breakfasts; here's mine. It's an ordinary story of a footballer who always did his best but minus the trappings of celebrity and bad behaviour. There's only a handful of superstars. But there are an awful lot of bread and butter footballers like me, Roger Eli.

1

On a Night in York

York is the last place you'd associate with football. It's a place of tearooms, tourists, museums, quaint streets, ancient walls, a castle and minster. It's a place steeped in history and medieval buildings. It is definitely not a football city. In fact it's more famous for horseracing. Football struggles to survive. Yet it will be forever remembered in Burnley and at Burnley Football Club.

'They came in their thousands, they're going home as champions,' said the commentary.

As far as Burnley fans are concerned those words are up there with Wolstenholme's, 'They think it's all over; it is now,' in 1966 at the end of the World Cup Final.

I could only watch from the sidelines; my knee hadn't responded to the cortisone injections as well as I thought it might. I'd had the injection before the Scarborough game in which I managed to play for 70 minutes. But the knee would lock for a short time then click back into place suggesting there was more cartilage damage. I remember the night so well but with feelings of regret that it would have been nice to have been involved. But I also knew that those lads down there were my friends and teammates who deserved everything that came their way that night. It had been no easy ride getting to that fortunate position.

The elation in the dressing room after the victory that clinched the title was amazing with the players' chants and the singing of 'Championee! Championee! Oh way oh way oh way,' all orchestrated by Ian Measham. Then there was the deafening familiar shout of, 'Get in you beauteee,' in that unmistakable Scottish voice of Micky Conroy.

Spirits were so high in the dressing room. Of course you felt out of it not having been on the pitch with the lads. But this was a special night for all, especially the supporters who had waited so long for something like this. Then there was Jimmy Mullen, the backroom staff at the club and of course Frank Casper who had assembled this squad. He must surely have had such mixed emotions that night.

To see the jubilation of the supporters, young and old, as they swarmed onto the pitch after the match was what you dream about as a player. The sheer numbers of them, like ants in claret and blue, embroiled in passion and disbelief that this once famous old football club was now back on the move after seven years of difficult times and frustration. And for me, it was marvellous to sit back after a number of difficult, injury-hit years and rejections, and think that yes I had played my part in this momentous occasion.

What's left today are the grainy, black and white pictures in old fading newspapers. But when you look at them you can feel the passion. To say it was an explosion of fervour and the end of years of frustration was an understatement. It was just wonderful. The wall of noise that erupted from the thousands of fans who cascaded onto the pitch was like the explosion of a volcano. It was the pent up emotion that had built up for seven years.

How fortunate I was that having spent just a few months with Frank Casper at Bury, he had taken a gamble on bringing me to Turf Moor. It must have been tough for him to convince his board of directors that I was worth bringing to the club as my career so far hadn't been anything to write home about. I'm sure the supporters wouldn't have been too pleased either, signing someone they'd never even heard of. But this is how it is with lower division clubs and this is what happens with unknown players who have been discarded by other clubs.

They will either come on free transfers or nominal fees will be paid for their services. But I was certain of one thing. Whatever anybody thought of me, I always had great faith in my ability and this was something that had been instilled into me from such an early age, whether it was at England schools trials, or captaining Nottingham Forest associated schoolboy teams, or during the four years I spent at Elland Road mixing with internationals and some of the best young players in the country.

Of course there were difficult times after that and confidence was sometimes low. But of one thing I am sure, I will always be grateful to Frank Casper for giving me a chance at the club I fell in love with.

'Football', as the old cliché goes, 'is a funny old game.' We were playing an FA Cup replay against Scunthorpe United on a cold, rainy night at Turf Moor. Striker Peter Mumby was injured and had to be taken off. Frank turned to me and said in that grizzled voice, 'Can you do a job for me up front?'

'You bet,' I said. It was as if I was released from my shackles now I had freedom to express myself. I went on and scored the equaliser, and made a few mazy runs and turns, to the astonishment of the Clarets faithful. They had only ever known me as a tough tackling midfielder or defender. I continued to play up front for the Clarets for most of the remainder of my time at Burnley.

The recognition for my performances at last began to arrive. Things were coming to fruition. The injuries were becoming a distant memory. Clubs wanted to sign me and managers who had discarded me were forced to eat humble pie. I shall be eternally grateful to fate, and the chance request from Frank Casper to play up front, that allowed me to be involved in season '91–92.

Because of injuries, heart is what kept me going on many occasions. I remember one occasion when Harry Wilson, then the youth team coach, said I had no heart. The other players had to hold me back from having a real go at him. Having no heart is something that certainly goes against the grain with me. You only need to have the catalogue of injuries that I had, and to drag yourself back to fitness through the monotonous rehabilitation routines, day in and day out, to understand that heart is exactly what you need and have in abundance. His accusatory label could never have been applied to me.

As a result of the goals I scored that season, the night in York owed a fair bit to me I can proudly say, and though I didn't play it surely was an unforgettable night. I had played my part through the season, played for a great club with some fantastic players, and played in front of one of the most passionate sets of supporters in the country.

There were other memorable occasions of course, certainly against Derby County in the FA Cup. Goals don't come much better than the bullet header that flew past Peter Shilton in the Derby goal in the first game at Turf Moor. It was a moment I really enjoyed; the fact that it was scored past a genuine football great. There are people who still talk about it.

Football is full of ironies. When I finally got into the ground at York there were people on the staff who remembered me. I'd once been a York player, only for four games, and it didn't work out. Now here I was a couple of years later having made my mark. I was greeted and welcomed warmly. It was nice. I felt proud and full of confidence now that I had a sense of belonging.

But the highlight: At 9.46 pm on April 28th, 1992, Burnley became Champions of the Fourth Division. It was a game re-arranged from March 10th, postponed because of the death of apprentice Ben Lee in a tragic accident at the club. Coaches and cars crawled and inched their way to the ground, held up in endless queues there were so many of them. Promotion was in the air. They wanted to be there. They'd waited seven years. Something like 5,000 or even 7,000, depending on which story you heard, descended on Bootham Crescent, most of them coming from the same direction. It was not an all-ticket match so in effect it was a free for all. It was a Burnley night out; the support was unbelievable with endless singing of 'No Nay Never', the Burnley anthem that took the mickey out of fierce rivals Blackburn Rovers.

When they finally got there, the queues and lines of supporters stretched away from the ground and past the end of the streets. I wasn't on the team coach, but followed behind in my car. I didn't even have the excitement and anticipation that filled that slow-moving bus; didn't join in the banter. In a situation like this you feel a degree of anger and resentment at the hand of fate that decided that an injury should deprive you of another moment of glory and participation in such a game, after all you've contributed so far. So much of any footballer's career is beyond his control.

Once in the ground, news filtered through that the game was delayed in order to squeeze everyone in. The police pushed and shoved them into the ground. They wanted everybody in not wandering round the pubs of York. This was a bonanza pay night for York City and people crammed into corners of the ground like sardines in a tin. There was no away end. The whole ground seemed filled with Burnley supporters. In one corner there was a small flat-roofed hut. A bunch of fans shinned up onto the top of it until the police brought them down before it collapsed.

Not until after eight did the game kick off but it was pretty clear that the players were nervous. York had the better of the first half. The swagger with which we had earlier taken Cardiff apart had gone. The team couldn't get their moves together. The nerves on the terraces grew; anticipation replaced by worry. Surely Burnley wouldn't let the chance slip?

York scored just before half time. It was scrappy and undeserved. McCarthy hit a shot, goalkeeper Williams didn't hold it and Blackstone put the rebound in.

Burnley came out in the second half with a greater purpose. The skilled moves increased, and slowly but surely Burnley increased the pressure. Conroy was in the middle of everything. John Pender headed the ball to Conroy who punted it for Painter to chase. He raced after it towards goal and attempted the world's lowest header. As the ball fell free, John Deary thundered in to his left and crashed it in without any hesitation. The Burnley fans exploded. An hour gone, 1–1 and suddenly Burnley were back on track.

Kiely, annoyed with himself kicked out at Robbie Painter who was celebrating. Deary immediately abandoned his own celebrations to intervene and grabbed him round the neck. That was typical John. If someone picked a fight with a team-mate, he was quick to get in there and give support. We loved him. Every team should have a John Deary. As everyone else went mad, John swung Kiely round and into the back of the net and the two of them were joined by the referee. Appreciating the occasion, and the fact that Kiely was only half strangled, not quite dead and still breathing, the ref only gave John a yellow. Another day it could have been a red. We'd already had a few of those that season.

In the previous game at Carlisle we'd already clinched promotion but a win at York would give Burnley the title. The fans wanted it badly, needed it. Time was running out, the point would do; nothing wrong with that but a win would make it special. Then, in injury time it happened. Joe Jakub, who'd had a great season, cleared an aimless York ball out of defence to Mick Conroy. Just over the halfway line he brilliantly spun away from his marker and ran in to the penalty area on the left. John Francis meanwhile was steaming in at full pelt into the box. Mick played the ball across low and hard. No-one was quite sure in the craziness that followed which part of his body it hit, or how he bundled it home. Few people actually saw the ball hit the back of the net. The ground erupted, the terraces fell apart. There was a mad rush to the front on all sides of the ground. The emotion and reaction was what makes football the greatest sport in the world. 5,000 fans and all of us that were part of the team were utterly jubilant. The fans were disbelieving. We'd done it after all these years. It was insane. There were seconds left. Burnley were champions.

Afterwards in the calm of day you can watch the video of the season, or the news film clips of the night. The goal was scruffy. The build-up was good but the scoring moment was no classic. The ball hit some part of John Francis's leg, thigh, knee, shin … it went in, who cared then what part it hit or how he did it. It didn't matter; John, an instinctive striker was there, on the spot, in the right place at the right time.

But there was still that little thought in my head, that little feeling of envy, that it could have been me. I could, should, have been out there. I didn't begrudge any player their glory that night, or John, still my close friend, his magic moment, just the knee that didn't see me through the season.

There were still several seconds of the game left. There was the ritual kick-off, but supporters only had one plan and that was to get onto the pitch. They poured on from all four sides and the police didn't attempt to stop them. Hopelessly outnumbered, how could they? This was like a human tide that buried the pitch beneath it. Those that got there first grabbed lumps of turf and divots or hoisted players onto their shoulders. All of them, players and fans, raced to the tunnel. They danced and sang 'Championees' Spanish style. Chants of 'Burnley are back, Burnley are back' and 'Jimmy Mullen's Claret and Blue Army' all of them long and loud. Some of us players might have had our personal opinions about him as a manager, but it was he who had marched us on towards that end of season triumphant night. None of us were stars, we were journeymen, but journeymen filled with heart and passion, spirit and belief. We were competitive and fought for each other. Some of that came from within ourselves and was self motivated. But Mullen brought us together as a team. Collectively, the will to win, the ferocious support for each other made us the best team in the Division. And at York we proved it and earned the right to be the champions. I'm proud of it still.

I can't begin to think what it must have been like for those supporters who hadn't had much to cheer about in the years before that, and had seen their club nearly fall out of the League in '87, and despaired of ever seeing success again. But that night, players and fans were as one. They celebrated together, sang together, chanted together. All of them hugged strangers, patted unknown backs and shook unfamiliar hands. Down below on the field they called for the players to appear. Shirtless they came out, Mick Conroy conducted the communal singing. The players beamed, waved, fists in the air sharing the euphoria; all united in the same cause.

But me, how did I feel? I was there, part of it but not part of it. I wasn't in my sweat-stained kit in the steam-filled dressing room after the game, I wasn't one of the gang, high as kites, that threw Jimmy Mullen fully dressed into the bath; you won't see me on the celebratory team pictures of that night. I was desperate to be part of it and nobody but a footballer can imagine the feelings when you are on the outside looking in on something like that. The news was so big that a local amateur dramatic society back in Burnley interrupted the performance to report the news to the audience. That's how important it was to the town. Sure, I'll be remembered in Burnley and years later people still chant my name but I wasn't part of that magical night. I drove home alone thinking of them all on the coach with the excitement running high, the noise and banter and all the good feelings that come when you have really achieved something. Driving home on my own was strange. I felt like an actor who had done the show but had missed the final curtain.

Jimmy Mullen had announced that six players would be released. How hurtful was that? No matter what anybody thought most of these lads had been part of the squad. They had travelled all over the country and taken part in many matches when we had got three vital points. Football can be so cruel at times, devastating when you are released.

One of them was Chris Pearce. He had been there for five seasons and had played a large part in the season. In his first season he had been an ever present and played at Wembley in the Sherpa Van Trophy Final. He was popular with supporters and his goalmouth dancing made him into a cult figure. He deserved better than this. The rest of us were taken on a tour of Bermuda as a thank you. Chris was left behind thinking about what to do next. Many of us looked at each other as stunned as Chris. In one moment your job is gone, your career on the line with barely a thank you. He had been first choice keeper in four of his five seasons. Football can give you glory. It can also kick you in the teeth. While we were sunning it in Bermuda Chris was suddenly out of work. Andrea, my partner then and now my wife, told me how at the final home game that season against Wrexham, how she had held his wife Michelle's hand. She was in floods of tears as Chris was making his final bow to the Clarets faithful.

We used to call Chris 'Skinny' on account of him being so thin for a 'keeper, even though he had fish and chips just about every day after training from Padiham Chippy. He was left off the list of players due to receive a championship medal. He was also denied his bonus. It took the PFA to sort it all out. He eventually collected his medal from the office in a brown envelope. It all demonstrated just how unkind football can be and left me sad that the club could treat Chris like this.

Driving home that night on my own, there was time to think and mull a few things over. We all do it. We get to a stage in our life or career and think about how we got there. Have we been successful? What have been the right and wrong decisions? I thought about managers, players and coaches I'd known, amongst them Eddie Gray, Billy Bremner, Peter Lorimer, Graham Turner, Dario Gradi, and Frank Casper; which ones had been helpful and good to work with; and the ones that it wouldn't bother me if I never met them again. I thought about the low spots and believe me there had been a few. From Leeds I'd moved on and wandered round other clubs. Images of goals flashed into my head, the header against Derby, the hat trick against Chesterfield — well I say it was a hat-trick even if John Francis doesn't.

And for sure up came the big question; what happens next? I was only 27, with a good few years ahead of me, or so I thought. I'd no need to think at that stage that injuries would more or less finish what career I had left at a decent club like Burnley. I knew I'd never been the greatest player in the world, never made a fortune, never made the real big-time but neither was I a poor player. I'd always been thoroughly professional and taken pride in being a conscientious player. At my best I could do a damned good job and had done exactly that over the previous two seasons. This last season there were awards for Player of the Season, and Goal of the Season.

Former manager Frank Casper must have had so many mixed feelings on that momentous night at York. Here was a man who had been a fantastic player for the Clarets, a coach and then manager. You could almost see the claret and blue blood in his veins. He had assembled the team that achieved so much that season but then left so disappointingly after the early difficult spell. Who was to say that Frank would not have achieved the same goal as Jimmy Mullen? Did we let him down? I think Frank would have turned it round and should have stuck around a little while longer. I know the players would have liked him to.

The club sponsors were now taking the playing staff to Bermuda. It would have been better if the club had organised my knee operation before the season had ended but they didn't. Jimmy Mullen gave me few opportunities to prove myself again in the new season. In the remaining time at Burnley I would learn how cruel and unforgiving football can be; so much so that 20 years later when we met at a dinner to raise funds for the stricken footballer Gary Parkinson, Jimmy Mullen would apologise for the way he had treated me.

2

Brian Clough
and Peter Shilton's Boots

From a very early age football had always been my passion. I could always kick a ball. All I ever wanted to do was play football and I kicked a ball around from the earliest days I can remember. I was never far away from a football. You could hear the constant pounding of a ball against any wall or garage door. At home we turned the front room into a football pitch and we used whatever we could find as a football, a balloon or one of my dad's rolled up socks.

I remember a meeting with our school's careers teacher, something we used to do once a month, telling him that I fancied joining the army. He laughed and said he was sure I was going to be a professional footballer. That made a change from the other teachers who used to say, 'Don't go pinning your hopes on a career in football'.

I supported Leeds United and that fantastic team they had. This was the one that progressed from 'Dirty Leeds' to the outfit that produced football that was a dream to watch with players like Clarke, Hunter, Lorimer, Gray, Giles and Bremner. We used to huddle round the TV to watch them in their all-white strip. The game was so physical in those days. When I showed my 10 year old son Jordan some of the footage of how it used to be, he couldn't stop laughing. He'd never seen anything quite like it.

With my brothers I used to try and emulate them in the back garden. I'd be Eddie Gray with hunched shoulders and socks round my ankles although the fact they were round my ankles was probably more to do with the elastic having gone. On other occasions I'd be Norman Hunter trying to scythe down my brother Rohan with a dirty tackle.

Revie was king. In the garden, in the street, at school, for school, I never stopped playing, never stopped dreaming. And as a kid I was good. Revie left, Clough came. He was booted out and other managers came and went.

The Don left for the England job and his boys, now men, were left fatherless. I didn't really take it in or understand how things would go downhill after that. Nor was I old enough to understand the daftness of the Clough appointment and the impact it would have. You don't when you're only ten, do you? I do remember the European Cup Final they played after Don Revie left. I remember watching it on our black and white TV. I saw the newspaper headlines and the back pages that described how Leeds lost. I remember the season well especially queuing for hours outside the Baron Hotel in Bradford to get autographs from the Barcelona players who stayed there like Cruyff and Neeskens before they played against Leeds. But in that Final in Paris, Leeds were cheated. A good goal was disallowed. A clear penalty was ignored. It was the middle seventies and as the decade went by, the glory faded, the triumphs ended.

Years later, watching the TV showing of *The Damned United* brought a real smile to my face. I don't know how many other actors were auditioned or were considered for the part of Brian Clough along with Michael Sheen, but I'll bet there wasn't a stampede to play the part of Billy Bremner. I had personal experience of both of them and if Bremner in real life had been more like the film version, I might have enjoyed my time at Leeds a little more than I did.

Looking back it was amazing to have been under the management of these two colossal footballing legends. If I'm asked to side, however, with just one of the two protagonists in the now legendary 44 days Elland Road stand-off, my choice would have to go against my West Yorkshire upbringing and roots and I'd be with Cloughie.

I grew up in Bradford knowing that there was a Bradford City Football Club; that it was the closest club to home, but I saw they continually languished in the old Fourth Division. Nevertheless, I had a slight affinity with them. The first team came to one of our school's summer fairs one year and I stood there in awe when I saw real, live footballers. I think I followed them round like a sheep all the while they were there. Fourth Division they might have been, but a footballer is a footballer to a young lad at school. As a family we once walked down to Valley Parade which was about two miles away from home. Somehow my dad had managed to get tickets. It was a game against Southampton in the FA Cup. Bradford lost. There was crowd trouble which put my mother off football for life. Bricks and missiles were being hurled around, we were on the terraces and the pushing and shoving was frightening. It was a good few years later when she eventually began to watch again. She came to Burnley with my dad and Aunty May. I met them after the match and introduced them to the manager Frank Casper. I swear to this day she offered him a piece of fried chicken from their packed lunch.

But for me, Leeds United were the only club in the region worth bothering about. Due to their standing in the game in the 1970s as former League Champions, FA Cup winners and European Cup Finalists, their matches featured on our regional ITV Sunday afternoon football highlights show, just about every week. Nearly all their players were household names; Don Revie enjoyed almost God-like status and to utter the words 'Brian Clough' was akin to swearing and might necessitate washing your mouth with soap and water.

When Cloughie became manager of Leeds United people really did despise him for his much publicised comments about Leeds and the players, about how they had kicked and cheated their way to their medals and Cups, and that these should be thrown away as they had not been won in the spirit of the game.

And yet, as a young teenager, I met the man, spent a week in his company and can only speak or write about him in the highest terms. If only things had worked out differently for him at Elland Road, if only he'd had Peter Taylor there with him. The players were not entirely against him when he was appointed and most were ready to reserve judgment and put pre-conceived notions aside. But with no-one to calm him, he shot himself in the foot and what might have been a glorious chapter in Leeds' history, with him at the helm, doing what he did later at Nottingham Forest, had no chance of ever happening.

I first met him when I was 15 years old as an associate schoolboy at Nottingham Forest when I represented Forest in a Youth Tournament in Rome. Never in my life had I ventured outside the UK, but Forest were heading to Italy and I had been selected to join them. In truth my career never really took off, never really hit the heights but as a young lad, as a developing teenager I was as good as anyone around and had real belief in myself. But that's football; fate and luck, be they good or bad, helps some and doesn't do a great deal for others. Some young lads fall by the wayside simply because they lack the temperament, mental strength or the truly competitive edge. Others just don't give it the single-minded effort that is needed. I had the latter in plenty. Whatever the reasons, the drop-out rate was, and is, enormous.

When I first joined Leeds they were in the old First Division and the manager was Allan Clarke. After a defeat against West Brom they were relegated. Leeds had been tracking me from a very early age so I trained with them as well as being an associate schoolboy with Nottingham Forest, something that mum and dad were opposed to. That arrangement ended when I was found out although no great fuss was made when I managed to riddle my way out of that little deception

As a fifteen year old I wasn't lacking in any necessary qualities. I was the equal of anyone I ever played against and attracted plenty of attention from no end of scouts. I wasn't lacking in application, 'bottle' or ability. There were games against a young 'Gazza' and I more than held my own, although even as a tubby kid then, he'd nutmeg you for fun and then run off laughing. In my case it was eventually Billy Bremner who decided the direction I took. You could say he affected the whole of the rest of my life. That doesn't make Billy Bremner the bad guy. It just means that when he came he had ideas of his own and it would be curtains for quite a few of the young players who were coming through. I remember big Andy Linighan who went on to play for Arsenal coming out of his office and telling us that Billy had told him he wasn't his cup of tea. He eventually moved him on. There seemed to be a who's who of Doncaster Rovers players coming to Elland Road to have lunch with Billy.

But the trip to Italy had me in a state. First, there was the panic of flying for the first time ever; and worse than that was the prospect of Brian Clough being there. Brian Clough—the great man, the legend, that larger than life figure—coming with us, a group of gangly teenagers. You must be joking, I thought. But the rumour was there according to the other lads. He would come with us and be in charge. Nobody believed it. Surely we were unimportant, just the youth players at the football club. Why would such a high-profile man want to come along to something like this?

The oddest thing however, was I had a pair of Peter Shilton's football boots in my bag. He was only the world's best and most expensive goalkeeper and I had a pair of his boots. The day before departure for Italy I'd played in a Saturday morning A team game at Forest and it was, shall we say, a lively encounter. When I came off I could see that my boots were pretty much wrecked with a huge hole in the front of one of them. Maybe it would have been possible to get somewhere to buy a new pair but panic set in until the youth coach Liam O'Kane stepped in with the solution. He was linked with the first team coaching set-up as well so he had access to the hallowed boot room. Every club has one and more often than not they are more than just that, they are a sanctuary and a place for a sit down and an unwind.

Anyway, Liam waited until the first team game was over in the afternoon and raided the boot room to find me a pair. I was size 9 and out he came with a decent pair. But then my heart sank. Trouble is they were Peter Shilton's, not just any goalkeeper but THE great Peter Shilton, the legendary Peter Shilton. I've no idea if they were his best pair but they had the No. 1 inscribed in black marker pen underneath so they were definitely his. It was agreed we would sneak them back in when we returned to the UK so that he, we hoped, would never notice. Word went round that he did eventually find out and as far as he was concerned I was just a little toe-rag but nothing was ever said to me. They were fantastic boots, Puma Kings, far and away superior to anything I could ever afford. They did the rounds at school and among friends. I wore them in the outdoor PE sessions and when I played for the school team. Everybody wanted to touch them. My brother Rohan kept offering to buy them from me so that he could keep them and put them in a glass museum case in our front room and charge other kids 10p to have a look.

Shilton and I met 12 years later. It was a cup-tie game at Burnley. There was a moment in it when he barged me so hard in my shoulder as we waited in readiness for a corner to come over, I thought there'd be a moon-sized crater in it. 'Blimey he's remembered the boots', was my first thought. 'Surely he can't have remembered after all these years'. I stared at him; the shoulder feeling like a tram had hit it. He was a big, powerful man and dished the physical stuff out just as much as any hardman centre-forward to him. He just coldly stared back at me as if he was looking straight through me. The shoulder ached for days but the reward was the goal I stuck past him in a 2–2 draw. Presumably he wasn't best pleased with conceding two goals and suffering the embarrassment of nearly being knocked out of the Cup by little Burnley. In the players' lounge afterwards he blanked me. I very much doubt it was anything to do with me taking his boots all those years earlier, but more to do with trying to out-psyche me for the replay.

We'd stayed overnight after the Saturday youth game and then reported to the City Ground to get the club coach to take us to the airport. It stood in the car park, impressive, spotless; all black and red with the large Forest sign emblazoned across it. Believe it or not I had only ever been on a coach with a toilet on once before in my life and that was a Wallace Arnold coach that took us down to London to see Aunty May. On this trip I was about to get a huge shock when I was staggered to see Brian Clough sitting in the front of the coach with his son Nigel and his wife Barbara. I tried not to stare but couldn't help notice he had loosened his trouser belt and buttons to make himself more comfortable. I was too much in awe to speak even just to say hello or good morning. What would I have said anyway? But there he was, large as life. All I wanted to do was get on the coach without tripping up on the steps and making a fool of myself. There's an old cliché about the hair standing up on the back of your neck; I imagined it's what happened to England players making their debut at Wembley, when they heard the National Anthem played for the first time. It's what would one day happen to me the first time I played for the Leeds first team and did the raised arm salute to the crowd in the middle of the pitch. It was something I dreamed about from a very early age. The hairs rose on the back of my neck this time at the mere sight of Brian Clough.

Cloughie stories have been plentiful down the years. It's possible more football books have been written about him than another football person. Good and bad things have been written but I only have good things to say about what a privilege I felt it was to be with him for a week. He was at the peak of his powers at the time and probably one of the most famous men on the planet as he was so high profile and forever on TV.

We might have been just a bunch of teenagers over there in Italy far removed from the importance of the first team and their achievements but you would never have thought so from his conduct with us. His standards, professionalism and attention to us were the equal of anything he gave to the big names in the first team.

He exuded and instilled discipline. They had just won back to back European crowns and he was a God. Yet here he was with us. His wife Barbara was with him and his son Nigel although he didn't play. We always saw Mrs Clough at mealtimes.

The image people forever have of him is his baggy green sweater and black, crumpled track suit bottoms but there at the check-in desk he looked immaculate in a very expensive looking tailored suit, perfectly cut. He treated us like adults and set the tone straight away as he stood there and addressed each of us individually as we approached him and the desk with our passports and bags. There were no handshakes or pleasantries but as we edged closer he addressed each one of us in his inimitable voice:

'Each of you represents Nottingham Forest Football Club and I expect you to behave in an appropriate manner.' At that moment I felt like a complete professional, not that I was, but for a little while I could dream I was a Brian Clough player, as long as he was standing in front of me.

The manner and tone of the statement, the firm, demanding look he gave you, told you immediately that if you stepped out of line that was the end for you. The man had charisma and a presence. There was no way I would have been tempted to disobey that command and for the first time in my life I took my hands out of my pockets. He noticed the smallest things; the length of your hair, the state of your shoes, the details of your appearance, the way you stood or slouched. He was famous for addressing many people as 'young man'. With me it was, 'Young man, take your hands out of your pockets'. It was something I had the habit of doing when I was nervous. Just seeing him made me nervous.

There was the temptation to try to make conversation, even ask for a photograph with him or an autograph. But such was the aura of the man you didn't dare. The England manager's job was the big topic at the time. I would have loved to ask him about it, but my mouth went dry. You spoke when you were spoken to and even big-name first teamers knew that rule, people like Shilton and Trevor Francis.

I'm not sure he knew all of our full names but he decided to call me Chalkie. I didn't think it was wise to debate it with him or ask him why. There was no malice in the name and he bestowed different titles on different players as the trip gathered pace. If he hadn't given you a name, he simply called you 'young man'..

The professional role he exuded he never let slip all week. Only once did he become angry during the time and it wasn't with us. There is no end of Cloughie stories but here's one I doubt has been told before. It was the time he took us on a sightseeing tour of the famous sights of Rome on one of the days when there was no game. We set off on foot; imagine a line of schoolchildren following their headmaster on a school visit, and that was us. We tagged along behind him in an orderly and civilised manner. The usual banter and fooling about between young lads was absent as we took in the Coliseum, the Tivoli Fountains and then eventually headed into St Peter's Square. I'm not sure if Cloughie was a religious man, but by the end of the afternoon we were fully aware of his respect for people's faiths and different beliefs.

St Peter's Square was filled with crowds of people, not to mention pigeons. At the head of our line Clough was in no way trying to attract attention or publicity. He was just being responsible and 'in charge'. We went where he went. We did as he told us. And we were thoroughly enjoying the day. We had all seen him explode on matchdays at bad behaviour and here he was just the same.

Suddenly a loud voice blurted out from nearby. 'Hey Brian, never mind the Pope behind those gates; it should be you the masses have come to worship.'

If this man thought he was being funny or that Brian Clough would appreciate the raucous compliment or that he would smile or think it funny, he was very badly mistaken. He went bright red and beckoned the culprit over to him. Then, in those familiar, nasal, slow monotones, he spoke. (Remember his famous TV clip where he balls at one of his Derby players in a training session who has just missed an easy shot: 'You are a bloody disgrace—for missing the target from there you want bloody shooting.')

This time Cloughie simply ordered the bloke: 'How dare you'. Intended joke or not, he was furious at being compared with someone as eminent as the Pope one of the world's great religious leaders. Maybe he was playing to the crowd who realised something was about to kick off. Had cameras or recorders been around, another famous chapter in the Clough story would have been added to all the others, and filmed as well.

Cloughie in the right circumstances would not have minded

being told he could walk on water, especially the Trent, but this was different. The Pope was being made fun of. He fixed the victim with a stare and then bellowing, laid into him.

'Get over here now sir,' he ordered the man. By now he was playing to the crowd and started wagging his finger. 'Show some respect and be mindful of where you are. I don't mind the odd pat on the back but being compared to the Pope is totally unacceptable. The man has a hugely responsible and difficult job and whilst we are in his surroundings we will all behave in a dignified and respectful way.'

The man walked away red-faced, embarrassed and crestfallen. It hadn't quite turned out the way he expected. His banter had seriously backfired. It was a typical Cloughie put-down. All of us stood there open mouthed. Put a foot wrong and that could be one of us. He was in headmaster mode from start to finish. His message to the bloke who'd upset him was a veiled message to all of us.

His next victim could well have been me. In the game against Juventus the ref made several dubious decisions. Five of us were sitting on the bench and after one daft decision I yelled out something like, 'Use your eyes ref,' or, 'I can't believe that.'

Cloughie turned round and fixed us all one by one with his glowering stare. If he'd known which one of us was the culprit he would have exploded. If looks and his disapproving stare could kill, we wouldn't be here today. It was half-time when he addressed us all and told us in no uncertain terms he'd have no more of that. To this day I can still hear that distinctive tone of Brian Clough ringing in my ears.

The Juventus game was the first one we played and he made another point. It went without saying he had such a tremendous will to win, complete professionalism, and a desire to produce outstanding players and teams; and not only that but teams that also played in the right way with respect for others. With him in the room there was never any raucous behaviour, fooling about or loudness. If he wanted to make a point he stood in the centre of the room. On this occasion, yes, he had a point to make. We were preparing only for a youth game but it was clear he had a real bee in his bonnet about something. Some time earlier when he was at Derby there had been an infamous semi-final against Juventus. Derby lost and it was more than likely that the officials had taken bribes.

The speech came: 'Most of you here will be aware that I have two European Cup badges at home. If it hadn't been for these buggers and a bent referee I would most certainly have three. Today we are going to show these buggers how to play football the right way and how to do things in the correct manner. If these younger buggers are clones of the older buggers they will nip you, tug shirts and even spit at you. If they wish to resort to these despicable tactics then let them. Do not retaliate. We will rise above it.'

'Good luck Chalkie,' he called out when I went on against Juventus. Even as youth players they were so cynical and as the game commenced his theories as to how they would play were spot on. They were as horrible as he said they would be. You couldn't deny their technical quality and playing up front I could tell how disciplined and drilled they were in the art of defending. But the nasty side was always evident. I had a good game even though I went down several times under their challenges. My man marker was skilled in the art of niggling and tormenting. Some tackles I skipped over, with some I just took the knock and got straight back up again.

Without Cloughie on the touchline we might not have been so restrained but his orders were clear: 'Do not retaliate.'

I was being knocked around so much it did occur to me that surely somebody on their side would eventually be sent off but the referee seemed to have no concept of fair play. Following one incident my shirt was nearly ripped off my back by one lad. The same lad spat into my hair.

At half-time it was Liam O'Kane who did the team talk. Cloughie just said one thing to praise us on our behaviour and restraint so far and that we would continue to do our talking on the field with our passing and superior manner.

The Italians were at it immediately after the break. My marker nipped me constantly and grabbed the hairs under my arms. Since the game started I'd been knocked around from pillar to post. I'm sure that Italian coaches instil this side of the game into their defensive players from the very earliest age.

One of them called me a 'Neegero,' and at last this opponent went too far. The referee eventually sent him off. I'd lost him with a neat turn and once again was chopped down cynically. The lad had already been yellow-carded and this time he had to go. With great restraint I just picked myself up and stood there hands on hips. Praise from Cloughie was rare but this time he called out, 'Well done Chalkie brilliant son.' I felt so good. At that moment Cloughie got up from the dugout, took a couple of steps to the touchline and gave me the trademark thumbs up gesture he used to do. I knew I was having a good game the longer it went on but didn't know that scouts from the Italian clubs were noting my name.

He didn't mix with the Juventus people at the end of the game but remained seated in the dugout. He didn't come into the dressing room and the next time I saw him he was already sitting on the coach in his usual position behind the driver's seat. He actually spoke: 'Hey Chalkie your conduct was fantastic today. I knew that you were in for a torrid time against those defenders but well done for not reacting.' That was it. He didn't want to get involved in any conversation or listen to my version of the game. I moved along the bus and sat down feeling just brilliant that one of the greatest ever bosses had praised me personally. Only then did the aches of the bruises begin to set in.

At the dinner in the evening he addressed the whole team and underlined his satisfaction at the way we had respected the officials and hadn't fallen for any of the intimidation we had experienced. He ended by stressing that he would never tolerate dissent or any backchat to officials. Thinking back to that I can fully understand why he so disliked Don Revie's Leeds United.

We came third in that tournament without losing a game. And Juventus were dreadful. They knew every trick in the book. It was the most fierce, bruising, physical game I had ever taken part in and gave me a rude awakening as to what football could really be like. Lazio and Fiorentina were two of the many Italian clubs who had scouts at this tournament. On the strength of how I had played they were interested in signing me. Their representatives spoke to me twice at the two civic receptions that took place. 'Come and play in Italy,' they said. Both Coach Liam O'Kane and Brian Clough knew I was asked. I was actually shocked to be asked.

'Chalkie take it seriously,' said Clough. But I didn't. What did I know? It was the first time I'd ever set foot in another country. I was just 15 just a young lad. We didn't have agents in those days; maybe now I'd just say, 'See my agent'. But it was recognition. I was a good 15-year old, strong, had pace, wasn't frightened, could play a bit and showed the Italians a few tricks of my own.

What a privilege it was to be there with Brian Clough. It's a memory that will last forever. Lavish praise was never his style so that just one word from him was worth all the more. His wife Barbara and son Nigel were there. At that age you might have been suspicious of having the boss's son there but he mingled freely and took all the banter. Many things have been written about Brian Clough, some that are not so flattering. But to this day I'm still so proud to have played for him, even if it was only at youth level and my own memories of the man are just magnificent, that he was a gentleman and a football genius.

In '82–83 I went back to Italy again to play in the same tournament. This time it was with Leeds United to another youth tournament. I felt like a seasoned traveller. This time it was some of the other lads who had never flown before and I was the experienced one. There were lads like Peter Swan, Scott Sellars, Tommy Wright, Terry Phelan and Dennis Irwin. Another young lad was Mark Russell. He was as good then as any of us and great things were expected. Injury though ended his career early typifying the casualty rate in professional football. The dropout rate is frightening. Again the tournament was in Rome and there were four teams; Leeds, Inter Milan, Udinese and Roma and what a contrast to the games with Forest. There was no Juventus pulling every underhand trick in the book.

How smart the Italians were, what a contrast to us they were. We had the old Admiral sweatshirt tops and polyester Umbro track suits. Roma, staying in our hotel, had wonderful training gear; everything matched even their bloody pyjamas, and they were so good looking with their dark swarthy looks and terrific kit. They say clothes maketh the man. There was a difference however. They had sponsors who kitted them out. We didn't. They seemed to look so much older than us. But we had the last laugh and won the tournament even though it began with us having a secret meeting to complain to Tony Fawthrop and Syd Owen who were both with the team, about Coach Keith Mincher who had been very critical of some of the players. It was unheard of for youth players to complain but we felt so aggrieved and were a very close group. Syd had been a great player and had been Don Revie's right hand man. With me he was superb. He gave me advice and coaching. When I broke my leg later on and was out for many weeks he wrote me a marvellous letter of encouragement. Such things don't happen that often in football.

On this trip there was no Brian Clough to put the fear of God into us. But just as with Cloughie we went to St Peter's Square, except this time we went with Leeds United. All four teams were loaded onto buses and we seemed to have special treatment as we sat in an area near to the Pope's podium from which he would deliver his blessing. From this seated vantage point we could see crowds that looked like they were there in their millions, just a sea of faces stretching away into all the corners of the vast Square.

It was a very hot day, and in truth it went on and on in a language we did not understand so of course boredom set in, but being a Catholic I felt I had a duty to look interested. My mind wandered back to the incident in St Peter's Square the year before with Brian Clough. Eventually the endless talking and blessing stopped. The Pope said his final words and then got into his 'Popemobile' and began to drive slowly round stopping once in a while to shake hands and gently pat people on the head. We had been told that when someone shouted 'LEEDS UNITED' we all had to stand up. The car approached, we all jumped up on command, and the Pope got down and walked along the line a little way. Suddenly Peter Swan leaped up, went down to the front and shoved his hand out to touch the Pope. Swanny swears the Pope took his hand, looked into his eyes and said: 'Bless you my son.' If he'd done that with Cloughie in charge he'd have got a clip over the ear for not staying in his seat. In fact he wouldn't have dared move. Personally I felt very priveleged that I'd had the chance to see the Pope first-hand. On our itinerary it said we'd be having an audience with him. I didn't realise it would be with 10,000 other people. I have to admit it made my mother very proud that I had been blessed by the 'second in command' even if it wasn't one to one.

Another tour was with Leeds to Switzerland. I must have been going through my period of being colour conscious because I remember it being another time when I preferred to stay in the hotel rather than go out for a drink with the lads. But what made up for it one night was meeting Celtic's wizard Jimmy Johnstone in the bar. He was there with Bobbie Lennox another legend and they were managing the Celtic youth team. These were two of the players that had won the European Cup in Lisbon. I was totally overawed when

Eddie Gray introduced us and I chatted away with them probably talking tongue-tied rubbish. Jimmy Lumsden, Eddie's assistant, had been youth team coach at Celtic so he knew them well. It was moments like this, rubbing shoulders with the greats that I sat without any thoughts of failure or leaving Leeds.

3

Early Days and Leeds United

When I was growing up, Bradford was in such a state of change. This great industrial Victorian city had once been so prosperous with most industry based on the wool trade. It was known as the wool capital of the world. It had such wonderful buildings and such pride. Mind you whilst millowners lived in splendour their workforce lived in poverty. Slowly the wool industry declined and through the sixties they ripped the city down and rebuilt much of it. Some of the old, great buildings have been restored; the Town Hall, Midland Hotel, the Wool Exchange and the Alhambra Theatre. But you'd have no real idea now of what Bradford used to be like back then when it was such a thriving city when it used to have electric trolley buses. These were buses connected to overhead wires by two long poles. We'd hop on them to go down and see our Pakistani doctor. Dr Rafi was his name and he always seemed to prescribe the same pills for everything. 'Take Paracetamol, twice a day, next please.' We eventually began to wonder if he was a fake. But because he always had gorgeous, blonde, buxom receptionists who always made our tongues hang out we never minded being ill. The barber was Pakistani as well but we hated going to him for a haircut and would do anything to avoid a visit. Dad used to have to drag us there because we knew we'd get the most brutal basin haircut. He either scalped me, Rohan and Rupert, or gave us a basin cut that made us look like Moe from The Three Stooges or a new three piece band, The Black Beatles.

Today something like 20% or more of the population is of Asian origin making any West Indian community almost insignificant. In fact it never did have a particularly big West Indian community. The city has produced its fair share of famous people, J.B. Priestley, David Hockney—oh and the Yorkshire Ripper. That was a dreadful time in the seventies when women in the city just did not dare leave their homes alone. I still live in Bradford and it is so easy to get to other areas of beautiful countryside that are close by; Ilkley, Skipton, Wharfedale, the Dales and Bronte Country.

I was blessed though and had a lot to thank my parents for. In the early sixties they'd come over from Dominica to Bradford as part of that influx of immigration from the West Indies. Dad went to Preston first but then visited Bradford to find work because he knew people there. He had two jobs on offer straight away. There was no shortage of work in the early sixties. They still visit the island if ever the cruise ship they happen to be on stops at the island, and still live in the same Bradford house that they moved into on the Swainhouse Estate after they'd spent a few years in the Manningham area.

Swainhouse Crescent, back when we were growing up, was smart and well cared for not at all like so many run down council estates today with overgrown gardens and so much neglect, poverty and hopelessness. There was a sense of pride and care. We were mischievous and had fun. When the rag and bone man came with his horse and cart he'd park it outside our house. That was our chance to untie it and move it to the other side of the road while the ragman was foraging for metal and scraps up and down the street. He'd come back and scratch his head puzzled. Sometimes we led it down the other end of the street. The nearby estate at Wrose was rather posh and the kids from there would walk by our house on their way home from school at 4.15 every day. The four of us, me, Rhona, Rupert and Rohan would do battle with them. Stones and mud bombs would hurtle back and forth but it was all in good fun and today we still know some of them and laugh about it. It was the norm to be chased to school. There was one particular tall, skinny, white kid called Ian Smoggy Smith who was particularly keen to beat me up. It wasn't racist; he just wanted to have some sport at my expense. Smoggy would chase me to school every day a bit like Road Runner in the cartoon. Thanks to him my running improved enormously.

If Rupert and me ever ventured over into the other estate we'd be taunted by Big Terry. 'Oi Rastas get here you little black bastards,' was the usual shout. I got called Kunta Kinte and Chicken George more times than I can remember. I began to believe it was my middle name. 'Run,' Rupert would shout. More running practice followed. More brick throwing followed because our kid was a dab hand with a brick and there was one girl who used to taunt him and call him

Golly. When we got back to the sanctuary of the back garden mum would give us 'the look'. She knew we'd been up to no good.

Back in Dominica dad was a carpenter and also a top cricketer representing his country against the MCC in the sixties. Mum was a seamstress but her first job in England was to work in a chocolate factory. For years that's where I told my younger brother Rupert he was made. Dad worked and worked, eventually becoming a site agent with one of the biggest building firms in the country. Mum and dad worked damned hard to give us everything we needed and their support for me was fantastic. If we were naughty out came the shoe or the slipper. Mum could throw the slipper and hit a sixpence from 20 yards. Nobody was allowed to leave the table until they had finished their food. It was that kind of firm upbringing.

Rohan was a good cricketer like dad. When he needed kitting out with the full regalia that's what mum and dad did. If we had any sporting interest they did their best to provide the equipment even though money was so tight. I went through dozens of pairs of shoes. She even got me a pair of steel toe capped boots thinking I'd never damage them. They lasted a couple of weeks. Mum went wild, but there was always a replacement pair. If I didn't like the replacement pair, I would hide another pair out by the dustbin to change into before I went to school. We weren't short on brains but sister Rhona was the cleverest and went on to university and became a lecturer. Both Rohan and Rupert were good footballers and got as far as Bradford Park Avenue. Rhona too loved football and became a pretty good goalkeeper, but only because being a girl we wouldn't let her play in any other position. She loved cricket too and when dad took her to a Test Match at Headingley there was no one more proud when he took her into the West Indian dressing room and was greeted with smiles and backslaps because they all knew him. Had he lived and played on one of the bigger islands and played more cricket he might well have been good enough to play for the West Indies.

Thanks to mum we were such a well grounded family. The house was small but filled with love and discipline. We had this glass fronted lockable cabinet in the living room where the best china and ornaments were kept. If it was Easter or Christmas, if there were biscuits, Easter Eggs, or chocolate or sweets they were always locked in the cabinet and carefully shared. It was torture being able to see them. One day my brother and me were wrestling on the floor and being a general nuisance. Mum grabbed the shoe and hurled it. This time her aim was poor and it hit the cabinet. The glass was shattered. After that there wasn't much point locking the sweets away.

There were constant football battles out in the back garden on the lawn. The lawn became more and more of a mud-bath. Imaginary games were at Elland Road but cut short time and again when we were over exuberant and slammed the ball over either of the adjoining garden fences. Neither set of neighbours were too fond of us and were forever complaining. If the ball went over, which was often, we could forget about getting it back. One of them took particular pleasure in slicing them open with his kitchen knife. The remnants went in a grey metal bin that I can still picture. I did get my own back one day when I found a tin of black paint and in revenge poured it over the fence onto one of the two poodles that were the apple of one neighbour's eye. Danny and Bimbo were their names. God those dogs yapped and barked every time the ball thudded against the fence or even every time they saw it through the gaps. Let's just say they were immaculate until I found the paint. Unfortunately there were consequences weren't there? Out came the slipper.

But mum was fierce in her protection of us. She might have been small but there was nobody more protective. The neighbour on one side was a retired Regimental Sergeant Major. Trouble was he still thought he was one. There was one time he took a new ball off us and mum was incensed. She marched round with the intention of snatching it off him before he stuck the knife in. Round she went and confronted him; but then thinking better of physically accosting him she decided that she would march down to the nearest phone box and call the police. Now then, because of all the community work that dad did he was known and respected. Up came Inspector Ackroyd, community liaison officer, Christa Ackroyd's father, the TV presenter. He spoke to both sets of neighbours. Mum always said we had no more trouble after that. But whatever we did we could never get a smile or a thank you from him. If we saw him coming, for example, carrying bags of shopping we'd open the gate for him. In he'd go looking like Mr Glum without a word.

Dad was fantastic in all the work he did in the Bradford area for the community and local sports in the Manningham area and the Five Lane Ends area—both cricket and football. He played a lot of cricket and on many occasions we found ourselves in places like Preston, Huddersfield or Nottingham watching him play against other Afro-Caribbean teams. I say 'watch' but more often than not we'd end up with the other black kids playing our own game of cricket. It was initially for the community from Dominica that dad got involved but then other islanders joined in. I guess any sporting interest or success I have ever had is thanks to dad. I loved him then and I still do now. He has a wry and gentle sense of humour. When the coalman came to the door one day his face covered in coal dust dad looked at him and smiled and said: 'You look like one of us.' And all the time I was involved in sport it was dad who drove me around if it was long distance or mum who took me round Bradford on the bus. Bringing all of us up and putting food on the table dad worked seven days a week yet still somehow found the time to transport me and encourage all of us in our sports.

Childhood was safe and secure for us and mum and dad would tell us stories of their family back in Dominica and describe this small island with a population today of only around 110,000. Christopher Columbus named the island after the Sunday on which he found it in 1493. The population of native Caribs who were there before Columbus arrived was then later supplemented by the African slaves shipped in who worked on the farms.

Our early family history is not without interest. Dad says he thinks his great grandfather was African. Something like four million Africans were transported to the USA and the West Indies by slavers. Those that came to Dominica worked on the coffee and sugar plantations and came from an area that is now roughly Angola to Senegal. It was a French Island until taken over by the British and a common name is Elie. A register my sister found listed something like 60 slaves with the name Elie between 1817 and 1823. Their owners were nearly all French.

When I heard Dominica was such a beautiful place of mountains, waterfalls, springs, rivers, sunshine and blue sky; of lush rainforests filled with wildlife, including many rare species of plants, birds and animals, I used to wonder why anyone would leave such a place. The description 'island paradise' would not go amiss. But work was scarce and that was the reason people left. Sunshine doesn't pay the bills or put food on the table and there was this idea that Great Britain was the motherland with work for everyone. With Dominica being so mountainous there was only so much space for agriculture and food growing. Bananas were an important export. When mum and dad lived there it was hard to get around with few roads. At one time if you wanted to travel from Portsmouth in the north to the capital Roseau in the south it was quicker to go by boat. Today, tourism and the almost daily cruise liners are the biggest earners.

Mum would have stayed there but it was dad who wanted to come over. Her side of the family, of French origin, came from Martinique. Because of volcano eruptions some of her family moved to Dominica where, of course, she met dad. She still has four brothers and two sisters on Martinique. Mum joined dad later when he sent for her after he found work and a place to live. It was over here that they got married.

After First School where we stayed until we were nine, the next school was Swain House Middle School where a teacher called Martin Mitchell was the first huge influence in my life. He was an old-fashioned games teacher who would put himself out for any of his pupils. He worked for the love of sport not money. Memories of him are still strong especially the images of him driving back from a game somewhere in his battered blue mini-bus with us all bellowing: 'We're gonna win the league, we're gonna win the league.' Sport in school was a massive thing when I was growing up. Sadly its importance has lessened now. There aren't the same numbers of teachers who give up so much time to it like they used to every Saturday morning. From what I can gather they spend all their time on paperwork or bound by health and safety rules. The idea of being truly competitive has been taken away. Martin put hours of extra time into it in the evenings and Saturday mornings and taught us about respect and good attitudes. He pushed me at every sport and taught me how to pass a ball properly. 'Crisp, pass it crisp,' he would say.

The Deputy Head at Swain House Middle was called Dave Robinson and at this time I was good pals with Liam Robinson. We more or less grew up together and he also went on to play for Burnley. Dave Robinson was a fearsome person who could put the fear of God into any pupil with a glower or a word. There was one time that something like 300 boys and girls were all kicking footballs around, playing or running all over the place. At lunchtime one day the whistle blew. A total of 298 kids stopped but two didn't;

those two were me and Liam. Oh God he beckoned us over when we realised we hadn't heard the whistle and approached him in fear and trembling. We expected the worst. He looked at us with an unsmiling face and then spoke.

'Come here you two.' We obeyed him and waited for bad news.

'You are both in my under-11s team.' That was all he said. The word 'phew' was never said with more relief.

I did most sports, was Bradford Champion over 400 metres for two years; played football for the school, West Yorkshire and Yorkshire Boys. I played cricket for Bradford Schools and when I was 11 and 12 trained with Bradford City. There were some good lads in and around Bradford then—Jamie Hoyland, Paul Simpson, Micky Holmes, Neil Redfearn and Ian Ormondroyd as well as Liam. There were other lads just as good who fell by the wayside. I was Head Boy for a year; sport kept me out of trouble and brought me respect. I wasn't the kind of kid who slammed school and lived on the streets. I was too well brought up and was taught to believe in values that mattered especially doing the best you could at everything.

At weekends I played for Pudsey Juniors. It was almost an early Football Academy. If you joined them you knew there'd be scouts from a lot of clubs, and certainly Leeds, watching the games. A Headmaster called Alan Cowley was team manager and my first real mentor. I owe a lot to him. After that I went on to Hanson Upper School continuing with all the sport, by now playing striker and scoring goals. I left at 16 with a few O Levels under my belt. I would have been good enough to go on and take 'A' levels but football was what I wanted.

I got as far as Under-15 England trials. I met up with other kids who one day would make the professional game. It was these trials that opened my eyes to how good other kids could be. It was a chance to mix with lads from all over the country. On the final day there was a full match which was organised into a North v South game. As a result it became rather heated on several occasions; we disliked the cockiness of the Londoners. When the letter arrived saying I hadn't made the final 16 I was gutted and just a bit miffed because I'd had to play out of position in midfield instead of as a striker where I'd scored goals regularly for Bradford and Yorkshire.

Leeds noticed me whilst I was playing for the County teams and I went down to train with them a couple of times a week. But

I was in this odd position of also being an associate schoolboy at Nottingham Forest at the same time. Before that George Mulhall at Bradford City was interested and came round to see dad twice. Dad asked his advice. What should Roger do, go to Forest or Bradford. Mulhall was honest. Go to Forest he said there's no choice to make. For a while neither Forest nor Leeds knew what I was doing. Forest didn't know about Leeds and Leeds didn't know about Forest. My mum was not happy with this. Leeds had been watching me since I was 12. There used to be a local chap who watched every game, he was the classic flat-capped scout who watched all these games whatever the weather. In those days there used to be an army of them on Saturday mornings looking for talent. I only ever knew him as Mr Saunders and after every game he'd come over for a chat just to keep tabs.

Tony Fawthrop had already introduced himself and talked about Nottingham Forest although later he moved to Leeds. He was just making his way in the professional game as a scout and was a regular at our house along with Forest's John Stubbs. Tony became a real and trusted influence and lived off my mum's bread and butter pudding. Before Leeds could do anything official Tony jumped in and took me and my dad to Forest and there I signed the Associate Schoolboy forms. Tony looked after me really well and made sure I was never short of anything.

Money was short in our house; there certainly wasn't enough for me to be watching Leeds United on a regular basis. I can only recall three games that I went to. It's funny how things work out. The Leeds United team, were doing a pre season tour of Denmark and Stansfield Rovers were playing in a tournament over there. Stansfield Rovers were a local Bradford team that I played for and were asked to represent Leeds. We got to the Final and the United team watched the game. After that game Leeds were all over me and at the dinner after the game Leeds directors Bill Fotherby and Leslie Silver said I had to sign for Leeds. I kept quiet about Forest. By this time Tony Fawthrop was working for Leeds not Forest so he'd drive me to Leeds training sessions even though I was a Forest Associate Schoolboy. On Saturday mornings there'd be 'A' Team Forest games and sometimes there'd be a first teamer coming back from injury like Chris Fairclough or Peter Davenport alongside us. In the afternoons we'd watch a home game if there was one and Brian Clough would

47

have us sitting alongside the dugout so we could get the feel of a big occasion and a massive crowd. Training took place in the school holidays at a centre in Barnsley. And at the same time as all this was going on, though I hadn't signed anything, there was evening and Sunday training at Leeds.

Forest trainer Mick Raynor actually asked me one day if I was involved at Leeds United but I flatly denied it. Somehow they'd heard that as well as playing for them I was also involved at Leeds United. The association with Forest ended but not for that reason. Brian Clough watched the 'A' team one morning; it was the Final of a local competition and I actually got knocked out in it going in for a header. More bravery than sense maybe but that's how I was as a player. I'd done OK and trainer Mick Raynor assured me that I'd be offered an apprenticeship at Forest. Then later there was different news. Cloughie had decided I looked injury prone and didn't want to proceed further. Was he psychic or what?

The images of Brian Clough have never left me and he had such a huge impact. I remembered the short, sweet conversation we'd had when he'd seen me limping in the hotel in Italy.

'Are you limping Chalkie?'

'Yes boss.'

'Are you? Well if you are you'll be on the first plane home. So — are you limping now?'

'No boss.'

It came as a shock to be told I wasn't to be kept on. I'd been captain of the Colts team and had been told I'd done well and that I would be signed. I'll never know if Cloughie had made a spur of the moment decision as he watched that 'A' team game and changed his mind, or had studied me for a longer time.

Meanwhile Leeds knew all about the Associate Schoolboy stuff with Forest but they weren't bothered. They were still courting me. They were the ones who were the poachers. So, when Forest gave me the news that they wouldn't offer me anything, I wasn't too disappointed. Leeds were the team I'd always supported as a boy and dreamed of playing for. They used to do this routine of lining up in the centre of the pitch before a game and giving the raised arm salute to the crowd. That was what I imagined myself doing. So: I would sign for Leeds and by now Tony Fawthrop was working for them so down we went with my dad, me in my blue polyester suit, to see Allan Clarke in his office and there I signed.

My dad was never the most demonstrative of men but I knew he was so proud. He was pleased because at heart he had a soft spot for Leeds United and he trusted Tony Fawthrop. He'd come over from Dominica with lots of hopes but not much in his pocket and just one suitcase. And now his son had signed for Leeds United, faded yes, but still a big and illustrious club.

And me: I just felt ten feet tall. The things I was going to do; be the best, play for England and be a Leeds star. I had all the dreams of a 16 year old. I didn't know then that in the years to come I would experience all the pitfalls and disappointments that come with the professional game.

As an apprentice if there was a dirty job to do, we did it . . . so unlike today where spending half the time at college is part of being a trainee. The old style apprentice is a thing of the past and at the bigger clubs today with their academies they are well and truly cosseted and wrapped up in cotton wool. You won't see them today painting barriers on the terraces, sweeping the stands, cleaning out the toilets, mopping the dressing rooms. But we did these things proudly. It was the best job in the world. We were Leeds United and proud. Then there was work on the pitch with the groundsman, weeding and forking, and grass cutting and more weeding. The youth coach was called Keith Mincher and he drilled us like a sergeant major dishing out bollockings for the slightest thing. He was very strict and instilled discipline. But he was a fantastic coach, ahead of his time, looking at different kinds of exercises, introducing psychology, emphasising the passing game. He demanded that we stay behind for extra training in the afternoon, something I always enjoyed. The first teamers, set in their ways, didn't like him though because of his new ideas.

There was a great controversy however when the directors decided to use him to replace Eddie Gray as team manager. How he had got to that step up was beyond my understanding at the time. From youth coach to manager, that would have been some promotion. All kinds of stories went around about how he had engineered it behind the scenes. I'm told that Eddie Gray suspected what Mincher was up to and went to see the chairman to insist that he was removed from the club. Then when it boiled down to the 'him-or-me' situation, the chairman sacked Eddie. Maybe the directors thought that with Keith

Mincher being responsible for all these good young kids coming through he should be in charge of them at a higher level. But, it went down like a lead balloon with the first-team players. Club captain Peter Lorimer was incensed and there was a players' meeting. Player power really did exist that day. Ironically if Keith Mincher had got the job I suspect my career under him might have gone from strength to strength at Leeds.

I can still remember it. I was only a reserve but we were all there at the meeting. The atmosphere was filled with disbelief and panic as well. There was confusion and anger. Who on earth wanted Keith Mincher as manager in preference to Gray? We were just stunned. Eddie Gray was our idol. He was approachable, fair, but never soft. If you were injured he would come into the treatment room for a chat. We were only young lads but he seemed to treat us like men. Peter Lorimer somehow assumed control of the meeting, the pandemonium and noise subsided and an amazing decision was made, that the team would not play if Mincher was appointed. When Mincher and Silver came into the meeting Lorimer stood up and announced that the decision was diabolical. Chairman Silver, who had already had his car vandalised by angry fans loyal to Eddie, backtracked and the popular Peter Gumby, was put in temporary charge.

* * * * *

There were times when all we apprentices seemed to do was paint, paint and paint some more; we had to do it properly as well. On my very first day at Elland Road there were some walls that needed a coat. My mum laughed when I told her because she remembered how I used to paint our house and once did it pink. But even if it was only painting a wall at Elland Road I did the job as well as I could. After a while I heard a familiar voice down the end of the corridor. Hell, it was only Don Revie. He had called in to wish Eddie well for the coming season and both of them were coming towards me up the corridor. I was kind of mesmerised and stared at them. In so doing my foot slipped off the ladder and I ended up in a heap on the floor looking thoroughly embarrassed and awkward although somehow I still hung on to the tin. The Don gave me a grin and a wink. Have you any idea how it felt to be given a wink by the legend that was Don Revie? But, Eddie Gray looked at me as if I was an idiot and he must have been wondering who on earth was this he had playing for the club.

A close friend then was Dennis Irwin and we were boot-room boys together. Apprentices were paired up and Big Nose was my partner. He was such a likeable Irish lad from Cork and was about the most laid back person I knew then. It's a close call who is the most laid back, an Irishman or a West Indian. He was such a good player, a very good passer of the ball and we both played at the back in a very successful team. Even at that early age he was a sort of shop steward and skipper rolled into one and probably had more sense than the rest of us put together.

Six of us could well have got into big trouble when we jumped on the training ground tractor one day and took turns driving it round the field as fast as it would go. It was something we'd done before but this time no-one noticed that the blades were still lowered and with six of us piled on the grass got shorter and shorter until one or two patches were quite bald. At last someone noticed and horrified we all jumped off and legged it, leaving it parked in the middle of the field. It wouldn't surprise me if the groundsman John Reynolds knew all along what had happened.

If any of the lads did a job badly, then we all paid for it. A court case would follow. One person could mess up. But the group paid for it. You learned that way not to let your mates down. The skip was in a mess one day. The boots had been polished but the mud underneath on the soles was still there. A lad called Wayne Roebuck was the guilty party. It was a day of snow and was bitterly cold as well; the running track around the pitch was 12 inches deep in the stuff. Wayne was collared, but all of us were ordered to get out onto the track for 30 minutes running. We thought we'd get away with it on account of the weather. 'But it's deep snow,' we protested not even allowed to wear our tracksuits. It made no difference, out we had to go. Okay it was only 30 minutes but it, and Coach Barry Murphy, nearly killed us with the toughest ever running session.

So, the court was set up to try Wayne Roebuck. It was how any apprentice who screwed up was punished. A judge was appointed. He put a towel over his head in mock seriousness. I was a member of the jury. Wayne protested his innocence. 'I didn't know I had to scrape the mud off . . . I didn't see it,' and so on. He knew what was coming and was duly found guilty by the lads who had endured 30 minutes' torture in the snow and cold. He was given a choice of punishments. He could have his bollocks blackened with boot polish and Vaseline, with the Vaseline making it harder to get the boot polish off; or he could be placed in the bath in his kit and hosed. He chose the latter but don't think it was the lesser of the two evils. This was a high power hose we used for washing the dressing room floor and corridors. Boy it hurt and could slam you against the wall if it was on full. After that I can't remember anybody not cleaning the first team boots properly again. It certainly made us think, and brought tears to our eyes.

There was no chance of developing any airs and graces in those days. You kept your feet firmly on the ground. There was nothing glamorous about what we called the Pigsty. This was an old brick showerblock on the edge of the Fullerton training area at the ground across the car park. It was cold, draughty and there was never any hot water. Showering in that primitive place cured any notion of this being the good life. If you didn't muck in you were soon brought back down to earth. It's different now. Too many 16 year olds, but not all, think they've made it once they're signed on by a big club.

The camaraderie between us was terrific. A group of us, Dennis Irwin, Tommy Wright, Scott Sellars, Terry Phelan and John Sheridan always made a beeline for the city centre after training. We'd wander round the shops, check the talent and more often than not call into a coffee bar called the Farmhouse usually for a hot chocolate and a cream bun. God they were happy days, no cares, no worries, just young lads at Leeds United with the world of football in front of us and doing something we loved. In those days I had a wet look perm. I've had a few hairstyles in my time; it was cool at the time. Because of my elegant, sartorial clothes style they called me Shaft after the black private eye in the film that was such a big hit in the seventies.

We'd take it in turns to buy drinks and cakes and the drinks always had a large cream topping. On this day it was my turn so I had five frothy cream-covered drinks on a tray and all the cakes. For some reason I'd had to go upstairs to collect them and then bring them down the stairs. The floor was very wet and slippery. Yep, over I went head over heels down the stairs like a downhill skier with the tray contents flying everywhere. The staff were apologetic. Somehow with the staff's help I cleaned myself up and thought I'd got every last bit of froth and cream off my hands, face and clothes. But the lads kept sniggering, at first faintly, then louder until it was wild and hysterical. They were sitting out of sight of the stairs and hadn't seen the fall. I noticed them looking at my hair. I found the cloakroom and checked it in the mirror. My wet look perm was still immaculate—but covered in cream.

For a while in the reserves I played alongside Kenny Burns, who was there because he wouldn't take a pay cut. He was on a high wage and Gray needed to move him on to cut costs. He called me Harvey, as in Harvey Moon, rhymes with coon. You put up with comments like this, shrugged and laughed it off. What else could you do? Black players did back then. It was said in jest, a joke, just a laugh, but at my expense.

Kenny had two sides to him and was always courteous to mum and dad. He used to make a bee line for them if ever he saw them in the players' lounge. Neither mum nor dad were interested in drinking and used to sit quietly at a table by themselves. If Kenny spotted them he always took soft drinks over for them and made a big fuss of them. I think it was the first time my mum had ever encountered Glaswegian patter and she always found it comical when he went across and uttered: 'Hullo Patsy, how are yi?' I used to look across at Kenny talking, laughing and joking with mum and dad and felt so proud. Here was this legendary player taking time to chat with them.

Way back then 'this is it' I thought. I'd been there since I'd left school. Players were there who had been my heroes as a youngster and here I was training and swapping conversations with them. We had some great times and good, solid professional habits were drilled into me that would stay with me for as long as I played. I play for Leeds United, I proudly told myself. At that age I felt nothing could go wrong. One day soon I'd be out there doing what I dreamed of doing, giving the raised-arm salute to the crowd in the centre of the pitch before a first team game. I'm here and I'm going to be here for the rest of my career I told myself.

But I wasn't. It didn't work out. Billy Bremner arrived.

4

Roots

Cruising in my white XR3i up King's Road, Bradford, shades on, arm out of the window and soul music in the background. I see a policeman driving towards me on the opposite side of the road. As he drives by he has a fixed glare at me. I check my mirror to see in the distance that he is turning round with the blue lights flashing. I put my foot down. I want out of here. Now he has the sirens on. I slow down and stop because I hadn't done anything wrong.

'Is this your car sir?' he says.

'How can you afford something like this?' he says.

What does he mean? He must think I've stolen it. 'I save my money officer.'

He asks what's in the boot. 'It's just stuff officer.'

'What kind of stuff?' he says and then takes the keys out of the ignition and walks to the back of the car. I get out. He opens the boot and starts rummaging through my dirty football kit.

'I told you it was just stuff. It's football stuff.' He looked disappointed. He knew I was winding him up. I knew that he had stopped me for being a black man in a nice white car.

'Do you know what I stopped you for?'

'Is it because I am black officer?' is what I want to ask. 'Is it because I am not wearing a seatbelt?' is what I actually stupidly say.

I wasn't wearing a seatbelt. 'Yes,' he replies and gives me a £30 on-the-spot fine.

I jotted that down on a notepad some time ago. I know why he stopped me and so did he. I'll bet I was stopped a dozen times by the police back then. I seemed to get stopped more in Lancashire than Yorkshire, funny that. I was late for training once after being pulled over yet again. The lads asked why I was late. 'I'm Random Black, there was a police random black man check,' I said and they roared with laughter. But it's no joke when you're stopped yet again.

I happen to be black. So what you might ask? Is it important anymore? Ask the BNP. Ask Roberto Carlos now playing in Russia.

Ask Djibril Cisse. Ask him about the abuse he got in Greece. Ask any black player who plies his trade in Spain or Italy. Ask black members of the England team who played in Spain not that long ago. In the Premier League there were incidents involving Evra and Suarez; Anton Ferdinand and John Terry. Racism, or accusations of it, hasn't quite gone away.

There were times when it was horrendous and I'm not talking about as far back as the sixties and the fifties or before that when people knew no better. No: I'm talking about not that many years ago when I was a player; the eighties and nineties when you might have thought people knew better or had been educated and were more tolerant and less inclined to pass comments or shout abuse. But no, even in the late eighties, people threw bananas at the great John Barnes of Liverpool. 'Niggerpool, niggerpool,' Everton fans screamed at Liverpool in the first derby game that featured Barnes. In the late nineties Ian Wright was badly abused in a Burnley away game at Colchester. It left manager Stan Ternent incensed. The next Burnley manager Steve Cotterill fumed at Crewe when his black players were abused. Nor is it just colour prejudice; as recently as 2009 when Burnley played Tottenham in the Carling semi-final at Turf Moor, the anti-Semitic abuse was loud and clear in a section of the Lower James Hargreaves Stand. A group of 20 or so were shouting 'Hitler was right'.

I was regularly abused at away games. In one I was abused by people in the wheelchair area. That really took me by surprise. I'd have thought they would have been well aware of what it was like to be 'different' and to experience discrimination and hurtful personal remarks. There was always abuse when I took a free kick near the touchline or a throw-in. There were occasions when away fans made complaints to stewards about me, that I had actually abused them. On one occasion I was accused of spitting at the crowd. Anyone who knows me would know how absurd that was. At such times there would be a knock on the dressing room door after the game and a visit from a policeman coming to examine the accusation. If a fan complained about abuse from a black player it was investigated. If a black player accused a fan of abuse it was usually overlooked or the player was expected to take it lying down. Or 'just shake hands at the end of the game,' said Sepp Blatter as we wrote this book.

After the fourth occasion I received another visit in the dressing room. It then became a joke and we'd sit and wait for the knock, or when the knock came there'd be a shout of: 'It's for you Roger.'

Today, it's difficult, if not impossible, to find an all-white team. Africans, French Africans, mixed race and Asians are everywhere. Look at Chelsea. Look at every Premier team, every league team. But it was once so different. At Leeds as a youth there was me and Terry Connor. At Burnley 20 years ago there was just me and John Francis. Before us at Burnley came George Oghani and Winston White, and before them there was a player called Les Lawrence bought from Rochdale. Bob Lord, the legendary chairman, at a game at Sunderland saw a coloured player for the first time and is supposed to have said: 'Na then, what the 'eck's 'e doing 'ere?'

In 1993 Alastair Campbell wrote about racism in football in his *Daily Mirror* column. He'd seen that Stockport County's Kevin Francis in one game at Burnley, and then Sheffield United's Adrian Littlejohn had both been badly abused by sections of the Turf Moor crowd. Littlejohn scored and celebrated. Cries of, 'You black bastard,' rang round the ground with the usual monkey and Zulu chants. For this game I was on the bench, but came on at halftime. Kevin Francis happened to be extremely tall. That plus his colour made him the target of the 'oo oo oo' and baboon chants. Burnley's John Francis and Kevin Francis were related. We used to call them Little Gimp and Big Gimp. At one game the BNP used Burnley for distributing recruitment leaflets. Alastair Campbell was angry at the continued presence of this sort of behaviour in football:

> Let me introduce you to the real passion in my life, Burnley Football Club. It is a love affair made all the more intense by my having followed them from the very top of the Football League to the very bottom, and now a bit of the way up again. It is a marvellous club with phenomenal support for a small town Second Division outfit which takes more fans to away matches than Premier League Wimbledon manage to draw at home.
>
> But recent trips have been marred by an increase in racism, prompting the vile British National Party to target Burnley for leafleting and recruitment. Racism was a real problem in football a few years ago but seemed to diminish as hooliganism did, and as the number of black players increased. QPR for example fielded six coloured players against Norwich on Saturday. If opposing fans had emitted racist chants every time one of those players got the ball they'd have been hoarse by half-time.

Yet having coloured players in their side hasn't stopped some Burnley fans behaving in a racist way. Roger Eli, whose kit my elder son sponsors, was on the field when Sheffield United's Adrian Littlejohn came in for the monkey chant treatment. Another coloured player Louie Donowa was playing for Burnley when Stockport County's Kevin Francis was treated to, 'Oo, oo, oo,' and, 'throw him a banana.' These chants are supposed to be illegal.

It's all very well for Metropolitan Police Commissioner Paul Condon to make an impassioned speech warning he won't tolerate racism. His words were welcome. Yet never have I seen the police move when these chants begin. Racism, to me, is every bit as serious as the Manchester City pitch invasion, but when was the last time football authorities bothered to address it? At Burnley a group calling itself Clarets against the Nazis has distributed thousands of leaflets demanding a stop to the racism. Burnley supporters' fanzine Marlon's Gloves has also waged the fight against racists.

Fans have led successful anti-racist campaigns at Leeds, Leicester and Newcastle. But the real leadership should come from police, chairmen, directors and players. One word from an overpaid Premier League 'superstar' could have an immediate effect. Or, are clubs worried that if racists are rooted out, the turnstile takings will fall?

I didn't know that Alastair Campbell's son had sponsored my shirt.

It was at the Wigan game that the BNP descended on Burnley. They were filmed by the BBC. Normal fans were angry that it showed them and the club in a bad light. It was this that prompted a group of fans to distribute 4,000 anti-Nazi leaflets at the Stockport County game. The organisers wanted people to stop and think about what they were doing. But it was at the Stockport game that the chanting continued at Kevin Francis. 'We want people to remember that racist chants against players from other clubs are just as insulting to Roger Eli or Louie Donowa,' said Stuart Marsden one of the organisers.

Probably the most frequently remembered, most infamous instance of racial bigotry experienced by a Burnley player happened down at Plymouth in the second-leg of the play-offs in 1994. I was still at Burnley then but on the fringes of things. Plymouth had held Burnley to a draw at Turf Moor and were so confident of winning the return game, the story goes, that the club had gone so far as to organise the coaches for Wembley. But my pal, John Francis, spoiled the story. Against a background of dreadful racial abuse, monkey chants and taunting, he scored twice to destroy their pretentious dreams in the best possible way by ramming their prejudice back down their foul throats.

Maybe I've been fortunate. I have been abused in my time, but didn't suffer badly from it because I never let it affect me. But funnily enough when I went to Partick Thistle in Glasgow at the back end of my career, playing there was the same player who had called me Uncle Tom when he'd played for Tranmere against Burnley. I never felt that Kenny Burns calling me Harvey was genuine abuse. It came across as banter that's all. The nearest thing to feeling affected by anything was more to do with being confused rather than deeply upset. There was one instance of that when I was only 16 on the coach travelling with Leeds United reserves somewhere and on the TV at the front they were showing *Blazing Saddles*. There was me, a young lad and this was a reserve side with several senior players, some of them ex internationals of some standing and reputation. If you remember that film one of the central characters is a black sheriff. Now the humour in that is supposed to be the fact that in the old Wild West, there was no such thing as a black sheriff. It was also the first film I had seen where I'd heard the word 'nigger' being used so often and so blatantly. Everybody on the bus was falling about laughing at this idea of 'colour' and I just didn't know whether to laugh at it or not. It was as if I was part of what they were laughing at. It was a moment when I really didn't know how to react or what I was supposed to think or do. I talked about it with my sister and she had a totally different view of the film. She saw it as this black man winning over an ignorant town and becoming a hero in the process. Plus it made her laugh, especially the 'beans' scene round the campfire.

There was one coach on the management side at Leeds who'd say: 'Sing me an old nigger song Roger.' Maybe he too had seen *Blazing Saddles*. There's a scene in it where the sheriff is asked to sing an old nigger song. You expect him to sing something like 'Ol' Man River' or 'Camptown Races'. But instead he comes out with 'I get a kick from champagne.' Nearly 30 years later I can see the genuine humour and laugh at it. As a 16-year old I didn't know what to feel.

Many years later when John Francis and me went into a pub in Todmorden one Saturday night for a drink there was a '*Blazing Saddles*' moment. We hadn't played for years and we ordered a pint. We could feel the stares and the 'ey up what the 'ell are they doin' 'ere'. I swear that pub went silent for a few seconds at the sheer gall that two black men should walk in. If this had been a film the honky-tonk piano would have stopped as the tension grew. A cold silence would have descended. Then one bloke sidled up to the bar. He sort of stared at us. 'Tell me,' he said. 'Are you two Roger Eli and John Francis?' I have the clear feeling that if we hadn't been we'd have been lynched. We smiled and nodded. If there'd been a piano that would have been the moment it would have started again. Smiles erupted. The tension lifted. Conversations started again. The man's face said it all: 'Well that's alright then.'

Terry Connor was a couple of years older than me at Leeds and he never liked the racist banter. Some people can put up with it and others can't and the problem is that if you kick back against it, you're not 'one of the lads'. Banter in a dressing room is ceaseless and merciless. Howard Gayle at Liverpool later on never took to this idea that you had to go along with it if it pointed to your colour. He left. At Leeds the squad went to see Bernard Manning one night in a club in Leeds. Manning was a comedian who specialised in jokes based on crudeness, abuse and prejudices. And somehow whilst Charlie Williams told jokes about black people that were never really offensive; Manning seemed pure poison.

So in this club the squad were in the front rows and tables and Terry Connor was clearly in the firing line. And predictably Manning singled him out. One joke was all about giving Terry instructions how to get to Manning's own club in Manchester.

'So you come along the M62 and then go this way and that way and down this road and that road; but when you get there—just drive straight past because I don't want you fucking coming in.' How nasty was that, but Terry's done well since then, and had the last laugh, assistant now to Mick McCarthy at Wolves. Manning is no longer with us.

It was the TV series *Roots* that opened my eyes to the history of black people. I had no idea about how they were treated. It made a big impression on me and we used to watch it as a family. It was based on Alex Haley's book of the same name. Haley claimed to have traced his family history right back to the original slave transported from Africa. The founder of his family he traced back to Kunta Kinte, the African taken by slavers from Gambia in 1767. Haley went on to tell the story of each passing generation until he reached his own childhood when his grandmother told him all the stories that she knew that had been handed down to her by her own father who was freed in 1865.

For all I know my own history might well be something very similar involving all that you associate with slavery; mistreatment, beatings, abuse and cruelty. The programme took me aback and affected me deeply. There's me, a black kid in Bradford, and at school the only history I ever knew was about the Wars of the Roses. My sister had even told me in her history lessons how her teacher would tell them that they were all, 'but not her,' probably descended from Vikings. I'd no idea how badly the early West Indian people were treated when they came across to the UK in the fifties, or the way in which even in World War Two when they came across to fight they were as good as left at the back of the queue, because they were seen as inferior. It seemed they never had any thanks for fighting for the 'mother country'.

It was around the time that *Roots* was such a TV phenomenon and a few years before I joined United that Pudsey Juniors played an Isle of Man Select XI. I'd have been 12 or 13 maybe. For 90 minutes I was subjected to more taunts of Kunta Kinte and Chicken George, another of the characters. Early adolescent teenage years are difficult enough anyway without this kind of stuff. At school there was a lesson involving nursery rhymes. There's one that has a line about catching a nigger by his toe. 'Ooh sorry, I shouldn't say that should I,' said the teacher after she had let the word slip. It all added up to a self-conscious period as I grew up.

The awareness that I was 'different' continued when there was a football visit to Denmark. It was a time when black faces in Scandinavia were few and far between. I could see, sense, feel people looking and staring at me as we moved around. It got to the point where I stayed in the hotel. There was a youth trip to Yugoslavia. It was my black hair, slicked-back, wet perm look period. People came up to me and called me Michael Jackson. It was reasonable to assume they'd never seen a black face before. I could have become quite paranoid about it if we'd stayed longer or had it got any worse. Paranoid or not—it didn't stop us beating Hajduk Split in the final.

Was there a more racist set of supporters in England than those at Leeds United when I was there? I remember that all too vividly. When I was a 17 year old apprentice at Leeds United, they had the most racist element you could possibly imagine. They did Nazi-style salutes in unison and monkey chants at black players with a passion but I have to say never at me. But I was very wary and either made my mum and dad leave a game early in case anything kicked off, or got them into the players' lounge. I remember at that time being on £25 a week and spending £15 of that on a taxi home, instead of the number 53 bus, when I'd cleared up after a game to avoid meeting any of those people at the bus station.

My pal John Francis endured it as well. When he made his debut for Halifax at Darlington he was hit by a banana as he ran out. He'll tell you today how it all frightened him, the fact that people could hate him because of the colour of his skin. It affected his game badly in his younger days. The centre-half's first contact with him in that game was to kick him quite badly and call him a 'black bastard'. But it's Plymouth he remembers as the worst when they made appalling monkey noises even though they had two coloured players themselves. When we were together at Burnley we were often told that none of us would have played there if Bob Lord had still been chairman. We had problems within the club from a member of the staff who made racist comments and particularly upset a young Asian player. Maybe today he regrets this? It was over 20 years ago. Maybe he would argue that the things he said were not racist? I know I regret not intervening. At the very least it was bullying.

Of course I knew all about Albert Johanneson at Leeds. He was one of the great players who led the way for others being one of the first to come to the attention of the public and gain real prominence. But in fact there was another player at Leeds before him, also a South African—Gerry Francis. The trickle of black players into the game had seemingly come to an end after 1945 even though the number of Commonwealth immigrants was rising. But in 1957 Francis arrived in Leeds from Johannesburg. Until 1961 he only managed 46 games until Revie packed him off to York City. He would dazzle one game and then disappear in the next, helping the stereotype view that black players weren't really cut out for the toughness of pro football. Thus he would vanish into the reserves, get back to form, reappear in the First Team again, and then vanish again.

So Johanneson became the pioneer for the rest of us who followed. We owe him a lot. He made his debut four games into Revie's reign and provided the flair in a team of rough, rugged, physically combative players who were designed to hustle and prevent the opposition playing. It took just two training sessions for Revie to see the potential and he played for the next six years, becoming known as the 'Black Flash'. He eventually succumbed to self-doubt and big-match nerves. His feelings of inadequacy were always there to undermine his confidence on the football field and in his private life. One thing above all else contributed to this—his colour. When he first arrived at Leeds, apartheid reigned supreme in South Africa. At Leeds he thought he would have to bath separately from the other players until they threw him in the bath and joined him. Leeds fans took to him; he was the icing on the cake, on his day quick, strong, full of flair and pace with a strike rate of one goal in three games, a ratio that some centre-forwards would have been proud of.

It was a schoolteacher back in Johannesburg who wrote to Leeds about Johanneson, and for the price of an air ticket Leeds gained a player that today would be in the £10million bracket. Maybe Ashley Young might be the nearest comparison. He came for a three-month trial, settled in well once he had adjusted to a world where he could sit on any bus seat he chose alongside white people. If he was abused he rarely complained or mentioned it. Only once did he tell Don Revie that he had been called a 'black bastard' by an Everton player. Revie's advice was short and to the point. 'Well call him a white bastard next time.'

When I was a young kid I used to see Albert at Elland Road where he'd call in to see Eddie Gray. It never really dawned on me who he was and how significant he had been. If I'd known I'd have made the effort to talk to him and get to know him. There were no outward signs of what he must have been going through. Eventually he had been moved on to York City. He retired in 1971 and sadly alcohol took over his life.

At that time it never occurred to me that he was only the second black player to play for the club, or that after Terry Connor, I was only the fourth. It just never crossed my mind and didn't seem important. I guess I didn't let it affect me too much as my parents had done a good job of raising me in the right way.

One of my earliest black heroes and role models as a kid was the Bradford City player Ces Podd. Not that all my heroes were black. There were people like Kevin Keegan and Mick Channon to emulate as well and of course the Leeds team. Ces Podd's name might not be very well known outside of football but this was the man who led the way for so many more of us and in Bradford and within the game his name is revered. He should have a huge place in the Football Hall of Fame. And yet his story nearly didn't happen. He moved to Bradford with his parents from St Kitts and Nevis in the early sixties when he was nine and he had an obvious football talent. It was a time when discrimination was rampant. As a schoolboy he had pace and he started out as a winger. Scouts began to notice him in schools football and he was invited for trials at Manchester United and Wolves.

A friend then recommended him to Bradford City, the next club to give him a trial. He was disappointed not to be put into his best position on the wing but when volunteers were asked to play at full-back he jumped at the chance. Life is all about luck and being in the right place at the right time. He did okay in that strange position and began training with the club whilst continuing with his college course. His progress continued; he was in fact a natural footballer and still had that terrific pace. He turned pro when he was 18 in August 1970 and soon made his debut against Chesterfield and for over a decade he would miss few games. In two consecutive seasons he was voted into the PFA Division Four team of the season by his fellow professionals. For his testimonial season he organised an all black team to provide the opposition. When he was voted into the PFA Division Four team a second time, it coincided with promotion back to Division Three. Roy McFarland was manager. There was a run of nine consecutive wins. Podd was an ever present but sadly just as the team began to get even better in the following seasons he was passing his best and at the end of '83–84 he was released. He had been there for 14 years and through endeavour and honesty he found respect and acceptance in two decades when catcalls and abuse from the terraces could be appalling. Being a full-back close to the touchline and terraces made it even more audible to him.

I met Podd several times when I was a ball boy at Bradford City and he was a first teamer. I'd have been 12 or 13 maybe. I was incredibly proud of this and the night before a game I used to polish my shoes and put on my best brown tatty suit, a hand me down that mum had got for me from a friend. Me and a pal called John Bell, a good young footballer, would go down on the bus feeling so smart and proud to be involved on City match days. But, it was a polyester

63

suit and had 'pulls' and threads hanging out. A girl I knew back then made endless fun when she saw us. 'Roger you've got more "clicks" in that suit than any suit I've ever seen.'

Never mind her; in my head I imagined I was in the first team and heading to the ground to play the full 90 minutes. Ces was a truly decent fella, so polite. Years later we used to meet in a Leeds nightclub called Digby's. The ladies' heads would turn when they knew the footballers were walking in. I used to call it 'Grab a Granny' night because the women looked so much older than me. But Ces was so suave in his all white suit and white shoes, looking like one of the Commodores; and such a great dancer he'd have a flock of a dozen women dancing with him in unison like a chorus line. No wonder he became a dance teacher in later years. (I laughed when co-writer Dave Thomas told me he'd been to a dozen of his salsa lessons with Harriet, his wife. When Dave realised who the teacher was he went up to ask for his autograph.)

It was a time when inner city deprivation and high unemployment worsened any opportunities for black people; race riots took place in many areas, and against such a background young black men were hardly encouraged to find a life in professional football even if they were highly talented. Being abused and attacked in the street was no encouragement to set yourself up as a target in front of a baying football mob at every away ground you went to. There were many incidents Ces was subjected to. His mother would never attend any away games although his father went to them all. He remembers the south being particularly bad for racial abuse.

Clyde Best was another role model for black youngsters. He was an early hero of mine and I used to collect Clyde Best football cards. He made his first appearance for West Ham in 1969 and continued for several seasons. It was a time of increasing television coverage for the top teams and his exploits came to the attention of football fans everywhere. He was probably the first black footballer to feature regularly on TV. West Ham as a club, in fact, were pioneers with a number of aspiring black footballers trying to make the grade. But it was Best who made it to the top. He provided inspiration to others.

Clyde Best never reached the heights that his team-mates achieved—Moore, Peters and Hurst. At that time he was the only black player playing regular first-team football in the First Division and was constantly subjected to abuse and discrimination. Best was probably the best example of why it had taken so long for managers, coaches and the public to accept coloured players. He would be brilliant one game, bad the next; and the stereotype views about black players' stamina, power and determination were constantly applied to him. Meanwhile in my own efforts to become a footballer I had no idea that 'white' coaches had such negative views of us. It never occurred to me and I would have been amazed if anyone had ever said to me I was 'soft'.

The racist treatment given out to black players at this time by both players and spectators dissuaded many black parents from encouraging their children to pursue a career in football, but not mine. Best provided an example of what could be achieved, although endurance was a quality he sorely needed in order to cope. The MBE he received in 2006 was well deserved.

A hero of mine was Viv Anderson. In fact at Pudsey Juniors the manager Alan Cowley bestowed the nickname Viv on me. During the mid to late seventies as more black players slowly emerged Anderson provided a high profile success story. He played in the fabulous Brian Clough side that won so many domestic and European honours and also became the first black player to win a full England cap. Fifty years earlier, Jack Leslie, an outstanding Anglo-African player who had scored 400 goals was selected for England. The selectors had no idea of his colour; so that when they did discover he was 'a man of colour' his selection was overturned. 'They must have forgotten I was a coloured boy,' he said.

Laurie Cunningham and Cyrille Regis were two other people I greatly admired. Winger Cunningham was the first black player to win an England Under-21 cap and went on to add another five and then six senior caps. His career began at Orient but it was soon clear he was destined for better things. Ron Atkinson bought him for his West Brom side and he became the first of 'The Three Degrees'. I was fortunate to play against him as a Leeds youngster in a star-studded reserve game against Manchester United when he was on a short loan spell there. I thought he was a great player and used to roll my socks down to copy him.

But it's wrong to think that West Brom were the only side in the seventies to have three black players, Cunningham, Regis and Brendan Batson. As well as Clyde Best, West Ham had John Charles, Ade Coker and Clive Charles. Yet ironically the West Ham supporters were among the most racist in football at that time. It was West Ham who were the first team to have three black players in their line-up.

On the surface you might think that Ron Atkinson was another groundbreaker and proud of his Three Degrees, how ironic that much later he would be shunned for some comments on TV about a black player when he didn't realise the mike was still on. ITV sacked him but you wonder if that was only because it went public and they 'thought' they had to do something rather than wanted to do something. A while back there was a big fuss because ITV had no black characters in *Midsomer Murders*. Not long after a black postman appeared in *Emmerdale*. Funny that. You should read Stan Collymore's opinions about Big Ron.

'Ron Atkinson a pioneer. Excuse me while I wretch,' wrote Collymore and went on to argue that Atkinson in picking the three of them was simply doing what was best for Atkinson, not the three players. Okay they were black but they were also bloody good players and to leave them out would have been just stupid. Those three players, Collymore wrote, were so far ahead of everyone else at West Brom he could NOT leave them out. Black or not it was blatantly obvious they would improve the side. So Atkinson wasn't being brave, he was just being practical wrote Collymore. Real bravery was Graham Souness picking Catholic Mo Johnston for Rangers. So, says Collymore, it wasn't Atkinson being brave, it was the players themselves. And what did Atkinson say years later? He only called a superb player Marcel Desailly a 'thick, fat, lazy nigger' when he thought the mike was off.

Nevertheless, if they weren't the first, it was the Three Degrees that showed for the first time that a good side could be built round black players. They blasted apart any stereotypical myths. Regis in particular personified power, fitness and strength not to mention bravery and as a centre forward going in where it hurt. Batson was a tough, uncompromising full-back who destroyed the myth that black players were a soft touch. Cunningham went to Real Madrid but his career was tragically cut short when he was killed in a road accident. He was just 33. Somehow they had a certain glamour that the West Ham boys lacked.

Regis was all pace, muscle and determination. He too, like Podd, was one of the first real role models. Other black players, playing in the parks and Sunday morning leagues looked at him and thought if he has broken through why not me? It was a time when few members of the large black communities attended games because of fears for their own safety.

Vince Hilaire was another of the emerging black players in the seventies. But the more that made it into First Team football, the greater was the level of abuse from far-right wing groups that sometimes deliberately attended games simply to heckle and be abusive. Spectators frequently hooted at the players, threw peanuts and bananas; chanted, taunted and jeered them. He remembered the scene at Port Vale when he made his debut in 1976 for Crystal Palace:

'After about 20 minutes, the manager, Terry Venables, told me to go and have a warm-up. I came out of the dug-out and started jogging round the touchline. I couldn't believe the abuse that was coming at me . . . animal noises and all the names you can think of calling a black person, every name under the sun. And it frightened me a bit so I couldn't wait to get back to the dugout.'

Then he came as a Portsmouth player to Elland Road along with a player called Noel Blake. I was watching the game from the stands and the abuse was appalling. Sections of the crowd chanted different things: One section chanted, 'Shoot the nigger'. A different section would shout, 'Which fucking nigger?' Then they'd all reply, 'That fucking nigger'. I sat there aghast, wondering how they would react and what they would shout at me if and when I ever made my debut.

The list of names increased some of them assuming 'star' status — George Berry, Bob Hazel, Garth Crooks, Justin Fashanu, and John Fashanu. Justin was at Forest when I was there in the youth team. We'd see him driving round Nottingham on his own in his Jeep Wrangler, with a big eagle on the front, dressed up to the nines wearing his shades. His story is tragic and illustrates the pressure and stress of discrimination. But nobody messed with his brother John Fashanu in his Wimbledon days. He was known as 'Fash the Bash'. And that's what he did. Any opposing centre half knew they'd been in a game after they'd come up against him. He dispelled any notion that black players could be kicked out of a game. An integral part of the Wimbledon Crazy Gang, he was lethal and whilst his brother Justin's career faded after a meteoric start, his brother's just got better. He was macho-tough, super-masculine and had a 'street' status that brought him huge credibility. Not only that, he was articulate and well spoken. He became almost a cult-like, working-class hero figure; the Barnado Boy made good, and then had a prosperous, celebrity career after football.

Maybe it was John Barnes though, that brought the black footballer into the real limelight in the eighties but behind Barnes' rise to fame was the England manager Bobby Robson who stated publicly in 1982 that the colour of any player was irrelevant and wouldn't make the slightest difference to his team selection. He received hate mail for selecting Viv Anderson, Ricky Hill, John Barnes, Cyrille Regis, Paul Davis and Chris Whyte in '82 for U21 matches against Denmark. Davis, Whyte and Barnes were booed when they touched the ball. Robson was undeterred and for the next game chose Danny Thomas, Mark Chamberlain, Luther Blisset, Remi Moses and Justin Fashanu. The boos and abuse continued.

This was a time of poor international results, football riots, general disenchantment with the game and falling gates but assistant England manager, Don Howe, said something astonishing. 'The black influx might just be the saviour of the game in England . . . they seem to be the hungry ones.' Despite the monkey chants, abuse, aggravation, the future on the park for black footballers looked bright with Robson and Howe in charge.

Alan Hardaker, secretary of the Football League, made a firm prediction: 'There is a new brand of footballer who might well revolutionise the game in this country, the black footballer. It will take time for the strength and skill to be accepted but the black footballer will break through and may even dominate English football.'

It was ironic. Black players were now seen as the possible saviour of the stuttering national team as more of them made the grade; but on the pitch and on the terraces they were still 'black bastards'. The debt owed to those first players who donned an England shirt, be it at full or U21 level is enormous. Yet even recently, the taunts and abuse was still there in Spain directed against English players and then casually dismissed by the Spanish team manager.

If there was such a thing as an ambassador for the black footballer, then not forgetting Ces Podd, it must surely have been John Barnes whose profile was national and therefore so much higher than Podd's. He won a total of 79 caps and his 1984 goal at the Maracana Stadium, Brazil, when he beat player after player, was the stuff of which legends are made. It was in essence a 'Brazilian' goal of flair and phenomenal individual skill. And yet on the plane home he was taunted by the nationalist bigots who told him it wasn't a proper goal. Four of them sat behind the team heckling and calling out. In all probability their tickets, fares and accommodation were paid for by the National Front. In the stadiums they were clearly identifiable by their Union Jacks and the right wing slogans on them. Whenever I read about that I wonder how they got away with it on that plane. Did Barnes' teammates intervene or say anything? Did the stewardesses or the plane's captain not warn them?

Liverpool bought him in 1987 and Barnes tells the story of how he dealt with colour. At the training ground cups of tea were put before the established players but nothing for him. Barnes looked up at the woman who brought them and said: 'What am I, black or something? Everyone fell about.' Barnes explained: 'Dressing rooms are rife with humour and many of the jokes are racist. When I asked "Am I black or something?" it was because I wanted people to understand I am comfortable with it. If other players want to make racist jokes, I was fine about that.'

His book should be compulsory reading.

For sure I too am now perfectly comfortable being black but as a young lad if I had problems to do with my colour it was to do with trying to work out was I black or was I English? My parents made huge efforts to integrate. They didn't even try to teach us the French patois they spoke in Dominica as they said we'd have no need for it now we were in England. Most of my friends, as a little lad growing up, were white from nearby on the estate or from school. But, there was a period when we didn't know who to identify with. There was a time when I wondered 'who am I?' and did feel self-conscious. When I was about eight, I went on a caravan holiday up into the Yorkshire Dales on a farm site near Dent with my pal, Matthew Wilkinson; he was the same age as me. It was with a lovely family and they were friends with the farmer who owned the site. We played with his son who was a similar age to us. He looked at me when we met and asked if he could touch my skin. He'd never seen a black person before. Only a few years ago a friend of mine adopted a mixed race boy. The little lad came back in one day after he'd been playing on his bicycle. He went back out with his arms covered by a pair of long white socks. The other kids had been asking him why he was not the same colour as them.

When I got into the Nottingham Forest youth team we played against local league teams. One of them was a team of black kids. They gave me hell. I got dogs' abuse from them. 'Why are you in this team?', they asked. 'What are you doing playing for them?' They kicked me all over the park. They saw me as betraying my colour and yet I was English. They made me feel truly inferior as if I was doing something wrong. That was the puzzle for me when I was younger. My sister's friends were mostly white but it all conspired to produce an identity puzzle. And for all the white friends we had there were always occasions when you went into a room or a shop, and you were the only black face there, and you did feel the stares and sense the looks—just like when years later John and me went into that pub in Todmorden—in, believe it or not, 2011.

As my own career had that brief spell of real success in the early nineties I was one of an increasing number of black players but the numbers were nothing like they are today. And back then, the idea that a black footballer could appear on something like *BBC Question Time*, as Burnley's Clarke Carlisle did in January 2011, would have been utterly unthinkable. Legislation and various campaigns have done wonders since the days when managers and coaches truly believed that black players were no use because they were too soft or felt the cold too much. I'm proud of being one of the group that broke the stereotype.

5

Leeds United: 'You Have a Choice'

I loved it at Leeds United. With Eddie Gray it was like a huge family and the senior players were great with us; people like Arthur Graham, Kevin Hird, Paul Hart, Brian Flynn, Frank Worthington, Kenny Burns and Andy Ritchie. As a regular routine everyone would take part in a sort of five-a-side club tournament. The youths, reserves and first teamers were all thrown in together and the teams made up of a mix of all of us. As a raw 16 year old there I was playing with and against these seasoned pros. It was senior pro Paul Hart who I thought one day was going to knock my head off.

In one training ground tournament I'd got stuck into him with some very tough challenges. I could dish it out and frequently did. I hounded Harty and he came off pretty much black and blue. A little while later some of the lads said he was looking for me. It was in one of the corridors that we approached each other afterwards. He was limping. And then he shouted at me. 'COME HERE . . . come here . . .' He was big and I was petrified, fully expecting a right-hander. Get it over with, I thought. Don't turn away. He was big and strong enough to lift me up so that my feet just about touched the floor. He stared into my face close up. At this point it's possible I closed my eyes and prayed. And then he spoke.

'Don't ever change. Keep getting stuck in. This is how we want you to play.'

Frank Worthington was a fascinating man. He was the epitome of class and deftness of touch. If he gave an image of being laid back and never giving any effort, forget it. He was a model professional and after doing our jobs the apprentices would join in whatever was going on. There was always this effort to involve us when Eddie was there. Frank was constantly practising his skills. There'd be one-touch routines or 'two-touch'. He'd no airs or graces even though he was such a wonderful player and an England international. He'd tell us about past games and people he'd played with and against.

Sure he always seemed to have a nice lady on his arm and he was such a cool individual with his colourful clothes. But he was also modest and courteous. On many days he'd be there early to practise hitting a ball against a wall just to exercise his touch and feel for the ball. One of my jobs sometimes was to lay out his kit in the dressing room and it had to be just right, all laid out flat and neatly folded with the creases in exactly the right place. Some players were happy if you just hung the kit on hangers on a peg. But Frank wanted his precisely laid out. But he had the oddest habit. He'd cut a V in the front of the neck of every training top and shirt he had. I never found out why. All I knew back then was he had everything, superb footballing talent, and sheer class when it came to the ladies.

Kenny Burns was someone I ran errands for. He regarded me as his personal slave. If he had a chore that needed doing it was me he usually shouted for—'where's HARVEY?' There was me a young 16 year old West Indian lad (born in Bradford of course) and I was his golf caddy on the club's golf days. What did I know about golf? Absolutely nothing, but he'd ask me for advice on which club to use, which way to hit the ball, did I think he should do this or that? I've often thought since then if I'd taken up golf I might have been the first Tiger Woods.

It was common for United in pre-season to send mixed ability sides to local semi-professional teams as part of the fitness build-up. Lads like me relished the games and the chance to impress the coaching staff. However, for the smattering of senior pros who were sent along, as a favour to boost the home side's gate revenue as much as anything, these fixtures were probably nothing short of a pain in the backside. I was playing alongside Kenny in one of these games against a local non-league outfit, Ventus United. Playing next to him taught me a lot, not the least of which was how to become another Kenny Burns, and how to become impervious to pain. His face as we got changed was a picture: 'What on earth am I doing here?' You could see quite clearly this was the last place he wanted to be. He wanted to get some fitness and 90 minutes and then get away as quickly as he could. This sort of game was beneath his dignity or where he expected to be. What he didn't need was some cocky, give-it-large upstart giving him some grief. But that, alas, was exactly what he got in this game. The upstart paid the price.

An opposing player was putting himself around big-time

and proving annoyingly and insultingly vocal with it. He had a reputation at his club of being full of himself, and his personal assessment of his ability was way above what it actually was. But, all Kenny wanted was a leisurely incident free afternoon where he could stretch his limbs and limber up. He wasn't the type who spent his summer bombing round country lanes to maintain his peak fitness and pre-season friendlies against non-league sides were a huge inconvenience to his normal routine.

The encounter he had with this particular player therefore led to the almost perfect lesson in how an old fox like Kenny still knew how to inflict pain and retribution. Kenny politely asked the perpetrator to tone things down a little. His opponent became even more abusive. He then proceeded to clatter into Kenny while challenging for a high ball. Kenny said nothing but I could see he was raging inside. Young as I was, I suggested to this brave bloke that he really needed to calm down before Kenny responded in kind. The centre-back replied with a volley of expletives. I could see Kenny watching and listening.

The next thing I remember is Kenny needlessly putting the ball out for a corner; although in fact Kenny knew exactly what he was doing and why. As the corner came over, he was nowhere near in the right position to head the ball away. But he was in the right position to be in the general direction of his victim when the ball came over and this was nothing to do with zonal marking. Kenny came in like lightning from an angle which masked his actions from the referee. His victim received a forearm smash in the face which led to him being taken away with blood gushing like a fountain from the nose that was now re-arranged all over his face. In fact his whole face was so all over the place it looked like a Picasso painting. It was perfect, except unfortunately it was the wrong bloke.

The intended victim had at the last minute moved, ducked, been off-balance, whatever; it could have been any reason. But now, the wrong person was laid out on the floor. Kenny, being Kenny, knew exactly what he must do next. He lay on the ground quietly groaning and waited for our own physio to come on to give him some attention and cosmetic treatment that he certainly didn't need. He was fine of course but his target wasn't and this of course was the object of the exercise except for the unfortunate error of it all going wrong. It was a classic hard man's ploy. Kenny had made it look just like a natural collision gone wrong, in fact the whole thing had gone wrong, but those who knew him could only stand back and admire how he had dished out a lesson in etiquette, albeit to the wrong player, and that seasoned professionals like him should never be disrespected. The incident caused a real upset and Kenny had to write and apologise to the poor man who had his jaw wired up for the next six weeks. Gordon Raynor, the intended victim, got off scot-free. I still know him to this day and he was a very lucky lad indeed.

I used to wash Kenny's car for a fiver. Now that was a fair amount in the early eighties. He had a gleaming, black, shiny, Ford Escort XR3. I used to take my own shampoo and polish in and did it proud. If I did a job I did it well. It's the way I am. He was one satisfied customer. So much so that Paul Hart then asked me to do his car. This unfortunately was the day I did not have any shampoo and polish with me. I used to spend a lot of time in the laundry room chatting away with the two lovely ladies there, Liz and Cath, who both looked about as old as the washing machines. They'd been there years and were lovely with all of us. In fact sometimes I took my own washing from home for them to do. Laundry ladies are the same everywhere. They don't see stars and big names. They just see the blokes who need their washing doing and make a mess on their floor if they have their muddy boots on. Nobody brings a footballer back down to earth quite like a laundry lady. This laundry room was where I used to fill my buckets of water and in the corner they had a huge bucket filled with washing powder. 'That'll do,' I thought and piled several scoops into all my buckets of water. Big mistake . . . Oh God the disaster was epic. There was foam and bubbles everywhere. The car was submerged in about three feet of the stuff from end to end. A hose would have cleared it all off in seconds but there was no hose; only the buckets of water that I ferried out to throw on the car to dilute the mess. But the more I threw on the worse it seemed to get. I felt like the Sorcerer's Apprentice. And then Harty came out to find his beloved XR2 drowning in soap suds. He was furious, glowered at me and just drove off fuming. Bubbles and suds streamed behind him down the road like a jet stream and to this day I don't think he has ever got the smears off. I'd kicked him black and blue in a game and he was proud of me. I'd messed up his car and he could have killed me. Funnily enough he never asked me to clean his car again.

Eventually I got a car of my own; well, sort of my own. I shared it with my brother Rohan because he didn't quite have enough money to buy it so I had a small share in it. It was a Ford Capri. These were the first really affordable sporty looking cars and even though it was second hand, in silver, it looked good with red seats (plastic not leather). It was better than asking to borrow my sister's car. This was a car that sounded like a hairdryer and did nothing for my street cred. It took me a couple of years to pass my driving test largely because there'd be one injury or another which meant lessons had to be put on hold each time. But don't think this car was ever a babe-magnet. All I used it for was to cart six or seven hairy footballers around even though it was only a four seater and two of those seats in the back were hardly big enough for one.

As long as Eddie Gray was there I felt quite secure and confident. He was understanding, you felt he cared and he was approachable. My sister remembers the time Eddie came over to talk to her when she was watching me play in a youth game. She couldn't believe he took the time to chat, but was less impressed when he asked: 'You must be Roger's mum?' There's this myth that Eddie was 'soft'. He wasn't. There was a line with him you knew you could not cross. He could dish out the bollockings when needed. But what he showed was that you didn't need to eff and blind all day long. He had high expectations and he only wanted players he knew could play a bit. He loved the 5-a-sides with the emphasis on skill but they were also incredibly physical. Peter Lorimer (Lash) too was good with us. I learnt so much from him about passing, or when to release the ball. In training he'd stop you and tell you how to do things better or differently. We all had lunch at the club together and mixed well. We'd be able to sit with these players and talk to them. Former players came into the club from time to time. It was like a who's who of Leeds United. These were all the players I idolised as a young kid and they came in to see Eddie. Big John Charles was a regular visitor. I never saw him play but certainly knew about his legendary status.

The step up to the reserve side was dramatic. These were 3 o'clock kick-offs at Elland Road at a time when the teams were filled with senior pros. Today reserve teams are more or less youth sides. But back then if a game was against Manchester United for example you played against people like Mark Hughes, Lou Macari, Laurie Cunningham or Paul McGrath. The first reserve game I ever played was at Old Trafford when I came on for the last fantastic 10 minutes creating lots of chances and playing for Man U in this particular game was Peter Beardsley. It was classic Eli, run, chase, harry, tackle and put yourself about. Ray Wilkins approached me at the end. He was a gent and must have known what it was like for me a young kid playing in a place like that for the first time. 'Well played son,' said this England international and I felt so respectful towards him. Here was a top England player giving me a few pointers as we walked off the pitch, leaving me so pleased that he was impressed with me.

I was forever looking at the teamsheet when it went up to see if my name was on it. This was in the days of just one sub and on the teamsheet it would be number 12. Just sometimes my name was down there as number 14 but on the day I saw it at number 12 for the first time for the game on November 3rd, '84, I was wide-eyed. It meant travelling down to Charlton. I just felt this wild excitement, this sense of enormous pride and elation. The thoughts that go through your head are obvious enough and I couldn't wait to get home to tell mum and dad. It meant going down the night before on the luxury coach. It meant looking smart and I did have this smart suit. Or at least I thought it was smart. The other lads had top designer gear, they were immaculate; if they had top cars they also had top clothes. But me—yes I had a suit but it had come from the Grattan's catalogue. The Grattans catalogue is long gone but Grattans was a Bradford firm, employing hundreds of people, and their mail order catalogue was about 1,000 pages thick. You could use it to prop up a car if you had to change a wheel or stand on it to reach a tall shelf. My mother had a job there in the accounts department, and I'd got this great suit, or so I thought, from the catalogue and I was paying for it at something like a pound a week. But when I got on the coach wearing it the lads looked at me wide-eyed. Unfortunately it was far from being stylish in their eyes. It had these great wide trouser bottoms and the jacket had ridiculously wide lapels. They crucified me and told me I looked like Shaft and that was the name they called me all weekend.

Was I bothered? That weekend I had arrived; I'd made it to the first team, albeit as a sub. I loved everything about it, the luxury hotel, the meal, my room, the anticipation the next morning waiting for the game and the trip to The Valley. On the coach I remember having a bag of sweets I passed round. 'At home already,' said Frank

Gray. Just three words that made me feel so comfortable. A young lad, that's all I was, wide-eyed and just so thrilled by the whole thing.

Out onto the pitch for the warm-up I ran, wondering if I'd get part of a game, and then quite surprised and a bit worried when half a dozen lads ran onto the pitch from the Leeds end. They headed for me and there was I wondering what on earth they wanted. And then as they got closer it was a group of my old school pals. I didn't get on the pitch, but the day was made even better by a 3−2 win; I still remember coming back home on cloud nine from just being part of it. If these were labelled 'The Dark Years' at Leeds United I'm not sure why. There were steaks on the way back on the coach. The hotel room, sharing with Dennis Irwin, had been the best. This never felt like a club that was in trouble or broke, even though it was in the Second Division.

It was as sub against Wimbledon on December 1st, '84, that I actually came in and took Peter Lorimer's place. I'd managed to get over a broken leg at the beginning of the season. There were these feisty games of first team against reserves and in one of them I went in hard against John Sheridan. We were close off the field but on the pitch he too could put it about a bit. You would have heard the crack of the bone a mile away. What a dreadful time to suffer an injury like this. I spent 12 weeks in plaster and then more weeks slowly getting back to fitness and catching up. It was agony being on the sidelines watching. Without this injury maybe I might have won a place in the side much sooner. Looking back I can see my progress was a bit like a game of Snakes and Ladders. Up a few spaces and then slide back down again.

What a player John Sheridan was. In these practice games he'd put the ball through peoples' legs for fun. They saw him as the next Johnny Giles. It was just sod's law that I broke a leg at such a critical time of a young career tackling him. Managers need fit players and it put me back to square one in the pecking order. Before all that as a 17 year old I'd played in a testimonial game at Barnsley. Mick McCarthy played for them in those days. He was iron-hard. Even his arms were like tree trunks. All I remember of that one is he nearly broke my jaw with one of them. It was sort of a welcome to football from him as if to say 'there's plenty more where that came from'.

'Good luck son,' Lorimer said as we shook hands as I came on against Wimbledon for the first team at last. Leeds had been one of the first teams to make a ritual of lining up in the centre of the field and then waving to each side of the ground. I'd seen them do that when I was a kid, and then as an apprentice when we watched a first team game. Now I was part of it, at Elland Road, in the track suit. It was a marvellous experience and a 5–2 win. They were no longer enormous crowds like there had been in the glory days but it was still an amazing sight to stand in the middle of the pitch and see thousands of faces and hear the roars and the cheers that were all for you. A Bradford lad with parents who'd come over to England with nothing. I stood there in the centre of all this acclaim and felt like a hero.

But the knee was never right. It was such a stupid, simple injury that happened in a reserve game against Blackburn when I was 18 and playing well. All I did was stand up after a fall to the floor. But somehow in standing up I twisted it. Maybe my studs were caught in the turf. Maybe I turned too quickly before I was properly standing. But immediately the knee came up like a balloon and filled with fluid. There was an operation for a torn cartilage about three weeks after and it was a month before it healed properly. They'd taken me down to Park Row in Leeds to see the consultant. Park Row is an elegant row of buildings in the centre of the city. Going up those steps at that early age all kinds of thoughts went through my head about how serious it might be and whether it could be put right. The surgeon did the operation and I returned to training and fitness, but the knee was never really right even after that. They couldn't get rid of the fluid. The ice packs came out after every game for the rest of my career when the knee never failed to swell up again because there were still bits of cartilage floating around. That was nearly 30 years ago and even today on a bad day it's strapped up.

So all I'd known and learnt so far at Leeds was whilst Eddie Gray was manager. He was one of my boyhood heroes along with Allan Clarke, Mick Jones, Billy Bremner, Tony Currie and Peter Lorimer. Gray was a legend, respected, hugely talented and thoroughly popular. There had been games when he'd torn opposing full-backs to shreds, and a game against Burnley when he'd dribbled through the penalty area beating about seven players and then rifled the ball home. There were other games when the only way to stop him was when he was hacked down mercilessly and kicked black and blue. There was a bit of irony in that; he was on the receiving end of the kind of treatment that Leeds themselves dished out so often. Injuries took their toll on his career. That was the game then, there was so little protection. If you find an old video of the Chelsea v Leeds FA Cup replay at Old Trafford you'll see how bad it could be. It's possible today the game would have to be abandoned with player behaviour as bad as that. At least six players would have been sent off when they deliberately targeted each with the most appalling and cynical challenges. It was as if all they wanted to do was take each other out of the game.

When Eddie took over as manager the club had come down from its pinnacle and by the early eighties was in decline in the Second Division. You could almost argue that the club had never recovered from the ridiculous result of the European Cup Final several years earlier. Jimmy Armfield was manager then. The players liked him but always said of him: 'The manager's indecision is final.' Peter Lorimer said they took terrible liberties with him. But even so, he steadied the ship after Clough's brief reign. The European Cup Final in Paris was the club's swansong. Had they won it, who knows what it might have inspired? Leeds were only the second English club to get that far. It was still Revie's team with the likes of Lorimer, Giles, Hunter, Bremner and Allan Clarke. The Leeds players and the supporters who were there will argue to this day that they were robbed of victory by a referee who denied them at least two penalties. My older brother and sister remember watching the game on television and not believing the decisions that were made. Leeds dominated the game and as well as the penalties had several great chances and near misses. Then when a Lorimer goal was disallowed for offside the fans rioted. After this, Bayern scored twice. Leeds were then banned from Europe for four years, reduced to two. Armfield set about slowly breaking up the ageing team, the first to go being Bremner to Hull City. The decline began. When younger players like Joe Jordan and Gordon McQueen were sold for big fees to Manchester United you knew the club had little chance of maintaining its top position. Allan Clarke left to go to Barnsley as player manager. There was a malaise, things drifted, the heart had gone. It was as much a social club as a football club.

Armfield left, Jock Stein came in and began to gee things up but after not much more than a month left to take over the Scotland job. Next it was Jimmy Adamson. The players jokingly called him

Howard Hughes on account of they never saw him. Before some games it's said he could sometimes be found asleep after a few drinks too many, spark out in a chair in his room. He got them into Europe again in the UEFA Cup but when things became bad after that the fans hounded him and called for his dismissal. The joke that went round was that he was the Yorkshire Ripper. It was the time of the infamous Peter Sutcliffe and the brutal murders of 13 women. The impact in and around Leeds and Bradford was enormous. The streets at night were empty. Women were terrified. The detective in charge was convinced by a hoax tape that the Ripper was from the northeast. The tape was played round various pubs in Leeds by the police who would then ask did anyone recognise the voice. 'It's Jimmy bloody Adamson,' they used to shout back.

Allan Clarke came in, declared himself a winner and said if he did not win a trophy within three years he would be a failure. By now, out of my boyhood heroes, only Eddie Gray and Trevor Cherry were left. Players came and went, things went downhill and at the end of '81–82 United were relegated. Clarke had been a superb goalscorer but as a manager he put the emphasis on defence. It was a club in absolute turmoil with violent fans that caused mayhem on several occasions. And then in came Eddie Gray as manager.

Eddie Gray had his instructions, 'Get back to the First as soon as possible'. The mighty had fallen but a few big names like Frank Worthington, Kenny Burns and Peter Barnes had been brought in. They were pretty much over the hill and Gray was instructed to reduce the wage bill. Wages were high, Barnes was said to be on £1,000 a week, Clarke had spent £900,000 on him; it was wasted money, the debt was growing and attendances were falling. If a manager comes in on a 'high' his job is so much easier, but Gray came in when things were low.

And against all that was a background of supporter hooliganism that was amongst the worst in the country. At Grimsby in the opening game of '82–83 came huge trouble that followed on from incidents at West Brom in the final game of the preceding season. There was serious damage at Blundell Road. As a result the Leeds directors issued warnings of possible fines and even ground closure if behaviour did not improve. The warnings went unheeded. There were clashes with Chelsea fans and then attacks on Kevin Keegan and his teammates. I'd been there watching a game when Keegan had been viciously targeted by the mob. At one point he was felled by something thrown at him and was down for an age with the crowd yelling, 'Keegan's dead, Keegan's dead'. I saw at first hand when we came down to the tunnel from our seats at halftime how thoroughly shocked, shaken and hurt he was.

On November 6th the home programme cover was dedicated to a message for the fans. It pointed out that the future of the club hung in the balance; that this was no idle threat or exaggeration. The hooligans were referred to as the 'scab element', their behaviour labelled loathsome. 'The very existence of Leeds United is now in jeopardy,' it stated.

The FA closed the terraces for the next two games and the rest of the stadium was to be all-ticket. The next attendance of 11,528 was the lowest for 19 years. The attendance at the next game was a miserable 8,741. Other than incidents at Derby County there was very little trouble that season to the relief of all concerned. It re-appeared at Millwall in November '85. Millwall games were made all-ticket after that and Leeds fans were banned from all away games. It was impossible to implement with hundreds of fans still managing to attend games at Carlisle and Wimbledon. The ban was lifted but the all-ticket rule remained.

Some of the big names went in '83–84. Worthington went to Sunderland; what a character with his outrageous clothes and hairstyle. He'd come in wearing Stetsons and cowboy boots. But what he could do with a ball made your eyes water with envy. Trevor Cherry became player/manager of Bradford City. Brian Flynn went back to Burnley. But still there was Kenny Burns, Frank Gray, Paul Hart and Arthur Graham. Eddie Gray began to blood the young lads—but not me yet because of first the broken leg and then the injured knee. Maybe the only thing to write home about was the cup-tie against Arsenal. It was 1–1 at Highbury and 1–1 in the Elland Road replay. The second replay back at Highbury went 2–1 to the Gunners.

Arthur Graham, Kenny Burns and Paul Hart left during the summer and Derek Parlane in mid-season. Some of the players who wanted to leave would sit in the bath singing the old Engelbert Humperdinck song: 'Please release me let me go.' But Peter Lorimer came back. Eddie Gray knew he had all these good kids but no old hand to provide the steadying influence. It was my bad luck he played in midfield. Lorimer had finished playing in Canada but was still tremendously fit. The man was a legend and what an incredible player he still was when witnessed at first hand. The new season started badly and when Chester came and won 1–0 in the League Cup there was real humiliation. The second leg was won 4–1 but to lose 0–1 at home to Chester was rock bottom. In the next round though Oxford hammered Leeds and went through. Lowly Scunthorpe managed by Allan Clarke knocked Leeds out of the FA Cup in the Third Round. This was no longer any fight for promotion, this was a fight against relegation but Peter Lorimer was influential in midfield and the season ended with Leeds 10th on 60 points.

By the end of '83–84 Eddie Gray finally hung up his boots after 550 games and 12 Scottish caps. Without injuries he would undoubtedly have added another couple of hundred games. The new young players he had introduced had done well, with Lorimer keeping me out, and there were reasonable hopes for the next season.

But, the cost cutting continued in 84–85, with Peter Barnes leaving and the coaching staff reduced. I played alongside him in the reserves but he found it difficult to motivate himself. He was a top, top player with superb skills. You saw glimpses but he never did himself justice at Leeds. But at his peak he was everything you need to be as a forward. Leeds went top after winning the first four games. It couldn't last however and there was a lack of consistency. The good football on some days was followed by other games when the youngsters were just outmuscled. There was a real lack of 'beef'. Nevertheless even on the very last day of the season there was still the faint, unlikely, mathematical possibility of promotion. The game was at already promoted Birmingham but there was massive trouble. Leeds fans invaded the pitch when Birmingham scored the only goal of the game. There were confrontations with the home fans who also came on. The teams went off and mounted police broke up the trouble taking 30 minutes to sort things out. The game finished uneasily and a boy died when a wall collapsed under the weight of the supporters. It was as bad a day as any involving Leeds. A total of 96 people suffered known injuries and a staggering 110 people appeared in front of the magistrates. It became known as 'The Battle of St Andrews'.

It was an appalling day but received less than usual publicity because it was the same day as the Bradford City Football Club fire tragedy. It was a game I had planned to go to. I was on crutches with my broken leg and was back home in Bradford while it mended. I'd have been there at Valley Parade, but couldn't get a ticket. Though I didn't know her at the time, my wife Andrea was there. The rest is history. And it probably is true what they say; that everyone in Bradford knows someone who was there that day and died in the inferno. Bradford might be a city, but it was also a small, tight-knit community. The memory of it still reduces people to tears.

As apprentices a few of us would follow Leeds to away games. Four of us including Terry Phelan piled into someone's battered old car and went to Grimsby. The memory remains of the vicious treatment dished out by Leeds fans to Grimsby player Tony Ford. Tony is one of the very few players to have reached the 1,000 game milestone. But as a black player he was the obvious target for abuse. Every time he got the ball, and I mean every time, the catcalls and monkey hoots rained down. The worst were the Heil Hitler chants. Leeds fans had filled the stand where we sat and all of them were on their feet hurling this chant at Tony. Terry and I sat there fully aware that we were two black people as well, feeling like we needed to hide. We felt dreadful. It was one of the worst experiences I have ever had.

Money was still in short supply with nothing to come from the FA Cup in '85 when Everton knocked Leeds out in the Third Round. There was a £5,000 fine that the club could barely afford for the disgraceful scenes at Birmingham. The thugs were back with a vengeance and it continued into the next season '85–86. Frank Gray departed for Sunderland and there was not one win in the first five games. In the next eight there was just one defeat and it seemed that things were improving. Walsall were beaten 3–0 in the League Cup but then Eddie was sacked, the result of the split Board decision. Fans chanted for Gray's re-instatement and the resignation of the chairman. Eddie had served the club for 22 years but 14th place was deemed not good enough. There was no change of heart. The decision changed my whole life.

So, in came Billy Bremner, another legend from the glory days. Bremner immediately replaced Lorimer as captain. In his two spells at the club Peter had made over 700 appearances and scored 268 goals. Lorimer was released and Bremner rang the changes. It was sad seeing Peter hanging round the club but no longer with any purpose or function. He might have been 36 but he could still do a damn good job and we all looked up to him as the elder statesman. Some youngsters that Gray had introduced were now overlooked. We wondered what was going on. Hadn't Lorimer and Bremner been through thick and thin together as teammates? They had played together for 20 years including playing international Scotland games together. They certainly weren't best pals any more. In truth, we were just bewildered young kids baffled by it all.

Against Brighton on December 28th, 1985, I got a second chance with Bremner as manager and I played from the start of the game replacing Peter Lorimer. Bremner must have noticed me playing well in the reserves and in training so here I was actually lining up at the kick-off after the pre game warm-ups and wave to the crowd. You can't describe how it felt. This was Leeds United, the club of Revie and all those triumphs and marvellous players. Looking back now from a safe distance I wonder what that crowd thought of me; a long-legged black kid from Bradford with a giant wet-look perm, I must have looked like one of the Jackson Five. This was the time I did try to copy Jacko. It was around the time of his *Off the Wall* album so I sort of 'borrowed' my dad's dinner suit. Together with a white shirt and black bow tie I looked like MJ on the album sleeve cover. My brothers and sister insisted on a photo-shoot. Now they embarrass me by bringing out that photo on family occasions and having a good laugh.

But now I was part of it; I was inside the bubble that was football. I'd have been heartbroken I guess if I'd known then that it was going to burst. How could Clough have sensed that I would be injury prone? Maybe he saw the way I threw myself around and he put two and two together. This is a kid who will get himself injured a lot the way he plays, he must have thought. Recurring injuries would be the curse that followed me. Play, get injured, play get injured and more often than not play too soon after an injury with a cortisone injection because I was so desperate, too willing to play.

The pitch was icy and rock hard, a player's nightmare. It didn't suit me at all. I was like Bambi on a skating rink. After two minutes I should have scored. It came from a cross from the right hand side as I charged into the box. I met it perfectly and it went like a bullet— just wide. Snodin was on one side of me and Sheridan the other, looking after the rookie.

But then the dream ended. After 40 minutes cursed by another injury I had to come off at half-time. It wasn't the knee, this time it was an ankle. And that was it. Over: my time at Leeds drawing to its end. Bremner was unsure about me and I knew that. There was always a lack of warmth about him. I can't think of any encouraging words I ever got from him in total contrast to Eddie Gray. But in the background I knew that Wolves were watching me.

By now Elland Road had been sold to Leeds City Council for £2.5million in exchange for a 125 year lease. What was supposed to happen after that was an improved stadium and sports complex around the ground. It didn't. Nor were there any real improvements in Leeds' form. In the league there was a 14th place finish with 53 points and yet again in the FA Cup Leeds went out in the Third Round. It was another embarrassing defeat, this time at 4th Division strugglers Peterborough United by 1–0.

The 1986–87 season saw the club have what might be called a resurgence making the end-of-season play-offs and the FA Cup semi-final. But many of the kids introduced by Eddie Gray by then were moved out. Dennis Irwin and Terry Phelan went on to have great careers. Scott Sellars, once fed on brandy and raw eggs before training to build him up, was sold for £20,000 and later returned for £800,000. And as for me: it was the end at Leeds United and the beginning of an odyssey round half a dozen clubs forever struggling with a bad knee.

When a club's manager tells you that you can go, that you are no longer needed, they're the words that hurt and can even destroy. For some there's numbness, the feeling of disbelief, anguish, but above all, failure—'What the hell do I do now? Where do I go?'

Others just feel bloody angry, all that wasted time, all those false hopes. Other people decide where your life and career will lead you. It feels like you're a puppet on a string. Other people have made decisions about you and you have no control.

It doesn't matter if you're 17 or 27 or 37. Maybe at a later age you've planned what to do, maybe you've been careful and put some money aside. Or maybe not, maybe you've spent, drunk, gambled, and enjoyed the good life, the girls, with no thought of the future. Maybe mid-twenties is the worst time, you're in your prime, the world at your feet; there's adulation, the club does everything for you, travel, hotels, you're spoilt rotten. A bad injury then that ends a career is like a knife that suddenly cuts off a leg. Maybe the shock is all the greater if you've been injury free until then. But, one thing's for sure, the younger you are the less thought you've given it. And if you're very young you've given it no thought at all. Everything is ahead, it's all to play for, you dream of the first team, of making it, of playing with the heroes you look up to and watched as a kid just a couple of years earlier.

But when as a youngster you're told you are no longer needed, no longer in the plans, facing the ignominy of being released, that's when a footballer's hopes are shattered. What's it all been for? It's been wasted time, a bad dream, surely they don't really mean it; surely it's a mistake? Blank incredulity, a furrowed brow, staring at the bad news, room spinning round, the light from the window suddenly blinding; it's been a mistake, just hollow emptiness, and you walk out of the room wondering just what's ahead, where the hell do I go from here?

It wasn't quite as bad as that for me in that I was given a choice of what to do, I could stay or go, stick or twist; but it very much amounted to the same—or so it felt at the time. It was just another way for Billy Bremner to tell me I was surplus to requirements.

What Billy Bremner said was simple enough when we met in his office. He was sitting in his big chair and me in another one opposite him with the desk in between: 'You've still got your contract. You can be in the reserve team; you can be in and out of the first team.' He gave me the example of Mick Bates who had been an understudy in the Revie era, a great player but who only got infrequent games. Was that what I wanted? I was only a young lad with no agent and I had this huge decision to make. When I look back I realise now how massive the choice was that I made, at such an inexperienced age.

In other words I could hang around if I wanted to or I could go somewhere else to get regular first team football. That was it. The writing was on the wall clear enough. Young lads like me were just extras. Goalkeeper Mervyn Day was clear enough with his advice; he'd told me a couple of weeks earlier that he knew that Wolves were watching me. 'Go and get first team football', he told me. Brian Little who was at Wolves and Mervyn Day were pals and Wolves' Sammy Chapman had watched me in the reserves. If no-one had wanted me I'd have stayed at Leeds and seen out the contract. But that's how life works isn't it? You base your own decisions on the choices available at the time. Here was a choice of going to Wolves for what I believed would be regular first-team football, or just stay at Leeds and maybe get the odd game.

As I walked out of Bremner's office, by coincidence in walked a Leicester City player, David Rennie. It was like a revolving door. We'd played against each other in reserve games and battered the hell out of each other. Now I was exiting the club as he was coming in. Funny that. If Tony Fawthrop had still been at the club I'd have gone to him for advice but he had left. I didn't talk it through with anyone except one person—dad. 'Stay at Leeds,' he said. But someone I knew at Wolves, Micky Holmes, a mate of mine who was playing there, painted a glowing picture of the place. Unfortunately I believed him. The place in fact was in real decline.

It was a free transfer but not a free transfer. Though I wasn't in their plans, Leeds and Bremner in no way thought I was useless and in the expectation that I'd do well at Wolves and might be sold on, they slapped a sell-on clause on the deal. The perception of a 'free-transfer' is misleading. It doesn't always mean that you are not up to standard. It can mean maybe there's been a fall-out with management and they want rid; it can mean no matter how good you are you are just not in the new man's plans; it can mean that the new man simply wants his own faces in. What it taught me for the first time was that this football road was littered with barriers and hurdles that you don't think are going to be there. From the age of 11 everyone so far has told you how good you are, and that you're going to be a star. You believe them.

Managers have their own ideas and their own favourites. Most managers sell players and later we can all say they should never have gone and what a big mistake it was to sell. But Bremner could argue his changes were a success. Players moved out and players moved in—one of them was Keith Edwards for big money from Sheffield United.

The season was only barely started though when supporter trouble flared again. The FA had lifted the away ticket rule so that when Leeds played Bradford City at The Odsal Stadium the hooligans were not segregated and roamed around causing mayhem. A fish and chip van was overturned and set alight. The ground was emptied and the game finished with an empty stadium.

With me gone, but still following their progress, the season progressed well until a 7–2 defeat at Stoke. Out went Ian Snodin for £800,000 and three more new players arrived with the money. In mid-season it was a gamble but it worked and the gap at the top was narrowed. Not only that, but the Third Round FA Cup pattern was ended and game by game United somehow sneaked into the semi-finals. Thousands were locked out of Elland Road for the fifth round game against QPR and a 1–0 win. The next game was an away-tie at Third Division Wigan. The 2–1 win saw the city come alive with hope and excitement. Leeds in the semis; it was remarkable. The last occasion was ten years earlier. But it was not to be. In extra time Coventry scored the winner. Mercifully there were no crowd scenes.

United won five of the last eight games and finished fourth on 68 points. I sat and thought I could still have been there part of the excitement, but I'd chosen to go. The first play-off game ended in a 1–0 win for Leeds with a late Keith Edwards goal. At Boundary Park Oldham led 2–1 on aggregate with just minutes to go. But again Leeds scored. United hung on in extra time and advanced to meet Charlton Athletic. I was desperate for them to do it. But again, the nagging thought, if only I'd stayed.

A grim game at The Valley ended 1–0 for Charlton. At Leeds it was 1–0 to United. The decider was played at Birmingham and at the end of full-time was still 0–0. In the first half of added time Leeds took the lead but then Charlton scored twice in the final minutes to win the game. It was heartbreaking.

But memories of the glorious past had been stirred. The sleeping giant seemingly had woken up and with optimism high Bremner was given a new extended contract and Leeds became promotion favourites. Of course I wasn't part of it by then; I wasn't part of the end of season thrills and spills, the tension and nerves. Bremner had them within a game of promotion, within a game of Wembley. I watched at Wolves from a distance and wondered about what might have been had I gambled on staying and had still been there. Dad had firmly told me I should stay at Leeds. But headstrong teenagers don't take any notice of their dads do they? I should have listened.

In my own case there was the consolation of knowing I had another club to go to. Sammy Chapman of Wolves had been watching me for a while, so it was to Wolves I went. The wandering had begun. But my heart was at Leeds and when it was clear that I didn't figure in Billy Bremner's plans it hurt. But someone like Dennis Irwin had no club at all to go to and had no idea what he would do. For a while he was in limbo until Joe Royle at Oldham took him to Boundary Park and what a fantastic career he went on to have. Football is like that. Like Dennis you can be discarded heartlessly by one club but then blossom somewhere else. Look at Lee Dixon released by John Bond at Burnley and the career he went on to have, or Martin Dobson released by Bolton as a teenager, David Platt released by Manchester United.

So far three people had left indelible memories on me; Brian Clough, Eddie Gray and then Billy Bremner, the latter for the wrong reasons. Keith Mincher too I suppose because whether or not he was after Eddie's job he was still a damned good coach and taught me so many values. Eddie left me good memories. Clough left me crystal clear memories that are as vivid now as they were 30 years ago. Bremner left the bad ones. Who knows what Clough might have achieved at Leeds had he been just a little less like a bull in a china shop or if he'd had Peter Taylor with him.

One biography of Bremner skates over his time as manager of Leeds in just a few brief pages. I find that odd. *Keep Fighting* seems to gloss over a few things. It's bound to. It's written by a journalist who was a Bremner disciple. It doesn't give the same story that Peter Lorimer described; that when Don Revie left, the job was Johnny Giles' until Bremner intervened and threw his own hat into the ring effectively sabotaging the appointment.

'John Giles was mentioned. I was mentioned,' Bremner wrote. 'Make no bones I wanted it and if they had paired me and John Giles we would have worked wonders.'

I fancy there was more to it than that. It didn't tell the story Johnny Giles tells that after Clough was sacked, he was offered the job again, and again Bremner somehow let it be known he too was interested, so that the offer to Giles was withdrawn again.

Bremner disliked Brian Clough intensely for what he was doing at Elland Road; he thought he was dragging the club to the depths. So the story goes he demanded a face to face, one to one meeting with Clough. Clough, after mocking him and Revie, said he was to meet him on one of the training pitches. And so they met, Clough versus Bremner snarling and lambasting each other. Bremner telling him home truths, Clough exploding like a volcano at Bremner's affront. Spittle was flying from his mouth, said Bremner. They exchanged profanities and abuse. Clough laughed. Bremner walked away. Next, says Bremner, he saw Manny Cussins and clarified what had happened and that Clough was destroying the place. Within days, says Bremner's biographer, Brian Clough was dismissed.

Maybe Bremner's story was true, that Clough could be obsessive, manipulative, aggressive and arrogant but the Cloughie I remember is the dignified person who led us so proudly in Rome and spent a week with us. Whatever: the story portrays Bremner as being the main catalyst for Clough's dismissal. I would have loved to play for Cloughie, another 'if only'.

I suspect it's more than likely that Bremner was sounded out by the directors for the Leeds job before Eddie Gray was sacked. But that's the way football works. The whole thing was a mess though. Rumours flew around. Coach Keith Mincher travelled to Walsall to watch Leeds in a League Cup game, expecting to take over. But if that's the case, then Bremner was in fact second choice and was only offered the job because Mincher was then dropped like a hot potato when the players reacted so badly to the news. Ironically, when Bremner arrived, Mincher was sacked.

The decision to sack Eddie Gray set the club back. The young kids were there ready to come through. And then the Board messed things up. Keith Mincher was producing quality young players. Eddie was nurturing them at the next level. I have always believed that with a little more patience, and given a little more time, Eddie would have found success. There were too many good young players there for things to end in failure; and coming up behind us were David Batty, Simon Grayson and Gary Speed to name but a few. But out went Eddie and in came Bremner. The real life Bremner was never the same as the myth that I grew up with. The hero I saw as a boy was far different years later in the dressing room as a manager.

Years later at Burnley we played an away game at Doncaster when Bremner had returned there. I played a blinder and it was one of those days when you feel like an angel is guiding you through the game. I made a point of going to his office after the game to see him. We chatted. He told me how well I had played and I shook his hand just to remind him of Roger Eli, the bloke he once let go. I didn't need to say any more.

6

The Wanderer

In some ways I wish it had been Eddie Gray who had shown me the door at Elland Road and not Billy Bremner. Eddie had brought me up. I doubt very much he would have recommended any club on such a downward spiral as Wolves. I doubt Billy cared at all which club I moved to as long as I was shifted out. If a new manager comes in very often they can't see further than getting the old out and the new in. A player's welfare is the last thing on their mind. They simply want to surround themselves with the comfort of people they are familiar with or their 'own men'.

How was I to know that Wolverhampton Wanderers was in such a financial mess? Whilst Leeds continued with all their old values, Wolves were on the edge of an abyss. Looking back I might as well have jumped into a large black hole. I knew they'd once been a top side with a great history in that famous old gold strip. But, when I arrived it was a season when the gate for one game was just 1,618. I was signed by Sammy Chapman but then when Graham Turner arrived that was the end for me. In between was Brian Little.

Wolves were a shambles when I joined them on a free transfer in January 1987. It was a total contrast to the comparative five star luxury at Leeds. Nor was it any fun playing at a ground where on one side there was a fabulous new stand but on the other two sides the stands had been closed down. Leeds might have been broke but the players were still well treated. But I'd given that up. Not entirely willingly and to this day there is huge regret at not staying to fight things out. Now I was at a club where the milkman had stopped delivering the milk because of unpaid bills. The club was hanging on by a thread with two sides of the stadium decaying, shabby and condemned. Debts grew and grew. There had been three consecutive relegations in 1984, 1985 and 1986 that saw the club sink into the basement Fourth Division for the first time. Rock bottom came with an FA Cup First Round exit at the hands of non-league Chorley in

November 1986 just before I got there for the second half of the '86–87 season when I played barely more than a dozen games.

The name 'Wolves' might still have been big, but behind it there was nothing. And without a great goal scorer, Steve Bull, they would have struggled even more. Graham Turner signed him and at one point it looked like Turner might have been sacked because of poor results. It was Mickey Holmes who might well have saved Graham Turner's job in his early days when Mick went on to have a magnificent scoring sequence. It might be a record that stands to this day. Had that not happened and Turner been sacked, you wonder if in time honoured tradition a new manager would have shifted Bully out and Steve would then never have become the legend that he did. Later in my career I used to watch videos of Steve before playing a game. He was the perfect role model with his attitude to scoring goals. He was single-minded, determined, physical, willing, and game after game went in where it hurt. People said his first touch wasn't good. But his second touch was deadly and he would have the ball in the back of the net with it time and time again.

There was a near hat trick on my debut. It sounds crazy but to this day I can't believe that I didn't score three in that game. I'd never heard of Terry Hurlock until that game but that was who I was up against versus Brentford. I knew only one way to play and that was to put myself about, get stuck in, make things happen and never worry if I got hurt. Common sense might have told me at an earlier age that this was why I had so many injuries. Terry was likewise. He had various nicknames; 'Gypo' on account of the earring he wore, or 'Animal' due to his wild appearance. At Millwall he was known as 'Warlock'. There's a story that while he was at Millwall he was asked what he would do to Vinnie Jones when they met. Hurlock got up and pulled the nearest door off its hinges. And this was the opponent against whom I played my first Wolves game. The *Times* rated him as the 23rd hardest ever man in football. We lost 1–4.

Sammy Chapman really rated me. I could do no wrong. I only had to pass the ball and he'd say to the other players, 'See that. That's how to do it; that's how you pass a bloody ball.' I used to get ribbed by the others that he was my long lost father. He had the knack of giving praise and compliments. He had a bit of a dispute with a player called David Barnes though. David had been one of the players who had made me welcome at Wolves. Others hadn't.

That's understandable. A newcomer means more competition for places. The dispute was to do with Barnes' contract and he simply stayed away from the club for three weeks and just didn't turn up for training. To our astonishment one day he arrived in the changing rooms and proceeded to get ready. Sammy came in and stared in amazement. Then rage took over as he demanded to know where Barnsey had been for the last three weeks.

Barnsey just looked at him calmly as Sammy ranted at him and when he stopped quietly answered: 'Sorry boss I missed the alarm, it never went off.' It was hard not to laugh or fall about in hysterics and then it got worse as Sammy ordered Barnsey to follow him to the office. 'Walk this way,' he bellowed. But Sammy had a funny walk where his feet stuck out at ten to two which Barnsey mimicked as he walked behind the unsuspecting Chapman. There we were sniggering behind our hands like little schoolboys. It was the first time I'd seen this kind of disrespect shown towards a manager, so different to my Leeds days. Now I was in a dressing room with professionals, several with one kind of gripe or another.

There were several games in which I'd played well, so much so that Sammy Chapman told me that David Pleat was watching me. He was either at Tottenham or Leicester then; I can't remember which, but it was a time when he was a 'name' manager.

I had a really good relationship with Sammy Chapman until he left, and it continued with Brian Little when he took over. Brian had been a great striker but finished early because of injury. You felt he sympathised with anyone who suffered similarly with injuries. Some managers don't and as soon as you're injured they don't want to know. They feel you've let them down and that's why players hide injuries and say they are fit to play. I was certainly one of that group. Once out of a team it's often hard to get back in. Brian was easy to talk to, trained with us and told us stories of his experiences. He made you feel you were valued. If you weren't playing he told you why. But he wasn't there long. It was probably a change of ownership of the club that saw Little dismissed. Change of owner, change of manager, change of manager, change of players; it's one of the laws of football as sure as night follows day. Brian Little was extremely popular and well respected. The news of his sacking affected us deeply and for me it was far from good. I was actually gutted. He got us all together and his voice broke as he told us,

'Thanks lads for everything but I've just been given the old Tommy Tack'. For me it meant back to square one again with a new man to establish a relationship with and to impress. How many times had I already had to do this? It was start all over again.

At Leeds it was the change of manager to Bremner that changed the course of my career. At Wolves it was the change to Turner. I'd only signed an 18-month contract there so it was easy for him to move me on. Had I signed a longer contract the irony is there would have been no money to pay me off and I would probably have been kept on. A broken metatarsal didn't help. That's the bone in the foot that both Beckham and Rooney broke and within a day of their injuries everyone knew what a metatarsal was when it made front page headlines. When I broke mine it was just a little bone that nobody gave a second thought to. I broke it again after having had my foot in plaster for a month so any chance to impress Turner vanished, especially when I broke my nose on the comeback trail. It made me think again about what Brian Clough said about me being injury prone. He must have watched me recklessly throwing myself about and put two and two together.

The broken nose came in a reserve game against Peterborough. Turner was there watching. The defender quite deliberately re-arranged the nose all over my face. It was well and truly splattered. Off I went yet again. But I did something that I rarely did and vowed to get retribution one day. It came when I was at Crewe and this time it was a first-team game against Peterborough. He was there again. I bristled and was determined to catch him. Don't be shocked. It happens. It was the only time I ever did this deliberately. The conditions were damp, grey, greasy, and the pitch was just perfect for the classic, 20-yard sliding tackle that takes man, ball, and half the perimeter wall. They happened all the time in the fifties and sixties. They were part of the game and the reason why full-backs were a feared breed of player. He had the ball somewhere near the touchline and I set off, gathering speed and momentum. The slide was perfect, the impact like an M1 collision. It was out of order, unforgiveable and reckless; but boy was it sweet. He lay in a crumpled heap, hurt and stunned, except he was laid on Dario Gradi's lap in the dugout, not on the floor. Somehow he managed to play on. It was a game and a moment I truly enjoyed. Revenge is sweet.

There was a practice game at Wolves when I did well and Turner came up to me and said a strange thing: 'I don't really know why I'm letting you go; you're actually my best midfield player.'

But it was new broom time and one by one as contracts ended other players were released. How callous football can be. A new manager equals a new pitfall and I have this feeling that too many managers have this idea that players released on what looks like a 'free' by a previous club, can't be any good.

The move to Wolves had a huge impact and career influence. Of course I thought yes I should have stayed at Leeds and hung on there. Football is all about ifs and buts. But if Micky Holmes hadn't gone on a scoring spree in the space of just a few games resulting in a decent run of results it could well have seen Turner sacked at Wolves after he hadn't been there that long. He ended up staying for seven years and took them from the Fourth to the Second Division and also won the Football League Trophy. I'd like to say that Graham Turner was a joy to work with and inspirational. But no, I thought he was just the dourest person you could wish to meet. Football is like a precarious tightrope sometimes. Success and failure are never far apart. Nobody found that out more than me. It's about luck and good fortune. Turner went on to achieve great success but he had his share of luck.

So far I'd had very little. At Chesterfield I was carried off unconscious. It was a bad day all round. I'd driven there with some of the lads. Contrast that with luxury coach transport in the Leeds days and steaks. In the town centre we'd been distracted by a good looking girl that one of the lads spotted. I drove into the back of a car. To cap all that, we lost. Bad luck had a long way to go before it finished with me. Things would get worse.

I left at the end of the season, but had hardly played, and under Graham Turner they had finished in fourth place. In the play-offs they beat Colchester 2–0 on aggregate, 2–0 at Colchester and 0–0 at Wolves. However against Aldershot in the two-leg final, it was a defeat 2–0 away and a 1–0 defeat at Molineux. Close but no cigar as the saying goes.

It was also goodbye to the worst digs I have ever been in. Young lads back in my day at struggling, impoverished clubs had little experience of the pampered, cosseted lifestyle that Premier club kids enjoy today. Stories abound of permanently hungry apprentices and even first team squad players placed in digs that were just appalling.

It happened to me. Times were obviously different in the eighties but it still amazes me that any business would put their assets into such diabolical abodes. I must admit I was spoilt in my early days at Leeds, and I'd lived at home, but the Wolverhampton digs were horrendous. Truth is they were inexcusable.

When I was taken there the first time I half expected to encounter a tramp sitting in the doorway with a battered paper cup asking if I had a spare 10p for a cuppa tea. The bedroom had damp in all four corners, under the window sill, and wallpaper was peeling off all over the place. The house had only one gas fire in the main living room and it was made clear to us that lodgers were as welcome in there as a Blackburn supporter in Turf Moor's Bob Lord Stand. There were no Slade pictures on the wall but the landlady's voice had more than a slight resemblance to Noddy Holder if any lodger dared step out of line. She bellowed with the best of Slade and was more than a little scary. On the first night my roommate Steve Stout warned me that she came up with a mop and bucket to give new lodgers a wash. Having met her I half believed him. She was only contracted to provide breakfast and it was usually disgusting. In the morning you would hear her heavy thudding feet coming up the stairs, the rattle of the door knob, and a tray would be thrust into the room without a hint of a 'good morning'. There was a stained teapot with tea leaves floating all over the place and two chipped china tea cups. The milk was usually on its last legs or off. There would be two of the cheapest and thinnest supermarket teacakes. One day there'd be an inedible greasy sausage each, and on the next some wet cold bacon. Steve and I hardly ever touched any of it but she never got the message. I think we survived on Mars Bars.

There was never a knock on the door when she barged in regardless of what state we might have been in. Steve took particular offence at this and decided we should surprise her so he decided that what she needed to see was a large erection. His theory was that if she was shocked she might learn to knock on the door. So, when we heard the thud of her feet coming up the stairs he threw back the bedclothes and both of us revealed all. In she came, face straight as a poker, slammed the tray down, looked and walked out without any reaction. Our prank altered nothing but then Steve developed a guilt complex and began to worry that she would report us to the club for improper conduct. She eventually did but it was nothing to do with our manhood.

The place was so damp and cold that keeping warm was a real problem. One trick was to use the iron I had to iron and warm the bed sheets immediately before we got in bed and then we'd jump in while they were warm. But as it got colder and colder we both developed chest colds and decided enough was enough when we found icicles inside the windows. So, Steve knew someone who hung around the players' lounge and his trade was industrial heaters. Steve's theory was that they were so powerful that a quick five-minute blast would warm the room to our liking. Somehow we smuggled a heater up into the room and later that night put it on for five minutes . . . and then that became 15 and then 30 minutes until at last we were so warm and drowsy we fell asleep. When she came in the room the following morning with the customary cold bacon sandwiches the blower was still on and the tropical heat must have hit her like a hammer. She gave us the mother of all dressing-downs as she read the riot act. She practically frog-marched us to the front door, and then followed that by throwing out our cases and belongings. Last of all she threw the heater out onto the pavement whereupon it smashed. Steve had to compensate the bloke who had lent it to him. He spent several days on a mate's floor and I went home to Bradford to stay and drove to Wolverhampton every day for training.

I didn't tell my parents what had happened and said I was waiting to move somewhere else—which was true enough because the club found us another place with a wonderful couple, Jack and Olive Carr, who were Wolves daft. They were like the grandparents I never had because my real ones were back in Dominica and I never ever saw them. They constantly spoiled us. When we got back from training there'd be a cup of tea. The meals were enormous. Jack had once been a farmer and loved his food. He had the habit of standing with his back to the fire telling us stories until one day when the fire was full on there was the smell of singed corduroy and then suddenly he was hopping round the room with his trousers nearly on fire.

Goalkeeper John Burridge had once been there and Jack used to tell us how they'd move all the furniture and then Jack would throw oranges for John to 'save'. All the players at Wolves knew them and this lovely couple would spend hours at the training ground enjoying watching us. But when the management changed, the new regime told them they were unwelcome. They were heartbroken.

On the off chance that any other footballer from my era, or before, reads this he will know full well that these things happened and will have their own stories to tell of life in digs when they were young lads. We had great fun much of the time, but it was no joke if your digs and landlady were a nightmare and you lived perpetually cold and hungry. And that's before you even mention the problem of having to use an outside lavatory in the pitch black and pouring rain at night when you were taken short. Peeing in a bottle was the answer to that problem.

From Wolverhampton the record books say I went to Cambridge; that was in '87. It was the nearest I ever got to university. I was there just long enough to unpack and didn't even play a proper game. I was only there on trial with seven or eight other hopefuls looking for work during a trial month. How do you psyche yourself at a time like this? It seemed only months had gone by since I'd had steaks on the luxury coach returning from Charlton with the Leeds team, with what I thought was a bright career in front of me. Now here I was scrapping for a poorly paid job if I was lucky at Cambridge along with the other hopefuls. Where had it gone wrong?

Cambridge was a lovely place and I might have discovered more of it if I'd been there long enough. Sneeze and I'd have missed it. All that Cambridge wanted were six or seven non-contract players on the cheap because like most lowly league clubs they were broke. I met Cambridge fan Mark Saggers who went on to become a respected broadcaster.

Somehow after that, I ended up in Cyprus for a month at a club where Mick Ferguson was manager. When I landed at the airport there were the usual long queues at passport control. Mick and the club chairman marched me to the front to the annoyance of everyone there. The heat was so great however that we could only train in the evenings. The idea of sun, sea and sand sounds marvellous, I thought. But I couldn't speak the language and for most of that month I was so bored I just had to tell Mick I can't do this. So I was back at home yet again.

Then I got to wondering. I wanted more than this. I wanted some certainty, some kind of contract. I got in touch with Sammy Chapman again, obviously no longer at Wolves and asked him could he help to fix me up somewhere by putting a good word in at Crewe where Dario Gradi was manager. The knee was still bad but I played through the pain and the discomfort. Football was all I knew and all I wanted. I clung to the hope and dream that I would be taken on and given a shirt, a contract and even a first team place. Gradi did take me on even though again it was initially on trial after the new season had already started in '87.

So Crewe was better. This was '87–88 and 27 games. Funny how things work out; I shared a large old Victorian house with three other lads there, paid for by the club so at least it didn't eat into the meagre wage. I was pretty much the serious, sensible one. One of them was David Platt, (yes *that* David Platt), who went on to great things of course. Another was Wayne Goodison. Another, Aidan Murphy was the fourth of the Crewe Musketeers.

Life was good at last. What a mix we were and because we were 'footballers' we were quite a catch for any girl who wandered by. A lot of them knew this was a footballers' house and came by looking up at the windows hoping for a glimpse of one of us. A footballer is a footballer whether he plays for Crewe or Real Madrid. Footballers have a reputation for giving a girl a good time. These girls thought we were loaded—in all areas.

It was Aidan they usually saw. He was an insatiable sex machine. Sex was like food to him, or petrol to a car. Without it he couldn't function and would feel faint.

'An apple a day keeps the doctor away.' Or with Aidan it was a woman a day keeps the doctor away.

You'd be sitting reading the paper or having a cup of coffee and then you'd hear his bedroom window open. You groaned. You knew what was about to happen. You knew the words that would be shouted down as he leaned out of the window.

'Fancy a brew love?' Oh God, the trap was laid. If I hear those words today I immediately think of Aidan, who was, by the way, a great footballer.

All the girls who wandered by knew what those words meant. If they didn't, they soon found out. They'd get a brew alright but not straightaway. How many times did he lure a girl into the house with this simple opening line? Most blokes approach a girl in a bar, or a night-club or on the dance floor. Not Aidan he hung out of that window and reeled them in. He might as well have had a fishing

99

rod. We stopped counting the catches.

He was all smiles when a girl came in. The routine was always the same. Up the stairs they'd go . . . a bit of giggling . . . the door opening . . . the door slamming shut . . . more muffled giggling . . . ooooh Aidan . . . a bit of silence . . . and then the noise . . . oh God the noise . . . bed creaking . . . headboard slamming the wall . . . bang . . . bang . . . bang . . . moans . . . groans . . . ooohs . . . ahs . . . silence . . . and then conversation . . . fancy a brew love . . .

It was almost embarrassing. One or two were regulars. Young footballers swap stories and we got everything in graphic detail from him. You wondered how the human body could do all this so regularly.

It was Platty and Wayne who did all the cooking. Aidan and me did all the cleaning. It was, in fact, believe it or not, a well run house. Just once I cooked a meal and decided to do corn beef hash. It was a disaster and in fact made me so ill I missed the next game. If I wasn't injured I was food poisoned. You couldn't make it up.

Platty had a nice girlfriend from a well to do family. They had an enormous, grand house. On occasions we'd all go up there quite in awe of everything to do with it. Platty was quite at home but the rest of us felt like three urchins going up to the 'big house' in the olden days and having to touch our caps. Platty was always on pins when we went up that we'd show him up. The place was filled with antiques. It was his worst nightmare that we'd send one or more of them crashing to the floor. We did try to behave and sat nicely and quietly with our hands folded on our laps.

I shudder to think now what went on in that house in Crewe. It was bit like *Men Behaving Badly*. We could have called it The House of Pleasure. Years later Wayne got married and Platty was best man at his wedding. Trouble was, his best man's speech was so risqué, so cringe worthy and embarrassing, that it made the red top Sundays the next day. Now Wayne had a brother, Steve, and that brother was a teacher at a little school in South Leeds. And who was the headteacher of that school? Talk about coincidences, only Dave Thomas the person working on this book with me. Dave nearly rolled off the chair with laughter when I told him the best man's speech story because he remembered how embarrassed his deputy had been after the wedding.

'Bloody hell, I remember it,' Dave said. 'His brother Steve was my deputy head. I remember he came in on the Monday morning with the *Mirror* or *People*, I can't remember which, and proceeded to tell me about Platt's speech and how the guests didn't know which way to look and just shuffled and wriggled about in embarrassment and disgust. He said it was awful and had ruined the wedding. I tut tutted and sympathised with him and said people would soon forget. But, truth is, I thought it was hilarious and the minute he left the office I just fell about laughing.'

Dario Gradi was a believer in proper football and the passing game. Don't think I couldn't play football and was just a get stuck-in character. I'd been brought up properly at Leeds and had never forgotten what real football is all about. So Dario put me in midfield.

He called me into the office one morning and asked if I had a problem with the knee because he'd seen me icing it. I must have mumbled something but I never told him how bad it was. I hid it, said it was just a bit stiff, or I'd been kicked. How could I tell him it was really quite bad? Back at Wolves they'd given me a medical but I got through it because it wasn't that rigorous. There are all kinds of funny stories about the crudeness of medicals. I'd heard that at Burnley one new player was given a medical by their medical man, Doc Iven, and it entailed running up and down a flight of stairs. He passed. Afterwards when he played his first ever game they realised he was crocked. One of the directors was scathing and asked since when has football ever been played on a flight of stairs.

Dario didn't miss much though and had seen that I avoided striking straight through the ball which simply means you avoid using the front of the boot. You use the instep. If I hit a shot with the front of the foot I felt it right through the knee. The knee problem had changed all the dynamics of how I ran and struck a ball. I had a badly sprained ankle while I was there. I kept quiet. I bought my own strapping and played on through the pain. Boots the Chemists were thinking of giving me an award for being their best customer.

Crewe offered me a two-year contract but the money wasn't good and I kept stalling. It was another crossroads choice. Eventually they stopped asking and I was playing game to game without any contract. Again it's funny how life works out. If I'd said yes to the two years, the sensible thing to do, the career path would have been altered and it would never have led to joining Burnley.

York was next. 'This is getting worrying,' I thought. All I was doing was just fumbling around in the lower leagues. I used to wonder how it had come to this. And the worst was yet to come — Bury and Northwich Victoria, bloody hell. York was '88 and you could count the games I had there on one hand. What have Crewe and York got in common? They both have big railway stations and at both I was just passing through. I began to wonder if something was wrong. Was it my face? In fact my mum once said to me, 'Doesn't your face fit?'

Had I said something? The manager was John Bird. I lived in Bradford and drove over every day. It was a case of go anywhere to try to carry on and stay in the game. I wasn't ready to call it a day. There was always the thought in the back of my head that if I could just get rid of the injury, get a good run of games somewhere, I'd be OK. But it was only another trial period at York with no firm promise of anything. There were four games and one goal. But in the last one I was sent off, a red card for an incident with Steve Harper who was then at Port Vale. Our paths would meet later at Burnley, both of us in the victorious team of '91–92. But this time we had a set-to. The consequences were dramatic for me. With a three game suspension and no contract John Bird thought what's the point of him being here? And that was the end of that and it seemed like the bottom of the well for me.

If there was a low point that was it. If there was frustration I felt it. If there was depression I experienced it. If there was a sense of hopelessness it was then. For the first time I thought, 'This is it, football is finished for me.' I actually had tears in my eyes. From Leeds United to being rejected by York, it could get no more humiliating than that. Who the hell were York City? I doubt I could have felt more dejection. By then Dennis Irwin, John Sheridan, Scott Sellars and Terry Phelan, the lads I had grown up with at Leeds were all doing well and were established at their clubs. But me: I felt I was on the scrapheap, finished, just drifting without any idea what to do or where to go next. This was the world of football. There were hundreds like me.

It was a time of thinking about all kinds of things and the things I had been through to carry on playing, and wondering if it was worth it. Endless visits to physios whether they were club physios like Geoff Ladley at Leeds or private ones that I went to and paid for myself. I'd tried herbal remedies, and made dressings with comfrey. Much later I would even try a hypnotist. The ice packs were automatic. The swelling was part of my routine. I'd played games against advice to hide the situation. I'd endured pain and more pain. As a player I'd never shirked, trained properly, always given 100%, never held back from any tackle. With all that going through your mind, you ask why me? Why haven't things worked out? Where has it all gone wrong? Am I just not good enough? Do I not deserve better; do I not deserve just a little bit of luck for once? For luck is such an essential part of any football career; the luck of being with a good manager who has you in his plans, and the luck of keeping clear of injury.

Not many years later after I'd been named Player of the Season, and voted scorer of Goal of the Season by Burnley supporters, came the occasion that coach Harry Wilson told me as we were coming off at halftime, in a reserve game, that I had no heart. Everything I'd endured and battled through flashed into my head. Me: no heart, I couldn't believe what I was hearing. He'd actually grabbed hold of me while he said it. Me: no heart, I was totally incensed and would be today if anyone said that to me. Heart was what got me through games; heart was what kept me going when I thought I'd hit the bottom at York.

What did he mean? Was it an unintended reference to racial stereotype; black players are soft, black players can't stand the cold, black players give in when the going gets tough? Whatever he meant I was utterly infuriated and feel fury even today.

But after the ignominy of being released by York City, next up was Bury in '88–89 for just 2 games. Martin Dobson was manager; Frank Casper was there as his assistant and by great good fortune remembered me later when he was manager of Burnley. I could never quite work out Martin Dobson. The only thing I vividly remember is being balled out when I arrived late one day. Driving over from Bradford, the day was bound to come when traffic hold-ups would have me stuck in a queue. The day arrived and when I eventually got there I went into the team meeting to be yelled at: 'GET OUT.' From there it was out to Northwich on loan. So I couldn't work out was he trying to make me or break me; if it was the latter, why? If there was another low spot this was it. How can you not think about how it all started earlier at Leeds, a rising young star, everything ahead of me, good prospects, surrounded by great players and so much to learn and look forward to. And then years later you find yourself at Northwich bloody Victoria. I felt like I had my tail between my legs for some reason, feeling that I was being made an example of, scrapping for a low paid contract.

Money now was in fact a problem. I hadn't any. There was nothing spare to get new tyres for the car. By now the Capri had gone. I had a Cavalier. It must have had 100,000 miles on the clock as I'd done so much travelling driving backwards and forwards. The Cavalier, me and my Adidas Sports bag were inseparable. The Adidas bag was almost my home. In spite of the mileage the car was always clean and polished. Everything was absolutely immaculate except for one thing; well four to be precise. The tyres were absolutely bald. It was Kenny Clements at Bury who came in one day and looked at me with a horrified face. 'Roger,' he said, 'have you seen the state of your tyres?' I hadn't. I'd never given it a thought. Never even noticed that they were utterly, totally bald, in fact almost worn through. But tyres and age apart it was a class car. I've always liked my motors.

The recall coincided with Martin Dobson being sacked. Sam Ellis then got the job. It all left me in limbo with no part in anybody's plans. But Frank Casper who had joined Burnley, got wind that I was free via Dave Robinson, Liam Robinson's father. Liam too, my old school pal, would later join Burnley. Frank remembered me.

So, just as I was beginning to think nobody likes me, nobody cares, I landed at Burnley in 1989. It was timely. I could get four new tyres on the old Cavalier. My life changed forever. Truly it is no exaggeration to say nothing was ever the same after that. It was like I'd found my home and the place I belonged. I arrived there thanks to the fact they had no money and wanted cast-offs. If you cost money they couldn't afford you. I was the perfect fit. If they wanted someone really good they went to Poundstretcher. The minimum football wage had been abolished in 1961 but it looked like no-one had told them at Burnley. We joked they had one light bulb that they took from room to room to save electricity. It wasn't that long since one of the players had driven the club coach. There was the story that NORWEB had threatened to come in and cut off the electricity one Tuesday. What made it worse there was a game that night. So one of the directors came in, ordered everybody out and locked the ground so that NORWEB had no access. The takings from the game paid the electricity next day. Maybe it's a bit of a mythical story but if it were true it wouldn't surprise me.

Frank had been given the Burnley job ahead of bookies' favourite Martin Dobson. Dobbo had blotted his copybook by touting his services to clubs bigger than Bury where he'd had some success. Way back then, believe it or not, this was considered unprofessional. Today nobody would bat an eyelid; in fact an agent would do it for him. As a result he was sacked. Although my stay at Bury was brief I had got to know Frank well. He was warm, but calm and collected, always ready to pass on his striker experiences to you. I took to him and I felt he took to me. He sometimes wore a stylish Fedora. I liked that.

Mick Docherty, his assistant, was another warm and jovial character and his knowledge of the game was second to none. He was arguably one of the most passionate football people that I can remember. So much so that at half-time in one game he was so angry he had himself in tears of rage. The players sat and looked in astonishment. But the lads responded as we went out and got a draw in an FA Cup game against Scunthorpe.

My goals helped win Burnley a promotion so you could joke that the long road back to the Premiership season with Owen Coyle, dated back to the day I arrived. It's funny how things work out. When York told me I was not needed I was in the depths of despair. At Northwich I just felt what am I doing here? It was like playing in a fog. But what lay ahead would be the best two and a half seasons of my career.

You never know in football what's waiting for you. For me it was Frank Casper who was just around the corner.

7

The Eli has Landed

I thought maybe Frank Casper should have played me more. He had already been acting manager at Burnley in 1983 for a short spell. In 1989 he had been appointed again but at a time when there was little money and Burnley were just floundering around. We all knew he'd been a superb player, deft and skilful, yet still hard as nails. He had to be. In the late sixties and until the mid seventies when he plied his trade the treatment forwards got was brutal. He was a member of the team that is still remembered in and around Burnley; 'the team of the seventies' as it was known, except that it never got the chance to remain together. So, for that reason we admired him and we knew he had scored some great goals. His other claim to fame was that he was the first player that Burnley had bought for years. They just didn't buy players; they grew their own. But the production line was diminishing and Frank was 'discovered' at Rotherham. For £30,000 they snapped him up. From that point on he was to work for the club on and off for over 20 years. That too was another reason why he had our trust. He was Burnley through and through. Just before re-joining Burnley he had been assistant manager at Bury and of course that's where our paths met. For two years Frank did his best to get Burnley to where he wanted them to be. But fans are notoriously short on patience and eventually turned on him. Jimmy Mullen, then his assistant, would eventually replace him; and then he too would finally suffer from the wrath of the fans when he could not sustain his success rate and there was a miserable relegation.

For his first full season Frank recruited a number of new players; me, John Deary, Peter Mumby, Tony Hancock and a player who had been at Burnley before, Joe Jakub. Tony Hancock was a character. He was 6' tall with shoulder length hair and two large pirate-style earrings in each ear. He was forever telling stories about the days when he used to drive HGVs and all the antics he got up to in the cabin. Andy Farrell signed a new contract although he had earlier said he wanted to leave. Tommy Docherty was added to the scouting staff. His son Michael was Frank's assistant. Early results were good even after a first day defeat at awful Rochdale thanks to an own goal. Spotland then was the pits. A ground that was falling down and Rochdale were very much the butt end of club comedians' jokes. And they beat us. It doesn't get much worse than that especially in front of a huge following of your own fans in the away end. I played in that game but the rest of the season it was in and out, in and out; in the league there were just 24 appearances plus five as sub. It was a poor season for all of us, chairman, manager, players and supporters with a final position in the league of 16th.

Ron Futcher had been drafted in to solve the goalscoring problems. Supporters christened him 'Rocket Ron' on account of his 'speed' or lack of it as the case may be. It was a name that annoyed him even though it was bestowed affectionately. £65,000 was a lot to pay for a cash-strapped club like Burnley. Thanks to Ron we progressed to the second round of the FA Cup. For the previous four years Burnley hadn't got past the first round, a sad testimony to how low they had sunk.

It took three games to get rid of Scunthorpe in the second round. Frank won the toss to stage the second replay at Turf Moor and I scored twice. In fact it was a goal from me in the first replay that led to the third and deciding game. The win cheered up the supporters by now fed up with the autumn slump in the league. The Scunthorpe games changed the course of my career. It was a twist of fate and changed things dramatically for me.

The strangest thing happened though. We trained for the game and then with Peter Mumby I drove home before coming back in the evening to the ground. On the way home I drove over a black cat. Amazingly it was unharmed and as I looked in the rear mirror to see if it was laying in the road, to my astonishment it was running away. The cat was certainly lucky. It must have brought me some much needed good luck as well. I had a storming game that evening and for the next couple of years everything seemed to go my way.

It had been a gamble by Frank Casper to throw me up front as an out and out striker. 'Can you do a job for me up front?' Frank asked. 'Make a nuisance of yourself?' Yes I could do a job and grabbed the chance. It was as if playing up front freed me from the shackles of playing a more defensive role. It was a move from being destructive to constructive. I doubt Frank could believe the result of his request.

'ROGER AND OUT': said the headline after the 5–0 demolition in the second replay. Stand-in striker Eli's scourge of Scunthorpe: it makes nice reading 20 years later.

'Two-goal hero Roger Eli played through the pain barrier last night as Burnley won through to the third round of the FA Cup in stunning style for the first time in five years. Stand-in striker Eli, who scored the Clarets' first goal in last Tuesday's first replay against Scunthorpe, proved an instant hit when he netted twice last night. The summer signing also set up another goal for his co-striker Ron Futcher that sparked a devastating three goals in three minutes either side of the interval. And Burnley boss Frank Casper revealed later: 'Roger has been playing with a niggly knee injury for a while. He's the type of player who will carry on without saying anything and sometimes you have to pull the reins back a bit. That's why we took him off towards the end last night.' Eli received a standing ovation as he left the field.'

Frank was right about the 'niggly knee injury' and I did keep quiet about it inasmuch as I never used it as an excuse. It was there. It wasn't going to go away. All I could do was make the best of it and minimise it—and get out the ice pack yet again. That's what you do when you're desperate to play. A few days later there was even a Roger Eli mini feature in the press; fame at last.

Roger Eli's success as a makeshift striker will come as no surprise to one past master of the art of goalscoring. Sniffer spotted his goal talent. Former Leeds United and England ace, Allan Sniffer Clarke signed Eli on as a hitman during his spell as manager at Elland Road. But persevering with Eli as a striker was a bit of a tall order for Eddie Gray, who followed his former Leeds teammate into the Elland Road hot seat.

'Eddie turned me into a defender because I wouldn't stop growing,' explained Eli.

But the former Wolves, Bury and Northwich Victoria utility man has found a niche for himself up front again at Turf Moor after being thrown on as an emergency partner for Ron Futcher in the FA Cup-tie against Scunthorpe. Eli and Futcher hit it off immediately and have notched six goals between them in the three games they have played together since Eli came on for the injured Peter Mumby that fateful night at Turf Moor and went on to score Burnley's goal in a 1–1 draw. He scored two more in the second replay against Scunthorpe and laid one on for Futcher who also claimed a brace that night, as Burnley romped to a 5–0 win. Eli also had a hand in Futcher's first league goal since his arrival at Turf Moor in the 2–1 win over high-riding Carlisle on Boxing Day.

'I'm enjoying it,' said Eli. 'It's great playing alongside an experienced professional like Ron. We get on well together on and off the field and I just hope we can keep the goals coming and keep the partnership going. But quite honestly I am happy to play anywhere as long as I am in the side.

For the first time ever I'd heard a crowd chanting my name. Roars of 'Eli, Eli, Eli,' rolled down from the terraces. It was the first time I'd experienced anything like it. With mass chanting like that I felt like a gladiator. Commercial manager Joyce Pickles had Roger Eli T shirts produced. I still have one. 'Clarets secret weapon' it says on the front. But the picture of me was so unflattering I looked like a criminal.

But Chairman Frank Teasdale got a rough ride from supporters. He was a true Burnley supporter with claret and blue blood but he took some flak for the club's demise over the years. In truth the club had been dying since before he took over as chairman but supporters need someone to kick and in this case, it was Frank. He had, and still has, some awful stories of the abuse he suffered. Fans saw it as his fault that the club had no money. Players aren't always sympathetic in situations like this. He was good company off the field but in the boardroom he was a businessman and it always seemed to us he had a hard streak when it came to settling players' wages.

Four league wins had generated some excitement. Frank Casper was brave and splashed £90,000 on striker John Francis. I wondered what the impact would be on me. At the same time Chairman Frank lashed back at his critics telling them to get off his back and let him do the job, reminding fans of the mess the club had been in three and four years earlier. That had been a time of John Bond, John Benson, relegation, Chairman John Jackson. It lead up to Frank Teasdale taking over as chairman and having to endure the worst day of his life when in the last game of the season in '87 Burnley beat the Orient to stay in the league.

Two things collapsed in March. First, local man Graham White and Colne Dynamo boss finally pulled out of any attempt to ground share and bring much needed money to the club. And secondly the team just about collapsed. Between then and the end of the season there was just one win. I played in most of those games. It was grim with a dissatisfied, grumbling crowd who by then were well and truly fed up. There were rarely more than a few thousand and they'd had years of this. The atmosphere at the ground was dead. The most frequently used word was 'inept'. A poem did the rounds of supporters and appeared in fanzines.

The lad stood by the pearly gates,
His face was worn and old,
He stood before the Man of Fate,
For admission to the fold,
'What have you done?' St Peter asked, 'To gain admission here?'
'I've been a Burnley fan,' the lad replied, 'For many and many a year.'
The pearly gates swung open wide,
St Peter tolled the bell,
'Come in,' he said, 'and choose your harp, you've had your share of hell'.

Nevertheless I carried on playing as best I could, wanting the crowd to see me doing my best, doing my damnedest to gee things up, to get things going, to bring a spark to the team, to get a result. I didn't want the Eli chants to stop. I had grown to like them and wanted to respond and earn any praise I got from supporters. Supporters don't grumble at players who always give 100%. I saw supporters who were passionate. It was the least I could do to show it myself.

But after one game, over 500 fans demonstrated outside the ground. It was all aimed at Frank Teasdale and the Board. They were utterly fed up and wanted change, whether it was the Board, chairman or manager. Frank fired back again and told them that he, the Board and the manager would not surrender to the 'foul abuse' and that it was just disruptive. This might have been the game where fans embarrassingly chanted 'Eli for manager, Eli for manager'. I'd scored a few goals and they'd taken to me. As the fans demonstrated on Harry Potts Way after the game, the police kept us and the wives back. Some wives began to worry. 'We'll be alright,' said my partner Andrea tongue in cheek. 'Roger's going to be manager.'

Frank Casper meanwhile argued that it took time to sort out a team. It took time to get rid of players that he didn't want and then bring in the ones that he did. He told fans that within 12 months they would be completely sorted out. Players of course were aware of all this unrest. There had been some turbulent months and some ugly demonstrations and chanting. Of course it filtered through to the players and put pressure on us. Don't ever think that players are immune to it and just count their money on the way to the bank— not that Burnley players at this time ever had a lot to carry there in the first place.

Despite all the shenanigans in the background, at boardroom level and noisy demos in car parks I was more than happy to sign a new contract. Some security and a regular wage was a decent prospect, plus I'd regained all my enjoyment for the game:

Utility player Roger Eli is set to sign a new contract with the Clarets. Eli signed in the close season as a free agent after spells with Leeds, Wolves, Cambridge, Crewe, York and Bury, has had preliminary talks with Burnley boss Frank Casper about new terms after a series of impressive performances in recent games.

The boss has had me in and told me he is going to offer me a new contract but I have not signed one yet. My present one-year contract runs out in the summer and I am just waiting to go back in and see the boss,' said Eli. 'I would be more than happy to stay here at Burnley. Things have gone well and the fans have been great with me.'

I never liked the description 'utility player'. Exactly what did it mean? I thought it was almost demeaning. The demonstrations were frequent, the abuse hurled at Frank Teasdale incessant. During a game at Peterborough on the field we could hear the chants: 'Teasdale out, Teasdale out.'

Headlines like 'Sad Clarets' and 'Shambles at the Shay' were typical. But a footballer can only do his best. I knew I did mine. When the offer came of a new contract, despite the troubles, I signed. I'd played 30 games, the fans had taken to me, I'd struck up a good partnership with Ron Futcher up front, but when needed, I could play anywhere. Truth is I was more than happy. I'd wandered around for the last few years but felt now I'd found a club where I could do something. I knew I could score goals. I knew I could perform as long as my knee held up and had no bad luck with other injuries. I'd felt despair in that month at Cambridge. I felt I was messed around at Bury. But now, things looked really bright.

The next season, 1990–91, was the one of course where we came so close to automatic promotion but then blew it in the final games with a defeat away at Maidstone and only a draw against Rochdale. The only real additions to the squad had been centre-back John Pender and striker John Francis who were great acquisitions. Before that Frank Casper had suffered a blow when his assistant Mick Docherty left to join Hull City. But in came Jimmy Mullen just sacked at Blackpool to replace him. It's funny how things work out. Life I think is sometimes just a chapter of accidents. Stan Ternent wanted Mick to join him at Hull, so by chance a vacancy arose for Mullen to fill. Frank spoke to a number of people but chose Jimmy. Fate you might say. Jimmy then eventually gets two promotions for the club. Meanwhile I missed the first games of the season, not because of the knee, but with groin and stomach problems that were a carry-over from the previous season. Twisting badly in pre season work had aggravated them. Clough's words came back again, 'That lad will be injury prone'. Sometimes I sat and cursed my luck but so far had always bounced back.

Our paths crossed again years later when Burnley played Forest in the League Cup. It was a two-leg tie. My reaction was predictable; 'Brian Clough again,' I smiled to myself. An echo from the past, an ironic reminder of younger teenage days when there was everything in front of me, not a care in the world and no thoughts yet of a bad knee, endless frustration, operations, pain and ice packs. The first leg was at the City Ground. It was a strange feeling going out onto the pitch. There he was, large as life, green baggy sweater but the face redder and showing signs of strain. I'd sat there in the dugouts before, even sat alongside Clough in complete awe of him when he had the youths by the pitch during first team games. Memories of the trip to Rome came back and made me smile wistfully. What might have been? You could get quite hung up about it if you weren't careful. If only . . . It would have been good to start the game but I didn't. Good to play a blinder, show Cloughie what I could do, or what I could have done for him.

When the Burnley coach pulled up at the stadium for the first leg, a few memories came back. What would I do or say if I actually bumped into Cloughie face to face? But it didn't happen. I'd spent a fair chunk of my time there and rubbed shoulders with people like Martin O'Neil and John Robertson. But the dugout was where I started the game. With John Francis's arrival for £90,000 he was clearly going to be first choice. A £90k buy takes precedence over a free transfer as a matter of course. The 4–1 scoreline to Forest didn't reflect how well Burnley played despite being down to ten men when Steve Davis was sent off. I got 15 minutes on the pitch. Would Clough remember me? Could I score a goal to nudge his memory? It's hard to say what thoughts went through my head as I ran on. The last time in front of him I'd scored twice in a Junior Final. Maybe instead of playing against Roy Keane in this game if life had turned out differently I'd have been playing alongside him and Brian Laws and Des Walker. Des and I had been in the same youth side at Forest and then we went different ways. Des and I were the double of each other in appearance; it was uncanny but that's where any similarity ended. While he was at Sampdoria I was at non-league Northwich. It's all ifs and buts. If Bremner had been a different kind of manager . . . but he wasn't . . . I'll always think I was good enough to have played for him. After the game we chatted about the old times but even with his high profile status he was still the same level headed person. On the journey home there were more thoughts, not regrets, but possibly tinges of what if. But then you shrug them off. What else can you do? You move on.

Following the game, Cloughie was Cloughie, threatening to take legal action against Burnley because of comments made about the heavy tackle by Stuart Pearce on David Hamilton that put him out of action for months. I was in the dugout but even though the tackle was on the far side of the field I could still see David go flying up into the air. His leg was in plaster from toe to groin. He fancied himself a bit as a hardman but Stuart Pearce was formidable. He used to have his shorts rolled up so that you saw thighs the size of tree trunks. The power in his tackles was unbelievable. If he went through you it was like being hit by a ton of concrete.

It was also during this season I had a first encounter with the legend that was Billy Whitehurst. It was away at Doncaster and they also had a player called Brendan Ormsby who had been at Leeds. I had a real old fashioned ding-dong with both of them and on one occasion I was clean through.

'Don't let that bastard score,' Ormsby yelled at Whitehurst. For some reason; maybe I'd wound him up, Whitehurst decided he wanted me that day. I took him on. Nobody ever fazed me in a game. If someone whacked me then I whacked them and I was well skilled in the art of winding people up. That was what you had to do if you didn't want to spend a game being intimidated—retaliate first as the saying goes.

What makes a hardman? I grew up with David Batty at Leeds; he was a couple of years below me. As a kid you would never have known how tough he would become. But off the field he was a quiet placid lad. I guess I was hard but didn't flaunt it or deliberately present it as an image. It was just me because no-one frightened me. I knew how to do anything to get an advantage and was no stranger to winning free kicks. I knew how to fall to make a tackle look like a foul. Some clubs teach players to do this or at least they did do. I assume they still do it today. If a player was kicking me I'd quietly tell him I'd dive and get him booked if he didn't stop. Blackpool had a player called Garry Briggs. Briggsy knew how to dish it out and I was on the receiving end so much so that when he didn't heed the warning, yes, I got him booked. Their manager Billy Ayre yelled at me that I was a cheat.

But I never saw it that I was a cheat. You do what you need to do to get the advantage with a little bit of gamesmanship. You're there to win. Otherwise, why play? It's another football rule as well; it's only a foul if the referee sees it. You don't worry if you do something naughty and get away with it. And what is a cheat anyway? Is it someone who feigns injury to get someone sent off? Is it someone who deliberately gets someone sent off? Yes there were the occasions when I tried to get someone sent off but I always warned them first to stop their bad tackling on me and it was only when I felt I was getting no protection from a referee. In that respect I only saw it as self-defence.

Oddly enough when Jimmy Mullen became manager he took me to task during a game at Walsall for being too physical. My style was simple enough. Run, chase, harry and upset the other players but all that was mixed up with skill as well. I could easily mix it and stick my foot in but always walked off the pitch at the end with no hard feelings—unless it was Big Billy Whitehurst. I knew my limitations.

But: I never deliberately set out to injure anyone. Hurt yes, but not put out of the game. These are people with families and mortgages. But that's how Mark Monington's career was ruined. He started at Burnley as a junior in 1989 the same year I arrived. He had everything and was destined to become a top player in the Premier League had his progress continued. I was five yards away though when Mark was taken out of a game by an opponent with the most sickening over the top tackle where a player goes in high. It was a tackle that makes a watching footballer feel ill and in my opinion from where I was, looked to be quite deliberate. We were incensed by the tackle. When Southend came to Turf Moor later, almost all of us were left with a stud mark or two left by Dave Martin. Mark was never the same afterwards. He recovered to play something like 300 games but they were all at lower levels, places like Rotherham, Rochdale and Halifax. He was heading for the very top and could have been an England international but that injury stopped his progression.

Long coach journeys: uncomfortable seats, motorway holdups, monotony, drab landscapes, grey towns, trips to Torquay, Hereford, Peterborough, Maidstone, Cardiff, Darlington, part of the routine of a footballer's life. Card games, watching through the windows, sometimes rain lashing down the glass, a magazine to while away the time, the newspapers, motorway service stations, holdups, queues, very occasionally fish and chips on the way home . . . hours and hours . . . back home in the dark. Hereford 3 Burnley 0, another defeat at Peterborough, where's the glamour in that?

'The soft touches of the Fourth Division,' manager Frank Casper accused us of being after one game. There was a killer journey all the way to Torquay and we lost 2–0. It was only home wins that kept Burnley in touch with the top. A drag of a journey to Gillingham to lose 3–2. Not even sub again. If you're not playing you're on the sidelines, a bystander — you train all week — for what? You could get depressed but you live in hope that you catch the manager's eye. Some players will creep around the manager, suck up to him, but I didn't. But in truth you only get back in if someone is injured. Half of you wishes . . . no . . . you don't really wish injury on a teammate but sometimes it's the only way you get back in. Someone else's bad luck is your good fortune. Somehow Burnley stayed fifth.

It was January before I got a regular place and couldn't understand why it had taken until then. Come April things looked good. A crowd of 18,000 saw us beat Blackpool 2–0 with one of the goals from me. In the home game against Peterborough I scored twice. What a feeling that was. Only a footballer can ever know what it feels like to score, the elation, the adrenalin, the roar of the crowd. For a striker it's a drug. There are times when football is a joy. You wake in a morning and can't wait to start the day. It's the greatest job in the world. In fact it isn't a job and to top it all you even get paid for doing it.

By the end of the season fans were disappointed that there wasn't automatic promotion. Overall I suppose you could say it was a good season with a top six place, even taking into account the horrible ending against Torquay when we faced them in the play-offs. After all those years in the Fourth Division, to be in the play-offs was a massive event for fans. I have a hunch Frank Casper never really got over the disappointment of losing. So close, but then at the end so far away; all that graft and hard work to get there and then ultimately, it was failure—by just one point. Giant screens had been erected at Turf Moor so that fans could watch the first-leg away game. Torquay had only provided 700 tickets. Those fans, whether they were at Torquay or Turf Moor, squirmed and groaned as Burnley had long spells well in control but conceded two goals.

By then I had been shifted permanently to a striker's role. A total of 15 games, plus 11 as sub and 10 goals wasn't too bad by the end of the season. Eusebio, Maradona or Messi I was not, but I gave 110% and was happy enough even though I hadn't played every game. Whenever I was on I tried to make things happen, tried to gee things up, to get the crowd going. But the Torquay experience was a total let-down and Frank Casper did something that was so out of character. I didn't play badly at Torquay but he yelled and bawled at me in a manner that he had never done before. 'ELI, ELI, GET 'IM OFF,' he hollered. First I was baffled as to why he should haul me off, second it was the way he shouted at me. It all adds to the feeling I had that he wasn't himself that day and was far from well. Years later supporters who were there will say we gave a dreadful display. It didn't help that David Hamilton was sent off either.

Those back at Turf Moor who watched on the Big Screen were maybe even more disappointed. At least those who went to Torquay saw the sea. But at Turf Moor the Big Screen picture continually broke up, and those who were at the opposite Bee Hole End, could hardly see it. Those who stood on the Longside had a sideways view. Perhaps it's as well they didn't see much.

One young lad who was just 13 at the time remembers:

We had about 800 tickets for the open 'terrace' which had six steps and then a drop at the back. Anyway a few hundred turned up without tickets and managed to get in (so said a policeman as they didn't want them in town.) Poor game on a really bobbly pitch and it was really warm. Roger Eli had the crowd laughing when he threatened to punch a defender that was holding him at a free kick. Don't recall their first goal but their second was hit low and looked to take a nasty bounce and snuck inside the post.

Some supporters who got there on the Saturday, enjoyed the seaside in the afternoon, and then in the evening went to the Torquay United Supporters Club bar at the ground. The Torquay chairman paid for their drinks and there were sausage butties for supper. The unlucky ones were those who set off at five on Sunday morning, got there for the game and drove straight back home again. Our own journey back home was long and despondent. Torquay to Burnley; what's that, 350 miles? There wasn't even the consolation of thinking we'd been unlucky. We'd been poor.

It irritates me that the year before Burnley did actually win promotion in '92, we had blown the chance of a Wembley appearance and promotion with this game at Torquay. Even all these years later the circumstances are still aggravating. The Burnley history book *Clarets Collection* describes the result at Torquay with just one word— controversial. It doesn't go into details. The first leg of our play-off against Torquay United was the weekend of the Nottingham Forest and Tottenham Cup Final. That was the final where Gascoigne made the infamous tackle on Gary Charles and ended up seriously injured.

Players are asked all the time during their careers if they ever fancy going into management or coaching and I was no different. But, it never had any appeal for me and for sure the events of that Torquay weekend didn't exactly encourage me to rush out and find a UEFA coaching course. Management and playing has its pressures and many a good man has been wrecked by the stresses and injuries, and too often its victims find solace in a few drinks. The football drinking habit is well known and that is where too many people involved in the game unfortunately find comfort. Today it has lessened a bit, but back when I played it was in full swing and for sure when I joined Burnley I found a few lads who liked a drink. There was almost a routine of train, play, drink, train, play, drink but big drinking was never really my style. I had this idea that it was actually disrespectful to the supporters to go out and get bladdered whether it was before or after a game. I had enough problems with the knee, without affecting fitness going on benders. My idea of a good night out once I met Andrea, my wife, was a Saturday night at the Showcase Cinema in Birstall. The lads made fun of it. On the occasions the coach ever passed a Showcase Cinema the lads would shout out: 'ROGER YOUR STOP!' There have been stories that some of the players had too many drinks the night before the Torquay game. I can tell you now. Any such stories are untrue. There were just two of the older players who always had a beer with their meal before every away match.

At Torquay the bottom line was we had the biggest fixture of the season coming up and there was so much at stake in that game. The journey down by coach was buoyant, optimistic and expectant. There was good humour, laughter and when that happens a journey passes quickly and enjoyably. The hotel was pleasant and comfortable, a perfectly suitable base before the game. Torquay is the English Riviera; it's a nice place, in total contrast to the empty mills, grimy chimneys and line after line of terraced streets in Burnley. There was precious little renovation and regeneration going on in Burnley in the early nineties. Mention Torquay and it's likely you think of Fawlty Towers. Our hotel, fortunately, was nothing like that. There was no Basil or Manuel that we could find although we joked all the way down about it.

On the Saturday I lay stretched out on the bed. There was a portable TV in the room, the window was partly open, the curtains fluttered in the breeze and the sounds and smells of the sea drifted into the room. Sometimes being a footballer had its rewards even if the money wasn't that great. I remember on TV that Spurs and Forest fans were singing 'Abide with Me'. It's an emotional song and I had a lump in my throat thinking that in 13 days time it could be me walking out onto the lush Wembley turf. Don't forget we weren't 'star' footballers with bulging bank balances. We were journeymen and wanderers. We'd been around a bit and we'd had plenty of bad days when we struggled and wondered how much longer we could hang on to a career in football, or where the next pay cheque would come from. This was a big chance coming up to taste something really special.

I had an image of thousands of Burnley fans massed on the Wembley terraces and in the seats and boxes. That would have been so wonderful. They'd had a rough ride for the last six years with nothing to celebrate. What a wonderful chance we had to bring some glory to the town and club. You get butterflies in your stomach when you think these things especially when you imagine your mum, dad, brothers and sister there watching. A crowd of 80,000 had turned up to watch Wolves and Burnley in the Sherpa Trophy Final just a few years earlier. Of course I'd never turned out in front of a crowd that big. Blackpool were due to play Scunthorpe in the other play-off so a Burnley–Blackpool Final was a clear possibility. The whole prospect was awesome. You lie there thinking and mulling things over; maybe it would be me who scored the winning goal in the 90th minute.

But first there was Torquay United to take care of. In 2009 Burnley were playing the likes of Manchester United, Chelsea and Liverpool in the Premiership. Burnley versus Torquay United in 1991 was a million miles from that. You can't imagine a game against Torquay in their tiny little ground, parts of which were almost falling apart, being a 'big' game. But for us, on that play-off and Cup Final weekend, it was the biggest.

The contrast between the two games wasn't lost on us as we filled in the afternoon killing time. Wembley and Plainmoor, you couldn't get a bigger difference than that. The gap between the two sets of players so enormous it was almost funny. Theirs was a world outside of ours.

We settled down to watch the game. In the morning we'd had breakfast and then done some light training. Some of the team went swimming after that.

Captains Mabbut and Pearce led out the two Cup Final teams. Careers take people in different directions. Decisions you make yourself, but more important, decisions made by other people, map out your lives. Bremner had decided the course of my life. I'd never felt particularly bitter or resentful but I looked at the players coming out and thought again about what might have happened or where I'd have been if Eddie Gray had not been sacked and the players he was bringing through had been kept together.

Clough was on the TV screen. It was a day when just about everybody was willing his team to win so that he could at last win an FA Cup. There was the man and manager I had known and been terrified of during that week in Italy not that many years earlier. There on the screen was the man who had decided the course of my life when he saw me as injury prone so not worth keeping. He demonstrated that day just how it is other people's decisions that change your life. Who knows how differently things would have turned out if I'd had the chance to stay with him? The week in Italy was magical but there was more than just that. He was around the place when we cleaned out dressing rooms or swept the corridors. You'd bump into him when you weren't expecting it—not that you ever dared speak. We sat with him on the touchline during the first-team games. I couldn't help thinking; might it have been me out on that Wembley pitch in Forest colours?

But moping about things is no good. If things happen for a purpose then those are also the things that eventually brought me to being the successful businessman I am today.

Old Big Head's demeanour really struck me as he walked at the head of the team. The grainy colour picture on the hotel room TV wasn't the best but it couldn't mask Cloughie's puffy, blotchy face. Gazza's outrageous lunge was the big talking point for most people. But me; I was curious why Clough just stayed on the bench at the full time whistle with the score at 1–1. Surely he should have been down on the pitch talking to his players, firing them up, preparing them for another 30 minutes of passion and effort. The Cup was still theirs for the taking. Was it the drink I wondered? Sometime later he would come clean that drink had clouded his judgement if not even wrecked it. Two years later Forest would be relegated and the scenes on that day were tear-filled and emotional. The straight-backed, square-shouldered man who had taken us to Italy and marched us round to St Peter's Square like a headmaster was a memory by then. But people still loved him for what he had done in both Derby and Nottingham. His 44 days at Leeds were like a bad dream.

Des Walker's own goal settled the game. Gary Mabbutt headed his team up the famous Wembley steps. Of course I thought that could be me in a few days time if we sorted out Torquay United. Surely we could do it; Torquay—just a piddling little team in a ramshackle ground that was falling apart at the seams; how on earth had they even got as far as the play-offs?

With extra time and post match interviews and all the studio stuff it was quite late. The TVs in a dozen rooms were switched off; doors opened and we all drifted down to the dining room for the evening meal.

The chatter inevitably covered the Gascoigne tackle and injury, moved on to Clough's appearance and strange behaviour before extra time, then Walker's own goal. Football is cruel, how often do we say that, in this case for Gascoigne and Walker? The cruelty of the game and life afterwards would hit Gary Charles later. The more astute members of the squad dissected the game and the tactics with salt and pepper pots. John Deary was his usual self laughing away at other things. Football wasn't the be-all and end-all for John. I didn't want a big meal before the game that was coming up so had a simple meal of scrambled eggs on toast. We didn't see Frank or Jimmy until the morning.

Frank was someone I had massive regard for. He and Eddie Gray had several similarities. Frank was the manager who had faith in my ability in whichever position he played me. He was a top quality coach and for me was a big loss to the game when he turned his back on football and was replaced by Jimmy Mullen later in the year. He was the sort of boss you could talk to when you needed to, or share an opinion with. Some of the abuse he endured was downright vicious and cruel. These are people that do their best and being a manager means sticking your head above the parapet. That takes guts.

But Jimmy Mullen and I were never close in any way and he was someone I never really took to. He had the managerial ability to win two promotions and you can't take that away from him but in the dressing room it's fair to say he wasn't too well-liked with his brash and sometimes what to me seemed an intimidating manner. Maybe that's a quality a manager needs to be successful; the ability not to get too close to players, to be distant, ruthless and impersonal. But we were wary of him and, there was a groundswell of opinion in the dressing room that Jimmy wanted Frank's job; in fact the story went round that he told someone he'd have it within six months. That's football you say and shrug it off, although it takes place in the workplace everywhere I'd guess. There's always someone who wants the boss's job and thinks they can do it better.

It was a Saturday night but we turned in for an early night and at breakfast the following morning most of us plumped for toast or cereals. Bacon and sausages might have been tempting but we resisted. There was no sign of Frank or Jimmy. And coming up was the biggest game of the season so far with such a lot riding on it. Sometime in mid-morning the coach was prepared for us on the hotel forecourt. In dribs and drabs we filed on. Wembley was just a few hours away if we did this job right. Some of us were pumped up already. Others, the more relaxed, were casual and light-hearted.

With all of us on the coach Jimmy was sighted in the hotel reception area and we presumed that Frank wouldn't be far behind. Jimmy sat in his usual place at the front of the coach but of Frank there was still no sign. Some Board members had come down with us to the hotel. The others had arrived at the hotel having made their own way down and they too took their seats at the front of the bus. From where I sat there was no sign of Frank.

One or two of the lads began to look quizzically at each other wondering what was going on. The coach was ready to leave, the driver all set to get it into gear and pull away. Gently, he revved the engine. Jimmy Mullen remained in his seat with more than a few of us wondering should he not be going in to find the boss. By now it was getting embarrassing. Jimmy remained in his seat as the minutes ticked by and some players were becoming quite angry at both the delay and the lack of any inclination on Jimmy Mullen's part to go and find him. As directors too began to ask each other what was happening and why the coach was still there, at last Frank appeared. He looked unwell. He dashed though the doors of the hotel and hauled himself up the steps of the coach before taking his seat and telling the driver to leave.

This produced a strange atmosphere on the coach. The Board members looked a little bemused; the players were taken aback and exchanged glances and more puzzled looks across the aisles. David Hamilton was cursing under his breath at the delay. It was not exactly the best start to the afternoon and left us in a strange mindset.

The journey through the quaint palm tree lined roads to Plainmoor wasn't particularly far. A large group of Burnley fans were waiting outside the ground and applauded us getting off the bus. Fans do this and it meant a lot to us. Torquay was a hell of a long way from Burnley. Frank disembarked first and his appearance didn't go unnoticed by the fans. The players followed him to a ground that was one of the poorest in all the Divisions. Rather than spend any time in the dingy dressing rooms we went out onto the pitch for an inspection. I remember I had a slight hernia problem but I was desperate to play, desperate to win.

A number of fans were draping flags and banners over the

perimeter wall and one of them made a move to come over. 'Ignore him,' said David Hamilton. 'He probably wants to know what's wrong with Frank.'

Frank looked ill. This had never happened before. It was out of character. We felt protective. Footballers are like this and put the shutters up when needed. We stayed out as long as we could so that by the time we got back to the dressing rooms Frank was composed and looked a whole lot better. He looked more like the character that all the players knew and respected.

We lost the game 2–0. If you ask me now whether we were in the right frame of mind, if we could have done more, if we played at our best, if we were wasteful of the chances that came our way or if Torquay were better than us, I'd struggle to answer. But they went on to win promotion. The fans and the reports say that we were dreadful in that game. That was down to us, the players. But why were we so poor? Back at Turf Moor in the second leg, despite all the pressure we put on we managed just the one goal and lost 2–1 on aggregate. I look back on it now with regret. It was all so hugely disappointing. Way back in '91 a game like lowly Torquay versus impoverished, struggling Burnley was a non event to the outside world. But to us it was damned important. And we blew it.

The journey home: think of all of us in a confined space like a coach for ten hours feeling bloody depressed. There was no laughing and joking. Even the bubbly John Deary was quiet. In fact it was almost an unwritten rule that after any kind of a defeat if you showed any humour on the way home you were scowled at for not caring. Sure the cards came out but everything was mute, subdued; grim in fact. There were no stops; it was straight back all the way. You look for road signs, landmarks and how many miles to here and how many miles to there. You sit and stare out the window half in a dream. It was a journey when I sat and thought about exactly what I'd achieved in football. That journey by luxury coach from Leeds to Charlton when I was exuberant and full of hope, and sat with so many international players passing round my bag of sweets, seemed a hundred years ago.

On the way back to Burnley, as ever the knee was swollen, tender and throbbed all the way home along mile after mile of featureless motorway. We talked about winning at Turf Moor in the second game but mostly we were down, out and quiet; we knew full well we'd played so badly. A bit of management-inspired geeing-up before the game might have helped. Remember the Al Pacino speech in that American football film *Any Given Sunday* . . . the inch by inch speech? These things do work in a dressing room. But before our game there was nothing that set us in the right frame, nothing of note from either Jimmy Mullen or an unwell Frank Casper. If Frank was obviously ill why did Jimmy not step in? It seemed to us there was no-one steering the ship.

Torquay came to Turf Moor for the second-leg. They'd already been in April and we could only draw in the home game. Four straight wins after that did the job of more or less ensuring the play-off place; one of them the Blackpool game and there was a terrific Turf Moor crowd of over 18,000. That game, (with four still to play) was the last in which I scored that season. Hell, you break the deadlock and score in front of a crowd of 18,000 and it goes wild when you win 2–0. Feelings for any footballer don't get any better than that. When Manchester City had been earlier in the season for a third round FA Cup tie, there were just over 20,000 but a 0–1 defeat to a team that included the likes of Peter Reid, Niall Quinn, Colin Hendry and Gary Megson. I was desperate to play in that game but wasn't even on the bench. Supporters can never imagine the massive disappointments that players go through.

Burnley battered Torquay at Turf Moor in the second game. How they held out we'll never know. Even the goal Burnley scored in the final minute was a Torquay own goal. I have a hazy memory of them having two unbeatable centre-halves who dealt with most things. One of them was Matt Elliott who went on to have a fantastic career with Leicester City. We trudged off at the end so disappointed, heads down, shoulders slumped. Sure you applaud the crowd and acknowledge their support but all you want to do really is get off and feel miserable. One dressing room is jubilant. The other is despondent—and that dressing room was ours. At half-time the DJ played 'Sadness' by Enigma. It couldn't have been more appropriate. It was also the game when Blackburn Rovers supporters hired a small plane to fly over Turf Moor. 'Staying down 4 ever luv Rovers ha ha ha' it said. Nobody has ever really got to the bottom of who paid for and organised it. Rumours say it was their ex-player Simon Garner. But Garner, the former Rovers striker and self-confessed Burnley hater says it was the 100 Club crew, whatever that was, who were responsible. To this day Blackburn fans think it was Garner even though he denied it in the local paper. Never mind who it was; it was just a totally ghastly day. We'd had a fantastic home record that season. Played 23 games and won 17 of them and only lost just the one, scoring an average of two goals a game. That's good going by anyone's standards. We should have walloped them good and proper. But we didn't. The top four went up that season with Peterborough taking the fourth spot on 80 points. Burnley had 79. It was that close. You think of games that were draws and wonder 'if only.' It sounds dramatic but this tiny margin went on to affect peoples' lives and careers.

Ahead there was the prospect of another year in the basement; a seventh year in the Fourth Division, unbearable for supporters and directors alike. Would Frank Teasdale give Frank Casper the chop was the inevitable question. But the answer was no. He was given one more year to get what everyone wanted—Burnley out of the awfulness of the Fourth Division. No pressure there then. But it's one of the cruelties of football. When players don't deliver, it's the manager who inevitably carries the can. Eventually he would bite the bullet, missing out on being a hero by just one point. If Mullen fancied the manager's job then he got his wish; but with Mullen triumph would follow.

A little less than 12 months later, disappointment and dejection would be replaced by joy; not for Frank however who by then had been replaced by Jimmy Mullen. He'd got the job we suspected he'd wanted all along. It is 20 years on and the image I have is not of Frank's indisposition at Torquay but Jimmy sitting on the coach outside the hotel and, as we all waited, making us wonder why he didn't go to find him.

8

A Season to Remember Begins

One of the items I have in my collection of old bits and pieces from my playing days is the pennant we received before one of the 1991 pre-season games in Russia. I looked at it and couldn't help smiling. My career had touched a few depths since the days at Leeds United and in the most depressing of those depths Russia was the last place I ever imagined I'd play. For sure it was a hell of a long way from Bury and Northwich Victoria. But there it was; the pennant and it must have been 20 years since I'd last bothered to look at it. With the pennant was a copy of the programme from one of the games. I've no idea what it says. It's in Russian.

Then there are the three programmes for the Derby Cup games. They were memorable games, one of them especially so when Peter Shilton could only blink in astonishment when my header flew past him at 90 miles an hour. And at the end of the season there were two programmes when the club printed FOURTH DIVISION CHAMPIONS on the front cover. The first was against Wrexham. Life is funny sometimes. We lost it. Then there was the end of season friendly against Ajax, Dennis Bergkamp, Van der Saar and company. I was never a great collector of such things but just these few found their way into my box. My boys can have them all one day; my memories of a great season and the old Fourth Division.

Frank Casper was still manager when the new season, 1991–92, began; the Torquay disappointment forgiven if not forgotten. Frank Teasdale, battling against disgruntled fans, was still chairman, putting up with abuse and threats and demonstrations. Who'd be a chairman?

But, even though we'd blown it against Torquay, there was still a little bit of optimism, the kind of optimism that exists at every club in the land at the beginning of a new season when there is a new start and a clean slate. One or two players left as is always the case at the end of a season. One was the late Ray Deakin, a great fans' favourite. His epic long-distance clearances were accompanied by the fans uttering a loud and sustained 'whoosh'. But he was not unskilled and supporters remembered his wonderful performance in the 'Orient Game' when the club avoided the drop out of the Football League. Fans were very disappointed when defender Steve Davis Mk1 left. He went to Barnsley for £180,000, a lot of money back then that no doubt enabled the club to pay our wages. He was a good, solid defender and it left a bit of a hole at the back.

My strike partner Ron Futcher moved on and this was all to do with a new contract. Jimmy Mullen was desperate for him to stay. This much travelled striker was 33 when Burnley signed him for £65,000. Burnley became his 13th club and four of these had been in America. He was joint top scorer in his first season at Turf Moor with seven goals. In the 'nearly got promotion' season he'd scored 18. Despite those 18 goals he never quite managed to become a cult hero which was a surprise. Of all the many players I played alongside he was a real professional and really thought about the game. He had an exceptional knowledge of football. But he was also a joker or the one who was first to say, 'That's not right,' to Frank Casper or Jimmy Mullen. We respected him for that because his opinions were based on his vast experience in the game. But at the same time he was the first to groan when it was time to do a long distance run.

In his place Frank bought Mike Conroy. By the end of the season supporters would know who Mike Conroy was alright. He was a striker at Reading where he'd ended up playing at full-back. Ron went to Crewe and Mike came in from down south, although in fact he was Scottish and up there he'd apparently done okay. Mike says it was Jimmy Mullen who was behind the move. He knew him from when he was assistant manager of Aberdeen and Mike played for Clydebank. Mike always seemed to score against Aberdeen and Jimmy filed that away in his memory bank.

But then Frank pulled off a masterstroke. Out went Steve 'Swede' Davis and in came Steve Davis Mk2. The Swede got his name because he looked like a character in a Clint Eastwood film of the time. The replacement Steve Davis had been to Burnley already, on loan from Southampton. Back he came to Turf Moor and became one of the outstanding players of the nineties and bedrock of the team right up until the Stan Ternent team that won promotion in 2000. He was voted an official Burnley legend a few years ago. He cost Frank just

£60,000 and it was money well spent.

There was a summer tour to Russia. We never knew how this came about and wondered if a Burnley director had contacts over there. It seemed an odd place to go and the travel was draining. There was a 1- 1 draw with Stavropol and another with Asmaral which is something I thought you got from the chemist to cure piles.

It was the charms of Rotherham for the first proper game; God it was a dump back then against a backcloth of a giant scrap yard where old steam engines were broken up. Surprise, surprise Burnley lost to two late Rotherham goals. I didn't play because of an Achilles problem. Mike Conroy became an instant favourite with a goal and a celebration that saw him leap at the away end fence and cling to it for dear life. It was so insecure and flimsy it was a miracle he didn't come crashing down and break his neck.

There were quite a few fans at the away Wigan League Cup game. In those days few people actually ever wanted to go to Wigan. It was a place most people wanted to get away from. This was the Rumbelows Cup in another ramshackle place that a light breeze might have brought crashing down. The only Rumbelow I knew so far was Mr Rumbelow in *Are You Being Served*. I half expected to see him there somewhere. Behind one goal there was no terracing, just a grassy muddy bank where the Burnley boys gathered. We lost and I only mention this game because I played and it was an example of no matter how poor the ground or the conditions I always loved playing.

At last a win over Aldershot. I missed this one ironically not with an injury but because of 'flu. But the game counted for nothing as before the season ended Aldershot were wound up. They were in their death throes when we played them. Remember the Monty Python sketch 'This parrot is dead'? It was a bit like that when we played them. Officially the game never happened; the two goals were never scored. The crowd who watched were never there. But by now Mick Conroy was looking a bargain. Funny how a change of club can kickstart a career; it had happened to me as well a year earlier.

An old crumpled newspaper can bring back moments and bits and pieces of your career. There are a few odds and ends in my loft; just a few things I can show the boys one day to let them know who I was and what I once did. There's a report of the Doncaster game.

Dad back row third left. Football Dominica style.

Schooldays, me in front of Martin Mitchell at Swainhouse Middle.

Mum and family, me end right.
Dad no doubt at work.

Garden chores.

The teenage years.

Bradford Under 15's 1980/81.

Bradford Senior Schools 1982.

An Agreement

made the TWENTY SECOND

day of JULY 19 82 between KEITH ARCHER

of 95 GROVEHALL DRIVE, LEEDS 11

in the County of WEST YORKSHIRE

the Secretary of and acting pursuant to Resolution and Authority for and on

behalf of the LEEDS UNITED FOOTBALL CLUB

of ELLAND ROAD, LEEDS LS11 OES (hereinafter referred to as the Club)

of the one part and ROGER ELI

of 41 SWAINHOUSE CRESCENT, BRADFORD 2

in the County of WEST YORKSHIRE Apprentice Football Player

(hereinafter referred to as the Player) of the other part whereby it is agreed
as follows:—

1. The Player hereby agrees to play in an efficient manner and to the best
of his ability for the Club.

2. The Player shall attend the Club's ground or any other place decided
upon by the Club for the purposes of or in connection with his training as a
Player pursuant to the instructions of the Secretary, Manager, or Trainer of the
Club, or of such other person, or persons as the Club may appoint.

3. The Player shall do everything necessary to get and keep himself in the
best possible condition so as to render the most efficient service to the Club, and
will carry out all the training and other instructions of the Club through its
representative officials.

4. The Player shall observe and be subject to all the Rules, Regulations
and Bye-Laws of The Football Association, and any other Association, League,
or Combination of which the Club shall be a member. And this Agreement shall
be subject to any action which shall be taken by The Football Association under
their Rules for the suspension or termination of the Football Season, and if any
such suspension or termination shall be decided upon the payment of wages shall
likewise be suspended or terminated, as the case may be.

5. The Player shall not engage in any business or live in any place which
the Directors (or Committee) of the Club may deem unsuitable, provided that the
Club shall, at the request of the Player or his Parent or Guardian, allow the Player
to continue his further education or take up suitable vocational training.

6. If the Player shall be guilty of serious misconduct or breach of the
disciplinary Rules of the Club, the Club may, on giving 14 days' notice
to the said Player, or the Club may, on giving 28 days' notice to the said Player,
on any reasonable grounds, terminate this Agreement and dispense with the
services of the Player in pursuance of the Rules of all such Associations, Leagues,

First contract Leeds United.

With Dad signing at Leeds,
Keith Mincher in blue jumper.

Proud Dad with FA Cup.

Souvenir programme Italy.

Eddie Gray and the lads, left to right, me, Steve Livingstone, Eddie, Wayne Roebuck and Scott Sellars.

Switzerland youth trophy winners, Terry Phelan and Dennis Irwin front row end left, Scott Sellars front row fourth right, me back row.

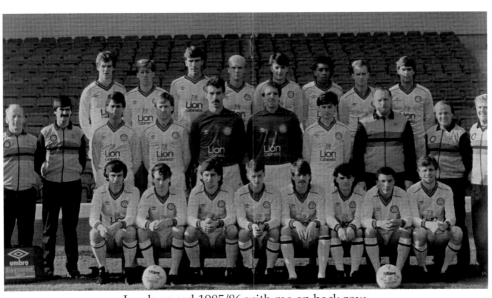

Leeds squad 1985/86 with me on back row.

BACK ROW (left to right): Keith Lockhart, Neil Edwards, Scott Barrett, Dean Edwards, Vince Bartram, Russell Turley, Andy Mutch, Steve Stoutt.
MIDDLE ROW: Geoff Palmer (coach), Matt Hallin, David Barnes, Darren Oldroyd, Peter Zelem, Nick Clarke, Roger Eli, Micky Holmes, Floyd Streete, Derek Ryan, Eddie Edwards (physio).
FRONT ROW: Henry Wright (now released), John Pardie, Paul Dougherty, Brian Little (ex-manager), David Haywood, Richard Wood, Matt Forman. INSETS: Top — Graham Turner (manager) and Ally Robertson.

Wolves squad, Brian Little manager.

Wolves debut versus Brentford.

Not my favourite picture.

Wolves versus
Reading 1986.

Burnley 1990/91 Frank Casper manager, me back row, Jimmy Mullen
end right middle row. Physio Jimmy Holland end left.

Video launch with John Francis. Not cheap were they?

Burnley 1992/93 Jimmy Mullen manager. Adrian Heath front row third right.
Mike Conroy back row second left.

In Stavrapol Russia.
Reproduced by kind permission of Burnley Football Club.

Frank Casper left and
Jimmy Mullen right.

Left to right Chris Pearce, Mark
Monnington and me.

John Deary front left socialising with the Russians.

Pre-game introductions, Burnley in white.

HITMAN ELI DOES TRICK FOR CLARETS

Treble top Roger guides Burnley into second spot

Fame at last in the local Press.

In determined mood.

Burnley versus Scarborough.

Typical me—fearless.

Goal of the season 1991/92 burying a bullet header past
Peter Shilton in the FA Cup.

Versus Derby and straight between the pair of them.

Did I score?

Getting the shot in, Adrian Heath watching.

Mick Conroy to the left and Steve Harper right.

20 years ago

Andy Farrell shows determination in this tackle that earned the Clarets a 1-1 draw with top of the table Crewe.

John Pender climbs with Crewe keeper Dean Greygoose as the Clarets apply the pressure.

Mike Conroy at full stretch to keep control of the ball as the Clarets push forward versus Rochdale.

A Crewe defender just fails to stop Roger Eli shoot.

Ian Bray times his tackle to halt a Rochdale attack.

John Deary listens to the referee calm things down.

Burnley versus Crewe.
Reproduced by kind permission of Burnley Football Club.

Snaps from Foshaan

Train journey.

Express taxi.

With the two
Scots lads.

My first shop.

In sickness and in health.

For better or worse.

Mum and Dad, cruise ship holiday.

Andrea stepping out.

Relaxing in Spain.

With my two boys Jordan and Ryan.

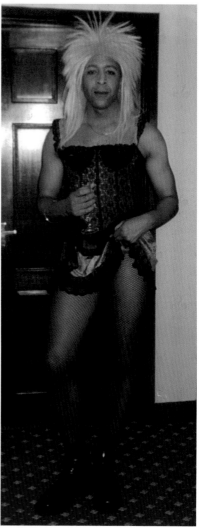
All dressed up and ready to go.

At the Potting Shed Café,
Woodbank Garden Centre,
Harden near Bingley,
checking the pages.

Big Billy Whitehurst still played for them. Ask anyone what it was like to play against him. I'd already played against him once the season before. He made Kenny Burns look like a kitten. In his pomp he was a striker and battered centre-halves mercilessly. It was funny: when I realised he was in the Doncaster team I thought this was still his old position up front, but to my horror he now played centre-half. In his old position he was big and terrifying. In his new one he was still big and still terrifying. Now I'd be directly up against him. You could hear my knees knocking from 20 yards away down the corridor as I got changed. There was real apprehension on my part. The thought of him coming through me if I had my back to him was worrying. The old faded newspaper has all the details. It wasn't exactly a walk in the park, but it brings a smile when I read about it now.

It was Doncaster 1 Burnley 4 and who was there managing them but Billy Bremner again. The clock in my head turned back a few years I can tell you. I looked across to him and knew he'd remember me. I was determined he wouldn't forget my performance that day. This was a game when I was playing not against Doncaster Rovers but against Billy Bremner. What a game to have a blinder. I didn't score. How good would that have been? Up and down, in and out; headers, brought down for the penalty, shots and tackles and passes galore; sometimes you play a game and you want it to go on forever. You're in the zone, can do no wrong, the ball sticks to your feet; shots are on target and Billy Bremner was there in the Doncaster dugout. 'Are you watching Billy,' I thought as I came off with a huge grin on my face? I went to see him afterwards to say hello. Yes he was sitting in his chair in his office. I'd love to remember exactly what we spoke about. I know there was some small talk. I'd love to think he said, 'Roger you should have stayed with me at Leeds'. But he didn't. I still went out feeling well pleased.

Doncaster were down to 10 men when Billy Whitehurst was sent off. He'd already clattered me in the penalty area and given away the penalty. It was hilarious how he was sent off. On the halfway line he was caught in possession by me and Mike Conroy. Setting off after us must have been like watching two sleek greyhounds being chased by a lolloping Rottweiler. Somehow, landing on all fours he stumbled over the ball and began a juggling act with it to stop us streaking away. He walked off the field before the red card was even out of the ref's pocket.

At my best they called me 'psycho'. Stuart Pearce wasn't the only one. There was one game when even with a damaged rib I showed what I was all about. Maidstone I think it was. There was a ball there to be won. If it was within reach, it was mine. I went in with one hard tackle and won it. It squirmed away. I went in with a second tackle as the next opponent came in for it. I went in and won it. Somehow it rolled away again and for a third time I went in hard and won it. It was gladiatorial. It was epic. Three tackles with three different opponents one after the other in quick succession. It was like a moment when a boxing crowd are up on their feet urging on their favourite as he batters someone. That's how it was. A crowd will recognise bravery. I had it in buckets. Years later you realise that this kind of daft bravery was the very reason you ended up on the treatment table so often. But I also had skill and knew more than a few tricks that I would always spend time practising, and before a game I'd often go back to my old school and practice touch and passing against the wall imagining myself to be in different situations on the pitch. If it was a Tuesday game I'd go on a Monday night. If it was a Saturday game I'd do this after training on a Friday under the stand. I just had to play with a ball before every match.

This book is no parade of every goal I scored but there was a hat-trick against Chesterfield in the very next game. John Francis and I still argue about it. Footballers do that, especially strikers. The one that John and I still laugh about was the third one that gave me the hat-trick, and soft goal that it was, there was no hesitation in me claiming it.

'Hitman Eli Does Trick For Clarets' said the local paper:

Hat-trick hitman Roger Eli was the hero of the hour as Burnley moved comfortably into second place in the Fourth Division at Turf Moor last night. But without taking any glory away from the Claret's sure shot striker, Eli was merely the final cog in a well-oiled goal-scoring machine that's netted seven times in two games.

Manager Frank Casper promised: 'We can play better,' after Saturday's 4–1 away romp over Doncaster. And so they did. From number 1 and goalkeeper Andy Marriott through to number 11 Mark Yates, everyone played with gusto and determination that's been inherently lacking in so many teams in recent years. The balance of the side looked better than anything Casper has had charge of since he returned to the club two and a half years ago. So much so that the Burnley boss never appeared to consider tinkering with substitutions. From the first second to the last Burnley's sole objective was to attack. Five, six or seven goals would not have flattered.

In all honesty it was a strange hat-trick. The first came when Mike Conroy surged forward with the ball. A linesman's flag went up for offside. The ball was slightly behind me but somehow my leg hooked round it and turned it into the net. Offside or not, it stood even though the Chesterfield players were not happy. Goal two came in the second half. A long ball from defence, flicked on by Conroy; it took me a couple of steps to catch up with it and then slam it, but alas straight against the goalkeeper. Sometimes your luck is in. The ball came back and I curled it inside the far post and in it went. Goal three was 20 minutes later. A corner, a defender's boot, another corner, the next cross only partially cleared, Johnny Francis lets fly from 20 yards. The ball brushes off my leg and in a second it's in the net. John Francis claimed it, but no way was he having it. The ball came off me, this was a hat-trick moment; this was my goal and nobody else's. It was me that went on the celebratory run that lasted the longest; but to this day John says it was his goal.

Afterwards I hung on to that match-ball and talked about the third goal. The quote is there in the paper to this day: 'This is my first ever hat-trick and I feel brilliant. John Francis fired in a shot and I had my back to goal. The ball just brushed my leg and took a deflection into the net. But whether John's shot would have gone in or not I don't know. But I'm claiming it.'

I read these two reports now of how well we played at Doncaster and then home against Chesterfield and I wonder how we managed to mess things up for Frank Casper. We were brilliant in those two games; so why not in the games to come when it went so badly wrong and Frank eventually resigned?

Meanwhile Frank had signed another goalkeeper, Andy Marriot, from Nottingham Forest. He was class and was to have a huge impact. After this there was optimism and cheerfulness. Doncaster was another ramshackle ground but when you've won 4–1 you don't care. It was the kind of ground where the 'Ladies' was a bucket in a brick shelter in the corner of the ground. It doesn't get more basic than that.

Supporters told me it was the first Burnley hat-trick since Kevin

Hird in 1885, sorry 1985. I was a hit, my popularity now secured. It was a wonderful feeling. It gave me energy and determination to give 110% in every game. I got the match-ball signed by all the players; it was a ritual set in stone that a player got the hat-trick ball, even if the club was hard up.

'For me,' wrote one fan Andrew Firmin, 'this was the first claret hat-trick I had ever seen. For that, Roger Eli will always have my thanks.'

Frank Casper played three central defenders and two wing backs. This was novel back then and Frank was keen to take credit for the masterstroke. Why not, he'd had plenty of criticism like all managers do, so when something works grab the credit. We all do it whether we're footballers or not. The win took us to second.

A glorious September sunny day and Ron Futcher was back with Crewe for the next game. He got plenty of stick which was disappointing. He had served the club well. Instead of merely smiling and absorbing it as all his years of experience should have enabled him to do, he got himself all worked up and lunged at Steve Harper. The referee found it very easy to send him off. With them down to ten men the way was clear for us to win. Alas, football never works like that. Yes Franny put us in the lead but then our own David Hamilton was sent off. He'd had an awful game anyway and was probably pleased to be heading for the bath. We all have games like that sometimes. Crewe had equalised by then anyway so the game petered out into a draw. Nearly 10,000 people went home disappointed, unless they came from Crewe. Yes there were a few of them, just enough to fill a taxi and a tandem. Before the game Dario Gradi had come over. We shook hands and he said he was pleased that my career was now heading in the right direction.

The wheels began to fall off at Hereford. The rot set in with a vengeance. Hereford is a beautiful place set on the River Wye. This ancient, historic town with its old charter dates back to 1189. The football ground looked like it was built the same year. Famed for Bulmers cider production and the Weston Brewery, some of the boys felt quite at home. The game was lost 0–2. David Hamilton was stretchered off. John Francis was sent off. John was a tough lad from a hard background and he allowed nobody to take liberties with him as one Hereford player discovered. If he'd ever discovered the name of the member of staff at Burnley who was giving a young and talented Asian lad a hard time he'd have separated his head from his shoulders.

From hoping to go top, the slide took us down to eighth and this was what was depressing to supporters. They thought Burnley Football Club was better than having to go to places like lowly Hereford—and losing.

There was even worse to come. Rochdale came to Turf Moor. Burnley goalkeeper David Williams had been allowed to go to Rochdale on loan. There was nothing wrong with that except he was then allowed to play against us when Rochdale came. Sod's Law decreed that he had the game of his life. He had never played like this before and never did again. He was unbeatable and stopped everything we could throw at him. So when Rochdale scored, yes, they won. A total of 8,630 Burnley fans were furious. The three Rochdale fans were incredulous. Fans asked by what daft lack of sense was Williams allowed to play? Probably because nobody in the Burnley admin or management team ever thought he could play like this so didn't think it would matter. That was why they had got Andy Marriott instead. The Rochdale fans loved it. They were minnows and remembered how the once great Division One Burnley fans had looked down their noses at little clubs like penniless Rochdale. They remembered every jibe and act of football snobbery committed over the last six years when Burnley came to Rochdale and took over the ground and had been so supercilious. Now they were on level footing. Oh how the mighty were fallen. Frank C and Frank T were screamed at by the angry crowd. Supporters were wildly seething. The mood was sour, bitter and vitriolic. The two Franks became public enemies one and two. Burnley had plumbed the depths with this result and oh how the Rochdale fans loved it and rubbed the Burnley noses in it. For Burnley fans it was a humiliation.

Frank Casper was on borrowed time. The next game, away at Scarborough, was lost 3–1. God it was a desperate game in wet, wild and windy conditions at a ground that had become a graveyard for Burnley. Frank Casper described the whole thing as 'horrible'. Fans who were there said it was appalling. And this was in spite of Scarborough being reduced to 10 men. I'd burst through, the way to goal was clear and I was a yard ahead of the nearest marker. An arm reached out and a hand nearly ripped my shirt off as a defender held me back. A goal then if I'd broken away would have changed things.

Maybe even saved Frank's job or given him something to help him change his mind about resigning. We were his team; he had gathered us. We could play a bit, and we'd shown that earlier only a few weeks ago. But the howls of abuse at Scarborough affected us. The louder it got the worse we played. Fans should realise that they do affect the players both in positive and negative ways. At Scarborough it was all negative. The longer the game went on I just wanted it to end so we could all get in the bath. And the fans thought I was one of the good guys. It was exactly how Frank described it: 'Horrible.'

In the dressing room after the game we sat numbed by the scoreline and the direness of the game. We could hear everything as the fans left the stadium, every bit of abuse, every bang on the walls and the doors, every catcall, all the boos and jeers. At a time like this you look to the skipper maybe, the manager, or the bubbliest players, for some sort of pick-me-up. But this time there was just silence.

Fans went home angry, resigned to more years in Division Four. Another bright start had descended into yet more dross. What we could hear so loudly was the result of the frustration, the bitterness and the fury at the prospect of another season in Division Four. But what they, the fans, or we, the players, didn't know was that this game marked the end of an era; the era of being not good enough. The pattern of failure was about to be shattered. Salvation was just round the corner. If only players and fans knew that this season would end with success, oh how much more we could all have enjoyed it.

We were shocked when Frank called us together on a pleasant sunny day at the Gawthorpe training ground and told us very briefly that he was leaving. We'd no idea why we'd been gathered together and this was the last thing we were expecting. There was no great long speech; he just said he'd get straight to the point and he was resigning. He was clearly choked and the meeting lasted only a few minutes. He thanked us and with huge dignity wished us luck. Moments like this are emotional. We were stunned. We were his players. Burnley had been his life. He was a Burnley man through and through.

This was the third time as a player I'd been part of an occasion when a manager had called his players together to tell them he was leaving. When it was someone you respected it was all the more hard to feel unaffected. First it had been Eddie Gray at Leeds, then Brian Little at Wolves and now Frank. Jimmy Mullen said that he had spent the previous couple of days trying to get Frank to change his mind. More than just a few of us looked at each other in surprise when we heard that.

We learned later he'd been deeply upset by the death of a good friend of his, Gordon Clayton, who had once been his assistant, and I'm pretty sure the funeral was the same week. Football can be a heartless, savage business and takes its toll on mind and health. As a player it's enjoyable. As a manager it's pressure and more pressure. And when you lose too many games and the supporters are on your back then it's just all stress and utterly thankless. Frank simply re-appraised his life and what he wanted to do. I guess he didn't want to go the same way as his friend. And who could blame him for that. He said it wasn't just the abuse he endured at Scarborough. To this day I regret that we didn't do more for Frank. Footballers don't play badly on purpose or not try. At Scarborough fans might have felt that was the case. The previous season Frank had got to 79 points and that in another season would have been automatic promotion. Fate, then, kicked him in the teeth.

Speculation abounded about who would be the next manager and don't forget that when there is a change it's a trying, uncertain and nervous time for a footballer. Martin Dobson had just left Bristol Rovers a couple of days earlier. It must be him, we thought. Other names were thrown into the hat, Mick Docherty, Stan Ternent, Brian Flynn and Leighton James, but it was Jimmy Mullen who was appointed caretaker-manager. We were not surprised.

His first game was at home to Carlisle and a quiet 2–0 win. It's the same at every club when a new man comes in. You wonder what he's going to do, who he's going to drop; what he's going to change. His training methods were nothing radically new. But they were simple and effective. We did plenty of possession work and teamwork. Mind you we'd done that with Frank. But everything was kept as simple as possible. Full-backs were ordered to get the ball to the wingmen as quickly as possible either to their feet or down the channels for them to chase and turn the opposition. He played with two quick wide men and me and Mick Conroy in the centre. Mick flourished with this service. But the start was a quiet one and there were no radical changes. No one on this day would have thought something big was to happen by the end of the season. It was a dour game but a welcome win. It was the same players and a return to 4–4–2 and in came a young lad Graham Lancashire who was to be a massive instant hit, in place of injured Conroy and suspended Johnny Francis. Graham would score a hatful of goals in his first few games but then his career would unfortunately fade. The ball in this game squirted to Lancs and he pounced from close range to score a predator's goal. Did it feel like a new dawn? A couple of thousand people from the previous game thought not and stayed at home.

Steve Harper was fit again. The club had issued a statement that he had broken his arm in training. In fact what had happened was he'd broken his hand when he punched a wardrobe door in Cheltenham where we were staying one weekend. There'd been a heavy drinking night and more than a few lads were the worse for wear. Back in the hotel there was some larking about which included someone trying to shave Steve's eyebrows off while he was asleep. Steve was not best pleased when he woke up and discovered this. Punching the wardrobe door so hard was not the best thing to do.

A new manager comes in and in the second of his games, away as well, against Wrexham you win 6–2. This was an incredible score and it was even after Wrexham had taken an early lead. But then our goals started going in and the first was that new man again— Graham Lancashire. He was only 18 and he went on to get two more for his hat-trick. His third was an audacious piece of skill, lobbing the ball over the keeper's head. (But hey, the assist was mine thanks very much). When you play well you enjoy everything. The sixth was me, chesting the ball down and sliding it in. Maybe not quite Jimmy Greaves but a goal is a goal and this was the season that was to be special for me.

The Board apparently did interview other candidates for the manager's job but after a 6–2 win away from home, and a new fighting spirit, Jimmy Mullen got the job on October 17th. They weren't to know it but history was being made. Graham Lancashire celebrated his 19th birthday with yet another goal in the third consecutive win. There was a definite buzz developing. 'A cocky little so and so,' said Mullen when asked about Lancs.

We continued with the Autoglass Trophy. No matter what the competition, I loved being involved and playing. A win was always good for morale and self-esteem. There seemed to be so many games in this tournament just to get to the regional finals. By the time you'd got there you'd played so many games that no-one seemed to care. But I cared. I scored twice. But there were only just under 3,000 there to see my two masterpieces. Lincoln, another wonderfully old city steeped in history with its castle and cathedral, were thumped next at Sincil Bank. Lancs scored again when I was taken off and he came on.

That night, back in Burnley I was collared by a supporter. 'Hi Roger you were rubbish today,' he said. Such moments certainly kept your feet on the ground.

So far we had won every game under Jimmy Mullen. In Burnley, away from the gaze of the media, people were starting to get just a little excited. The shape of the team was beginning to emerge. Marriott was damned good in goal. The defence, Measham, Davis, Pender and Jakub, was ominously hard to beat. Andy Farrell and John Deary were skilled and competitive in midfield. Steve Harper and John Francis played wide. Up front was Mike Conroy, scoring all the time, the prodigy that was Lancashire, and me. Me, bustling, all action, head going in where it hurt, chase everything. They said I even chased the crisp packets that blew across the turf. I could do no wrong. Fans made comments that reflected the way Mullen had taken the same players and got them winning. The next games couldn't come soon enough. It was becoming a side that people wanted to watch. Roll on November. But why hadn't we done this for Frank?

When you'd won, the dressing room was a great place to be. As we got back in after every game there was jubilation. Hugs, high fives, shouting and towels being tossed around, huge smiles and Jimmy Holland scurrying round trying his best not to show his delight, tending to the players' cuts and bruises. I'd grab him in a headlock and ruffle what hair he had left. Secretly he enjoyed all the players' banter. The gaffer would bounce in feeling pleased and want the attention of all the players to go briefly over the game. He'd raise his voice, the first words: 'Take a seat.' His voice would fall on deaf ears; you were still on a high, in a daze, thinking about the game, your own game, and if you'd scored re-living the sweet moment of scoring.

Nobody was interested in any negative aspects of the game if it was a win. That could come on Monday. The three points were the most important thing. In that dressing room the euphoria and adrenalin still pumping meant you didn't bother about a bad pass, the time you nearly let them score or falling out with a teammate on the pitch. A win was a boost, a shot in the arm, as satisfying as an addict getting his fix but then only until the next time. Scoring goals is like a drug. You need the elation again. Once is not enough. A win is the ultimate collective high in the game. The group is everything. For a little while it's like reaching the moon; the supporters are pleased, the manager is pleased. Everyone is buoyant. You are a star, for a day at least.

Some players would want to get out of the dressing room as quickly as possible to get to the bar and let off a little steam. Others wanted to soak and relax in the white-tiled bath where you'd let the pressure of the last 90 minutes disappear and gather your thoughts. And then Jimmy's last words as we left: 'Enjoy the victory tonight without going crazy, we are bang at it again next Saturday.'

Halifax and the Shay; round the perimeter was an old speedway bike track. The gravel and cinders used to fly up from the track and land on the pitch. A sliding tackle and you could end up with a cinder stuck in your leg. This was a club so hard up that one year the winter ice was so thick they used the pitch as a skating rink and charged folk to use it. This was the world I lived in; places like Liverpool and Man United were in another galaxy. But yet another win took Burnley to third. Halifax had two players sent off. Pundits say that sending-offs spoil a game but the other team thinks good, that's a bonus. And if it's a foul and a sending off in the penalty area, it means you're doing something right and they can't handle it. Halifax normally had maybe a thousand spectators and a few pigeons up on the stand roof. Burnley took a phenomenal 3,000 fans with them. It was six wins in a row, officially the best start ever by a new Burnley manager. It was game when I embarrassed myself before it had even started. Both teams lined up ready to come out but I was so focused, oblivious to everything around me, and had this habit of looking down at the ground when I came out. I followed the Burnley colour socks out that my eyes focussed on. Out I came. But it was the Halifax team I came out with; their socks were so like ours at Turf Moor. John Francis and Ian Measham were creased up laughing.

I had my trademark hairstyle, shaved to the skin round the sides and back so that only on top was there this mop of black hair. I must have thought it made me look hard, fearsome on the pitch but cool when I was out and about. I've had a few hairstyles in my time.

Make that seven wins on Bonfire Night against York. John Deary was having the season of his life and got a deserved goal; then Graham Lancashire again because I was injured. It was the day tycoon Robert Maxwell died. Funny the things you remember. Nobody will ever know if he fell overboard off his yacht or was pushed. There were plenty of people who would have been willing to help him over the side. The win set Burnley up for a top of the table clash against Mansfield. Nearly 12,000 people turned up. Chairman Frank Teasdale was by now beaming and the abuse previously hurled at him was silenced. I'd played in a new pair of boots that I was unused to. I remember that because I missed a golden chance and blamed the boots.

I'd drive to the ground from Bradford with loud music roaring away. I'd have had a pasta meal the night before and would always arrive early before a game; park the car and then walk along Harry Potts Way to the players' entrance. If it was a night game I'd have a sleep in the afternoon. At home I wasn't the easiest of people. I'd be irritable, anxious and tense. Andrea understood. She'd once worked at the Alhambra Theatre in Bradford and saw how short-tempered some of the 'stars' could be before a show. She knew all about pre-show nerves. Walking along, maybe someone would stop me for a chat and always: 'We gonna win today Roger?' Even an hour early there'd be people there waiting to get autographs by the entrance. The atmosphere and focus gradually built up.

The walk down to the dressing room at Turf Moor is down a long, narrow corridor under the Cricket Field Stand. The noises of supporters above your head up in the stand would be starting. I was usually the first in. The kit was there ready waiting for us in the small dressing room. Back then though you didn't get all the staff and subs that try to crowd in today. There was a brief period of quietness on my own. I'd read the programme and then begin to focus on what lay ahead. Jimmy Holland would be around getting his gear ready. One by one the other players arrived with their chat and gossip, banter and jokes; some of it nerves.

My boots were special to me. Nobody cleaned them but me. Other members of the team let the apprentices do theirs. This was a season we rarely lost at home, a season that was driven by the crowd as expectations grew. Jimmy Mullen would go round the players individually. I can't remember him being any kind of Churchillian orator before a game. But after a game he could dish out the hairdryer treatment when called for. Close to time and the referee would come in to inspect and check boots and studs. A bell sounded when it was time to go out—warriors, gladiators; psyching each other up, battle cries, hand-shakes, shouts: 'Come on lads, come on . . .' And then out into the light, the amphitheatre, the Coliseum, the wall of noise, eleven of us, one thing in mind.

It was a brilliant game against Mansfield, said to be one of the best Fourth Division games ever. The win, the eighth, was a tribute to a galvanised team with a never say die spirit. A bunch of lads comes together every so often and for some reason at some point they just gel. They win and win again and then a momentum builds up so that eventually they just assume they will win the next game, and the next, and the idea of losing just doesn't happen. You can't underestimate the confidence factor. When it goes you lose but when it's high you expect to win. If I related in detail the story of every game this book would be the length of an encyclopaedia but this one was a hell of a game. Andrew Firmin's diary tells the story of this one:

> In front of a crowd huge by the standards of the division, Burnley took on the leaders and beat them. We opened the scoring with a deserved early penalty. John Francis ran into the box where he was scythed down by a clumsy tackle. It was a clear penalty. Conroy made no mistake with the penalty sending the keeper the wrong way. One of the reasons it was such a good game was that Mansfield could play a bit too. Deservedly they made it 1–1. In the second half Burnley regained the lead from a fine Jakub corner and Steve Davis rose above everyone to head powerfully home. But five minutes later they were level again. It came from that rarest of things, a mix up between the two central defensive colossi. Davis and Pender banged into each other going for the same ball. It aimlessly looped into the box and in the confusion it fell nicely for Wilkinson to blast in his second goal.
>
> Mansfield could have won it after that. They had chances, none better than the shot headed off the line by Joe Jakub. It summed up a heroic performance by the little 5' 6' Scot. This was the moment the crowd warmed to him. He hadn't been popular before and had

laboured under the less than flattering nickname of 'Cabbage'. But at left back under Mullen, this 35-year old produced a string of terrier-like performances. Before long the 'Cabbage' taunts were shelved and the crowd was singing, tongue in cheek, 'Scotland's number three'. It was from another Jakub corner that Pender scored the winner. The corner was long and high and was met by the captain lurking close to goal. Conroy characteristically whooped it up at the Cricket Field End. We all did. (Andrew Firmin)

Joe had got the name 'Cabbage' because he'd once called the fans cabbages. It was on the coach in private to another player. Unfortunately it became public and it took a long time for the fans to forgive him. They frequently abused him after that and even used to knock on his door at home and then run off.

It was a barnstorming game; the win was a hard-fought and valiant one with relentless attacking and determination. It was one to send everyone home happy. 'We're on our way,' everyone thought but Jimmy Mullen tried to dampen the growing expectations. 'I'm not making any promises to anyone. This game has a knack of kicking you in the teeth.'

The wins wouldn't stop. The County Ground at Northampton was famously shambolic. Those who have been there still talk about it. It was where George Best scored six times in one game. Somehow Northampton went all the way up to the First Division... and back again. With the score at 1–1 they pressed and obviously fancied their chances of all three points. But they didn't take into account our attitude. As they pushed up they were punished by a superb goal. Farrell cleared a long ball forward to Mick Conroy. He controlled it and laid it to Steve Harper whilst he himself charged through the middle. Harper played the ball in front of Mick; he controlled it on his thigh and then buried it in the net. You could only stand back and admire his skill. And this was the player who was so unsuccessful at Reading they played him at full-back. He was on 10 goals already and it was only November. The goal showed everything that was good about us. When Steve Harper brought the ball forward, three Burnley players raced into the box against one of theirs. We were never beaten, always looking to attack, fast and skilful, imaginatively looking to use the wings. Another huge away following erupted.

But there was a downside. It was Andy Mariott's last game. Brian Clough wouldn't sell him to Burnley so supporters spilled onto the pitch and chaired him off the field. It was emotional and touching. When he got back to Forest he said something remarkable.

'I think of Burnley as my first club and Nottingham Forest as just somewhere I train.' It was an extraordinary thing to say. What Clough's reply was is not known. I can't imagine he didn't blast him to Kingdom Come. But later in the season he broke into the Forest first-team and even played at Wembley in the League Cup Final. He was a damned good keeper, and a great lad. We called him 'Beaver'.

Jimmy Mullen was rightly awarded the Manager of the Month award. He'd overseen seven wins and a draw during the month. Northampton was the ninth consecutive league win. He tried to be modest about it in public. The crowd chanted 'Jimmy Mullen's claret and blue army' long and loud. They thought they and we were invincible.

He had taken over a club when it was on a downslide. The remarkable thing was he still had to sign a new player. This was the same squad of players that Frank Casper had managed. All he had done was tweak the formation and tactics. There were no great sweeping changes and he had stuck by the same players.

But what was disappointing was that the phenomenal Graham Lancashire didn't really get the chances to develop further. If Mike Conroy was injured, then Graham was in the team. When Mike was fit he dropped to the bench. So the appearances and goals dried up. You wonder if that talent should have been nurtured just a little better. After his wonderful start, he never produced anything like it again and he slid down the familiar northwest slope, from Burnley to Preston, to Wigan, Rochdale and then non-league. If you'd seen one young kid in any team in '91 you'd have put money on Graham to make it to the big time.

Nothing lasts forever and the league winning run finally came to an end. Not away to one of the top teams but at home to Scunthorpe. It wasn't a defeat but a 1–1 draw. It had to happen some time and this was after nine astonishing consecutive league wins. Scunthorpe were no mugs and hard to break down. Having taken the lead, we assumed the win would come. I had a hand in the goal, my saved shot prodded home by Andy Farrell. The equaliser was bad luck for big John Pender, sometimes called 'Penderdog' by admiring supporters. To us he was 'Bison'. He went for everything, and doing that yet again headed into his own net. The bigger disappointment

142

was not going top which a win would have secured.

The club were meeting a firm refusal from Forest in more attempts to sign Marriott. Jimmy Mullen clearly had little faith in Chris Pearce and now brought in yet another loan goalkeeper Mark Kendall who had previously played for Wolves and Spurs. It sounded impressive enough. If we'd known Aldershot would be wound up by the season's end maybe we'd have chosen to stay in bed on 21st December. All that way for a result on a day that was beset by a howling gale, a win that was eventually expunged. But on the day Mansfield the leaders lost, and Burnley went top. Lancs scored again but it was to be his last for Burnley.

Going to a place like Aldershot was a lovely example of the quaint places in which we lower league players plied our trade. Supporter Tim Quelch described it beautifully:

> We will miss Aldershot with its quaint park entrance and herbaceous borders. You expected to pick up your crazy-golf clobber and your raspberry split as you squeezed through their turnstiles. Once you had climbed up the winding path up to the pitch, you were actually quite disappointed not to find a boating lake and a few ducks. When kept behind after an evening game you half expected them to ask you to turn off the lights and put the cat out as you left. Steve Claridge told us in his book Tales from the Boot Camp that one 'Shots' player qualified for a disabled sticker. Forget your Nou Camps and San Siros; this was a club with true class. (Tim Quelch)

Maybe it was struggling clubs like these, and the Rochdales and Torquays and Herefords which were at the heart of the game. These places were filled with the little people of football, the people filled with genuine heart. Half-time collections at Aldershot games had helped keep them going and pay the wages. This was the reality of Division Four football and not that many years earlier it could well have been Burnley.

Despite this rise to the top, Mullen was careful. 'We have to keep our feet on the ground and make sure we don't get smacked on the nose.' This was ironic. The after-match interview was delayed because Jimmy had a nosebleed, probably because we were so high in the table.

Unfortunately, we got smacked on the nose in the very next game. Boxing Day at Turf Moor and some of the laws of football transcend all others. Regardless of the circumstances, however well Burnley are doing, Burnley always seem to lose on Boxing Day and Burnley duly lost against Rotherham United in front of nearly 14,000 people, most of them filled with turkey, mince pies and stuffing. Fans used to say there was always a magic atmosphere on Boxing Day with the aroma of cigar smoke and the tang of brandy from hip flasks. Try doing that today. This one was the day that the 16 game unbeaten run ended. I remember us being below our best; this was so disappointing in front of such a big crowd. Fans said it was typical of Burnley to screw up when the pressure mounted and now that we were top was it this pressure that was invisibly weighing us down? No, we said, you can't stay unbeaten forever. However good you are, a defeat will catch you up one day. And we were still top because all the top four teams lost so there couldn't have been a better day to lose. People went back to their turkey sandwich suppers. We went back home thinking there was another game just two days later. We'd actually been in the day before on Christmas Day for a training session. Footballers don't get a Christmas. There was even one Christmas when we stayed overnight in a Burnley hotel and I took a voluntary breathalyser test down at the local police station to see if I was fit to drive. If not I would need to ask Andrea to drive me.

The last game of 1991 and it was back to winning ways. For the fifth time it was against Doncaster Rovers. Bremner was no longer there. The score in this game never reflected how well Burnley played and how dominant they were. There were so many chances one after the other. I cringed when I managed to miss in front of an open goal. It was total one-way traffic; we were always on them, always at them, pressuring and outplaying them. Mick Conroy scored early and then yours truly atoned for the earlier miss, latching onto a long pass and then chipping it over the goalkeeper. Lovely stuff but somehow they pulled one back nearer the end to make it a daft scoreline and leaving supporters chewing fingernails in a game where we might have had six. But we hadn't lost and at the end of the year there was Burnley at the top of the Division, leaving supporters blinking and Frank Teasdale and directors dreaming of triumph.

Jimmy Mullen set a target of not losing two in a row. Do that he said and promotion is possible. We didn't lose two in a row. Promotion was possible.

9

A Grand Day Out

When a footballer's career is over, for most it is then all about memories. When we finish we can draw on the good ones and smile. When we meet we can re-live treasured moments, and carry on playing if we can, wherever we can find a game. And yes we grumble about old managers.

Several of us who were in the '91–92 team meet fairly regularly to play in charity games in and around the Burnley area; there's myself along with John Francis, John Deary and Graham Lancashire. It's a good chance to puff and pant and enjoy ourselves. There are others from other years. They won't mind me saying but John Francis and Ian Britton compete to see who has the bigger waistline. I remember first meeting with John at Burnley. He had a little moustache and a black shiny suit with lapels so wide he could hardly fit through the door. He looked like the lead singer from the Four Tops. He suffered from bunions. If he fluffed a pass or mishit a shot we'd yell at him: 'Must have hit yer bunions John.'

It was Ian Britton who scored one of the goals in the end of season game against the Orient that Burnley just had to win in '87 to stay in the Football League. The only downside to these charity games is the occasional young buck you meet playing for the opposition who decides he wants to make his mark and leave a few bruises on an old ex-pro.

Of course we talk about our families, kids and jobs. We talk about who we've played for and who we've played with, about this modern player and that. We all have teams we watch. Manchester United is mine. But one thing we talk about is what makes a good manager. Between us we've played for dozens. Players don't ask for much but they do like fair, strong, decisive managers who inspire them. It's a big thing if you can look up to great ex players like Eddie Gray, Frank Casper and Brian Little as managers. But, great player that he was, I can't say I ever looked up to Billy Bremner as a person

145

but as a player he was always someone I aspired to be.

The way managers motivate players varies. It might come from great training sessions and intelligent tactics. It might just come from rousing words, a great sense of humour, an understanding of players' problems and their needs. Maybe it comes from a bubbling, enthusiastic, infectious and dynamic energy that a player cannot help but absorb. The best are good communicators and treat their players as adults. From this comes trust. But sometimes a manager has few, if any, of these qualities yet still the team succeeds. That's usually down to sheer good fortune when sometimes a group comes together by chance and gels as a team. We talk about how the same bunch of players failed Frank Casper, a man who had so many good qualities, but succeeded for Jimmy Mullen. In long phone calls I've had with Ron Futcher or John Deary, or whenever I meet John Francis, we've inevitably discussed Jimmy Mullen. With Mike Conroy it was in emails we exchanged. All of us I suspect, no matter who we are or whatever our jobs, talk about our old bosses.

It's as interesting talking to John Deary now as much as I ever did. We called him 'Loafy' and the remarkable thing was how little interest he had in any football outside of whatever game he happened to be playing in and never had a clue about who we were playing. Ask him about any opposition player and he'd say: 'Never 'eard of 'im.' He was a massive fans' favourite.

Sure, we'll remember the bad times and the disappointments too. Even if season '91/92 had been disappointing with no end product it would still have been remembered. Even without promotion, one series of games would have provided great moments that would become part of Burnley history. They were the three games against Derby County in the FA Cup. I played in all three and in one of them scored a goal to remember.

For someone like me where the chance to play at the real top level for any length of time never really happened, I'm just grateful that I managed to salvage something. I can look back fondly at my spell at Burnley where one of the seasons there was so magical. The fans took to me. When I go back now, I am remembered with appreciation and affection. I realised this not too many years ago at a book launch dinner at Turf Moor. Dave Thomas invited several of us to help celebrate the appearance of one of his books. One by one the football guests were introduced and from behind a screen we walked to our table. John Francis was there as well. As I walked in, the shouts and applause and chants for me took me totally aback. It was unexpected. The warmth was enormous.

Why do fans take to some players and not others? It helped that I scored goals I suppose, but it was more than just that. Maybe they saw in me a whole-hearted battler, a give-everything, chase everything, 100% player. What's clear in football is that skill alone will not make any player a hero. Some of the most skilled players I know could just drift languidly through a game, a pass here, a pass there, a moment of class, but there was still something lacking. Somewhere there has to be passion and spirit, guts and pain for a crowd really to identify with a player. Maybe John Deary is the perfect example, a real box-to-box player, and a real midfield ball-winner. There's an iconic picture of him standing and snarling over a fallen Bryan Robson. He had everything and the fans loved him and what he brought to the team; bravery, physical toughness, the teammate you'd want next to you in a real scrap. Fans today will say we could do with another John Deary. They can pay him no higher compliment.

The rapport between fans and the whole team on the pitch is something else. It's a chemistry, a bond based on raw passion. It's as if the fans on the terraces feel that the players out there are an extension of themselves. It's possible that every man on the terraces would love to have been a player. So we, the players, are their alter egos. When we hurt, they hurt. When we win, they've won. If the team gives 100% they will give the same. When we don't, or they perceive that we don't, then they are let down. They've been failed. They're angry. But when they're with you, you can feel it and hear it. They lift you, drive you on; raise you to the next level. And nowhere was this more tangible and visible than at Derby County in the FA Cup on January 25th, 1992. It was one of those days when people can say, and still say, 'I was there'. It was a game where the crowd was more important than the result. In fact we lost but there was an outpouring of support that made the national headlines the next day. It was truly remarkable.

It started at home against lowly Doncaster with a 1–1 draw. The game was tinged with a bit of 'after the Lords Mayor's Show' feeling coming after the terrific game against Mansfield. Cloughie had decided he didn't want goalkeeper Marriott to be cup-tied so back came Chris Pearce. Mike Conroy missed a penalty. Doncaster scored. Davis nipped down the other end and equalised. So it went to a replay. Just three days later it was Doncaster again in the Autoglass Trophy. There ought to be a limit you are allowed to play the same side in one season. This was getting ridiculous. Jimmy Mullen played the full strength first-team. A 2–0 win kept the momentum going. Few people were interested with fewer than 3,000 there. Who could blame them? The only reason I remember it is because I scored. You know what strikers say; all goals are good goals so it must have been a good one.

Doncaster again on November 27th, the Cup replay and third game played against them in just a few days. I didn't mind. I scored again. The name Belle Vue is a misnomer; there was nothing belle about Belle Vue. My goal was the third and in the papers was described as the 'flourish' at the end of a comfortable win.

So next up it was Rotherham at home in the second round. They were doing well and were just below us in the table. At stake was a potentially lucrative tie in the next round if the draw was kind and a big name came out. When you play at the bottom end of the football pyramid these things do matter. It's the one chance of a bit of that mythical glamour and limelight; a spot on Match of the Day maybe and a few newspaper headlines. We struggled a bit until Mike Conroy's goal and then Graham Lancashire's wrapped it up. I suppose you could say it was one of those routine home wins where the home team wins simply because they are at home and are just that bit more comfortable. The draw for the next round was sort of half pleasing. Yes it was a decent draw against a club with a big name. But Derby were no longer a First Division force; they were in the Second Division. But there was still an aura to the name and the game was at Turf Moor.

For the Rotherham win there had been a gate of nearly 10,000. The FA Cup back then was still a big occasion. It still had standing and prestige. Wembley to us and the supporters was a distant target that only big teams achieved—but there was always that tiny bit of 'well who knows?' People used to look forward to the Cup then and big teams did not play their second-string teams. It was still a special day in the football calendar when the Third Round arrived and the big teams joined in.

Turf Moor, Derby County, and 'we were up for it' as the saying goes. And they had Peter Shilton in goal. 'Should I ask him does he remember me and the boots I nicked?' I wondered.

We spent three days in Harrogate before the game. If team spirit wasn't already good it was even better after a couple of nights in luxury conditions at the Majestic Hotel. After training on the Thursday before the game we left for Harrogate. We did wonder if this was arranged for us the players, or the directors who came along. Never mind, such perks received no complaints from me.

Jimmy 'Mad Dog' Mullen got his preparations right and we were superbly relaxed. I shared a room with Ian Bray, a good lad and a good player but who couldn't manage to break in to the first team on a regular basis. A continual moaner, but he was happy on this occasion and within five minutes he was filling up the sunken Jacuzzi in our suite. I had to sample this. A cigar, a bottle of champagne, a fedora and a long legged blonde would have been perfect. Alas, when I looked across, all I had was Ian Bray, better known as Pod. All this was a million miles from Crewe, York and Bury and the way they used to prepare. I couldn't help thinking this is what it must be like all the time for the top teams.

We left The Majestic on the Saturday morning leaving elegant Harrogate behind us and travelled through the picturesque Yorkshire countryside. I looked down the coach and it felt so good to be a part of this team. Jimmy Mullen was in his usual place at the front of the coach alongside the chairman. The directors were a couple of seats behind. Hughie, the driver, calmly negotiated the twists and turns of the road over the moors and through Blubberhouses. I sat with my own little thoughts of Wembley and Cup Final day. This would be the closest I ever got to something I had dreamed of since boyhood.

There were always people waiting at the players' entrance for autographs and photographs. As ever Edgar was there. I never knew his other name but he was an older supporter who always greeted us. Every home game he'd wait and give me any cuttings or newspapers featuring me that he had saved. He was the kind of supporter who made me want to play, a true diehard who had supported his team through thick and thin. Such blokes are the lifeblood of the game, not the spoilt superstars who live in a different world.

The dressing room buzzed. You could hear the noise of the crowd above our heads and the stamping of their feet. This was a day that we were really up for.

What a fantastic game it was in front of nearly 19,000 people. It summed up all that was good about the excitement of the FA Cup. It was the sort of game that fans hoped for; that had them leaving the ground well satisfied and proud. Derby County, two divisions above us, twice had the lead but Burnley just wouldn't let go. We were a team of persistence with a never-say-die spirit. It was a team that never gave up without a fight.

But it started so badly. Martin Chalk scored after just 32 seconds. The crowd was deflated but we weren't. As a general rule a footballer is stunned when this happens but realises immediately that there are still 89 minutes to do something about it. A goal so early you tend just to shrug off, annoying though it might be. The crowd might think a rout is on the cards but players don't. We came back and within minutes Steve Harper put Burnley level, finishing off a right wing attack and slotting past Shilton. Joe Jakub had fed me the ball. I went past two Derby players, got to the line and crossed. Steve was on the end of it. Shilton had been given a good reception by the crowd but two and a half years later he would generate huge bitterness and anger when his team came in a play-off game and attempted to kick Burnley off the park.

Close to the end they took the lead again but Burnley equalised in the 84th minute:

> They had reckoned without Roger Eli. It had been in a Cup match little more than two years before that he'd become a striker. Now our cult hero produced something really special finishing off another Conroy cross. Eli's header was perfect, powerful and precise, truly bullet like. It must still be one of the best headed goals I've seen and Shilton didn't stand a chance.' (Andrew Firmin)

I can remember it to this day. It was a peach of a header and went in like a rocket from the cross that came over. If I could choose one moment to re-live, maybe this would be it. Every second is crystal clear to this day. If one moment was heaven in my footballer's life, then this was it. It was the perfect header, the perfect goal. Bill Thornton in the *Sunday Mirror* gave Burnley and me a rare bit of national publicity when in just a few paragraphs he told the story of my fragmented career. I'd like to think that Eddie Gray saw it, along with Billy Bremner, Graham Turner, Dario Gradi and Martin Dobson.

No one at the Baseball Ground this Tuesday deserves to grab some Cup glory more than Roger Eli. The Burnley striker has been shunted from pillar to post in a career crammed with lows and no highs until recently. Now just the replay at Derby stands between Eli and a date with the big-time and a possible confrontation with FA Cup holders Spurs, Gary Lineker and all.

'It would be quite something wouldn't it?' ponders this 26-year old veteran of six clubs, not one of whom have paid a penny in transfer fees for his services. 'There is the small matter of beating Derby first. But it's hard not to dream about meeting Spurs or Villa. Either will do me fine.'

Eli notched his tenth goal of the season for the Fourth Division pacesetters last Saturday to take Derby to a replay. If Burnley can go one better on Tuesday they will bring one of the First Division giants to Turf Moor in the fourth round. It is heady stuff for the player who has faced an uphill route since a broken leg and cartilage problems crushed his hopes at Leeds six years ago. He joined Wolves, broke a foot and was rewarded with a free transfer. Then Eli was booted out by Crewe after 30-odd appearances as a non-contract player. A trial at York lasted only a month before he was shown the door again.

'I had a successful trial with Bury before Frank Casper brought me to Burnley two years ago. The town is buzzing with football talk. It's all very exciting and it makes all my struggles worthwhile. The easy way out would have been to quit. But I absolutely love playing football. I just hope that at the end of the day, the effort is going to pay off,' says Eli. (Bill Thornton)

With the game level we went home happy. It was the perfect day for fans and team alike, and certainly the chairman and club treasurer. Maybe we even felt disappointed as it was a game Burnley could have won if Graham Lancashire had been two inches taller when going for a header in the dying minutes. However, nobody was more disappointed than my sister Rhona who had been dragged away early by my dad. He wanted to avoid the rush of fans leaving at the end of the game. They missed my Goal of the Season equaliser.

I was named Man of the Match. I got quite a few nominations in my time at Burnley. When awarded Man of the Match, players met the match sponsors in the sponsor's lounge to be presented with the award. On this occasion it was a top Panasonic hi-fi outfit, a Brixton briefcase as the players called it. Nice. Sometimes it was a crate of ale or a bottle of champagne. You'd feel great on such occasions. Man of the Match, compliments, back slaps, warm greetings, applause, smiles, you're feeling fantastic; well, at least until the next game. Me: the player who in earlier years scrabbled for a contract in a trial at Cambridge. I loved the attention. What footballer wouldn't?

Ted McMinn was in the Derby team and on his day could turn anything and anyone inside out. On this day the crowd gave him some stick. Not long after he would become a Burnley player and another cult hero. In the post-match interview (after some games I just couldn't talk) Steve Davis called him a cheat, forever trying to con the referee. Not much later they'd be teammates in a Wembley play-off final.

The games by now were coming thick and fast with the replay at Derby just three days after the crunching 5–2 defeat at Blackpool. The daft thing I remember about this game was the fog. Derby cruised to a 2–0 lead but bit by bit the fog came down, and the fog thickened . . . and thickened . . . and thickened. Into the second half and from one end of the field we couldn't see the other half. The humour of a football crowd is something mystically wonderful when they chant in unison, seemingly spontaneously; and this time the Burnley fans chanted for the weather and fog to intervene. The Derby fans joined in and cheered imaginary goals.

Then, 'you only sing when it's foggy,' they chanted. It was hilarious and all of us on the field hadn't much of a clue what was going on more than 10 yards away. With 14 minutes to go the referee, Ken Redfern, blew and abandoned the game. By this time from the centre circle we couldn't see either goal. The Derby players must have been praying it would get no worse. We prayed that it did, desperate for it to be called off. We left the field delighted.

Mark Kendall didn't chuckle though. After the game Mullen wasted no time in making sure he would play no further part in the season. He was sent back to Swansea. It's a sad thing; maybe Mark was a perfectly good and competent goalkeeper nine times out of 10 but at Burnley he will be remembered by supporters and the history books solely for a 5–2 defeat at Blackpool. As soon as he had gone Chris came off the transfer list.

The replayed replay was set for fourth-round day. Everyone else was one step ahead. Burnley enjoyed a little more than usual publicity and attention. The old Baseball Ground was less than impressive and had always been known for its mudbath of a pitch. There was a curious hotchpotch of stands. They bordered the pitch tightly, almost dangerously but because of this the atmosphere the place generated was second to none.

Derby set about the match as if they were determined to prove that this replay was an unnecessary irritation. Somehow it was still 0–0 at halftime but in the second half they quite comfortably went 2–0 up from a goalkeeping muddle and then a deflected free kick. Their win was routine and expected.

But this game passed into the Burnley history books because it was a game during which a most extraordinary thing happened and this was nothing to do with the players; it was all to do with the supporters. And because it was so special, so unique, I've included supporter Andrew Firmin's marvellous account of the day:

The fact that we went out of the Cup was not what this game was all about. This isn't why this game has passed into legend, why it forms such a key part of Claret history, why those who were there were proud to be, and will talk about it to this day. And even better, it wasn't the players who made that day special. It was us. We did it. If I look back at other memorable games of our time, I remember the part the supporters played in them of course, I remember what it felt like as a supporter to be there, but mostly I remember a goal, or a tackle or a save, a piece of outrageous skill or a colossal blunder, or some action or other by a player. But here, the players and what happened on the pitch are incidental to the story. This is how it should be. I have long maintained that the only thing that matters in football is the supporters. We are the only thing to provide continuity to a club that elevates it beyond the status of a mere business. Players, staff, managers, directors and chairmen all come and go. The history of a club lives in its support. Without these keepers of the flame, Burnley is just a local business that plays football and sells shirts. Well—this was our day.

The chant crept up on us halfway through the second half. It started gradually, in a defiant response to the second and decisive goal. I wonder who started it. I wonder who starts any of these chants. It was taken up: Jimmy Mullen's Claret and Blue Army. By now it was a familiar chant. The bloke's stock was set at an all time high. His Messiah status seemed assured. The chant had first been aired during the two months after he'd taken charge during which we'd gone unbeaten. The club had even taken up on this and slapped it on a T-shirt. It was a good chant too; because it started slow and orderly, then sped up, sent the handclapping all over the place, got breathless and lost the words in a blur.

So it went . . . and went on . . . and on and on and on. After a while everyone knew that we were going to keep this up for the rest of the game. That was the challenge and we must not fail. We kept it going. People stood up and joined in. The events of the game grew unimportant. We were losing, so what. The chant kept going.

The game took an air of unreality. Balls flashed across our box, or went out for a throw-in on the halfway line. The response was identical. The chant continued. They attacked, or we threatened to break away. It didn't matter. The noise was the same noise. There was one moment when the chant gave way. Somehow by a process unknown, it was communicated to us in the bottom tier that Andy Marriott was sat watching the game from an upstairs seat. Our love for Andy was strong and unconditional. Here was a young lad who had come on loan from Brian Clough's Nottingham Forest, who had come to Burnley an unknown and left three months later a hero. It wasn't just his all-round goalkeeping ability that had endeared him to us, or his agility, reflexes and bravery. There was all that of course and almost from the first game we'd been demanding we sign him on. To the club's credit they'd tried too, and had offered rising sums of money far in excess of anything we'd ever seen bandied about before. But Quixotic Clough had insisted that there be no sale, and when the three months loan had run its course, Marriott had to head back. He'd been chaired from the pitch a hero after his last game, away at Northampton. But beyond all that, what made us bond with him is that he had clearly bonded with us. If we wanted him to stay then it genuinely seemed he wanted to stop. He'd repeatedly declared his desire to sign in the local Press, even taking the fairly extraordinary step of announcing that he now regarded Burnley as his first club and Forest just a place where he trained. I wonder what Clough had to say about that.

There was only one thing to do in the circumstances: sing. We launched into our familiar song, 'Swing Low Sweet Marriott' and invited said keeper to give us a wave. Formalities acknowledged; one of our own properly greeted. Now back to 'Jimmy Mullen's Claret and Blue Army' with a vengeance.

I suppose I had half an idea we would stop chanting at the end of the game, applaud and then quickly abandon the away end. Not a chance. The final whistle passed as though trivial. A little applause to greet the end was not allowed to interrupt the momentum of the chant. We went for it with renewed vigour, louder, faster. Some people stood on seats to add emphasis. Hardly anyone left the away end.

The home fans, meanwhile, had run through a range of reactions.

At first they had ridiculed us and attempted to patronise us, as fans of a higher club in a higher division always do. Then the brighter ones had started to twig that something uncommon was happening here. By the end they were frankly gawping at our show of support. As they left, some even gave us their applause. This was tough for the police and the stewards too. They would have been expecting us to leave quietly at the end. The fact that we stayed and kept on singing left them bemused. Trained to intervene in crowd unrest, nothing in the handbook prepared them for a crowd simply enjoying itself too much to go home. They talked into their walkie-talkies and left the initiative to each other. They had no idea what to do. They might have had experience of protests at football grounds before. Certainly they would have been veterans of picket lines and student marches. And demonstrations at football matches are nothing new. But this was an odd one. It was a demonstration in favour of a manager not opposing him. It was an affirmation of undying support, of belief in the club, of willingness to stick with them. Who ever heard of that kind of demo before?

Eventually the team and manager emerged to take our tumultuous acclaim. It was by now about 15 minutes after the game had ended and apart from the stewards we were the only people in the stadium: the team, the management, and the supporters. A strong connection was forged between us that day. On a couple of occasions that season the team pulled off unlikely results through late goals and who knows how much of that never-say-die attitude was due to a determination not to let these fans down. One also thinks of several of the players from that day, who, long after their Burnley careers had ended, would express their continuing affection and support for the club.

Then at the end of the season when at York we sealed the title, moments of pure joy there had their grounding in the extraordinary unity between players, manager and supporters that was created at Derby. Although we lost this particular game, who knows what value the manner of the defeat had in us winning the title?

Finally we filed away, conscious that we had played our part in something quite special. This was confirmed by the Press coverage which abandoned any pretence of reporting the game to concentrate on our show of devotion. I would never give houseroom to the *Sun* but even I would admit that John Sadler's piece from the following Monday is something that needs to be read and preserved.

It was a day that will always be remembered by any Claret who had the privilege to be there. Often, when Burnley fans of my generation are asked to name their moment when they were proudest to be a Claret, it is this day they think of. There have been countless games when we've played a lot better. There have even been times, usually at Cup games, when we have played superior opposition, when we've attempted to sustain a chant as long and loud as this, and there have been many times when we have come close, although of course it's always lacked that spontaneity and the sense of surprise in the achievement of surpassing ourselves that we had at Derby.

But this day was special. It always will be. Derby had won their test series of games against us 1—0. Whichever way you look at it we had been beaten. Yet we remember it as a victory. How many other games could you ever say that? (Andrew Firmin)

John Sadler's report in *The Sun* two days later confirmed all that had happened:

Burnley took 4,000 Lancashire lads and lasses to the Midlands. And they were sensational. Soon after goalkeeper Chris Pearce dropped his dreadful clanger they set up one of the loudest, sustained chants I've heard on a football ground anywhere in the world. The Burnley crowd's chant of 'Jimmy Mullen's Claret and Blue Army' totally drowned the home support.

'Jimmy Mullen's claret and blue army' was the chant from the terraces and double-decker stand that housed Burnley's admiration society. Over and over they chanted it. Clapping and stamping their feet and drumming on the advertising boards in perfect rhythm. On and on for 20 minutes until the end of the match and another 15 minutes afterwards until I urged the chairman to get his manager and players to leave the dressing room, return to the pitch and wave their appreciation. The bedlam was almost deafening.

Those who kept up that incessant, thunderous chant were real fans; genuine football people with a deep love of their club, no matter the result of a single game. They had nothing to do with the executive box brigade and corporate hospitality merchants to whom football is pandering in the modern era. They stood in the rain, sat in the cold and screamed their allegiance to a game which, at the highest level, continues to turn its back. (John Sadler)

It all left Jimmy Mullen open-mouthed and amazed: 'In all my 23 years in the game I've never witnessed anything like that. It left my players feeling they were prepared to die for those people.'

Never mind what Jimmy thought. It left us, the players, amazed and confirmed my view that I still hold today, that supporters are the most important people at any club. Without them there is no club. The roar of the crowd puts wings on a player's boots, gives him confidence and puts determination into his heart. To this day memories of the Burnley crowd and the passion and noise of The Longside are crystal clear. I can't begin to explain how that Burnley crowd gave me such a marvellous feeling.

10

A Time to Remember Ends

The party was subdued that Christmas. It was late and didn't take place until after the Blackpool game that was well into January. In previous years they had been riotous affairs thanks to party animal and chief organiser Winston White. A stripper and body lotion usually featured at the annual bash at The Hawthorns in Nelson. A stark naked player who cavorted round one year shall remain nameless. But this year after a defeat it was low-key and subdued. It was organised by the Club and it certainly wasn't a stylish Christmas Dinner event. This was Burnley not the Ritz, and it was Pie and Peas. There wasn't even a sprig of holly stuck in the pie. But, anyway, none of us were in any mood for festivities after the Blackpool defeat. The Club had laid on a karaoke machine for us, the wives and the girlfriends. It went down like a lead balloon and when Andrea and I went up to perform the Lionel Richie classic 'Hello' it was more a case of 'Hello and Goodnight'. It was embarrassing. Just sometimes I'd jot a few things down on paper. I found this. It could have been written after any defeat.

Defeat: the end of the world, crushing every feeling of positivity at that very moment. Walk off the pitch in a daze. If there's booing, negativity from the terraces, you don't hear it. Carry on walking down the tunnel. Kick the dressing room door open, sit down, all the players are sitting down, hunched shoulders, staring at the floor. Kit thrown all over the place, nobody speaks. The gaffer walks in. Face showing the strain. Helps himself to a mug of tea, decides to have a sip; decides against it. His eyes start to roam round the room. Who will be the first to get it?

He looks across at me; the defence mechanism kicks in. I'm ready to deflect the situation; ready to deflect the moment the manager has a go. You learn to find ways of avoiding the tongue-lashing, 'But gaffer I had two men to mark.' The gaffer looks for the player who allowed that to happen. His eyes move on. This way you get away with it this time. The inquest seems to go on forever. It seems like a lifetime in that room. It smells of sweat, damp and mud. You cannot switch off. You have to pay attention in case he comes back at you again and you need a decent answer to his criticism.

The door opens. It's one of the apprentices. 'Out!' yells the gaffer fuming with anger. He hasn't finished yet. It goes on. As if you didn't feel bad enough already he then rips into you saying that you've let the side down, you should have done this, you should have done that. You should have tracked the runner. That was a chance you should have scored.

Deflated, depressed, the lads are quiet. The gaffer leaves and says, 'See you in the morning.' Shit that's the day off we've lost and we'll go through all this again. The dressing room starts to breathe, starts to move; bit by bit livens up. Muffled conversations start. The apprentices come in collecting boots and kit from all over the floor not daring to say a word.

We get into the bath, sit and soak, contemplate things. There's always the next game.

The seventh away league win in a row came on New Year's Day at Chesterfield. Apparently it broke a record that had stood since 1919. But then for the next away game at Blackpool goalkeeper Chris Pearce was gutted to be dropped again as Mark Kendall was the latest goalkeeper to arrive on loan. It did nothing for his confidence. It was a feature of an outstanding season. By the end of it, Jimmy Mullen had used five goalkeepers. I'd guess this was a record; that a club with so many goalkeepers actually won a title. Chris asked to go on the transfer list without knowing that Mark would not last long following the game at Blackpool.

It was just one of those days and it all went wrong at Blackpool on a wild, wet and windy day. It all went wrong for Mark Kendall. Everything about going to Blackpool was unpleasant that day. Back then it was a shabby place and the ground was a crumbling, unimaginable dump. It looked like someone had got hold of an old, decrepit, non-league ground, thrown it all up in the air and it had landed badly. The rain that day lashed down and the wind almost lifted you off your feet. Jimmy Mullen was nervous and edgy as he always was when there was a game against the Tangerines. He had previous history there. It transmitted itself to us. Inside the ground, being a former manager, he was given some dreadful abuse. Even the stewards joined in and celebrated every goal that Blackpool scored.

I was on edge too. I had a kicking from Garry Briggs to look forward to. Almost every time we played them, our talented full-back Ian Measham would do his best to wind him up calling him, 'Gringo, el Bandido' on account of his thick, black, Mexican-style moustache. It was Ian who goaded him but it was me who felt Briggs' scything legs whipping into the back of mine. I had played against hard players many times, but this guy was like a silent assassin. He never said a word and would give you his welcoming crack to the back of your head with his forehead just to remind you to be on your guard.

Maybe we were suffering a reaction to the exertions we had put in against Derby at Turf Moor in the Cup a few days earlier. But we certainly underperformed; none more so than our unfortunate goalkeeper who to put it mildly had one of those nightmare games that one day afflicts all footballers. And when it is a goalkeeper there is, alas, no hiding place. Everything about the Burnley display was off-key but supporters' fingers pointed accusingly at Mark Kendall. But I missed some good chances as well. By the end it was a horrible 5–2 defeat and no amount of team spirit or fight-back could make up for so many errors, one of which included a cross that went straight through the goalkeeper's fingers. Yet, in an earlier game he'd saved a penalty. Twice we looked to be back in the game, at one point the score being just 3–2 to Blackpool. But overall it was calamitous and the first away defeat under Jimmy Mullen. I felt for Mark; a goalkeeper makes mistakes and they are remembered. A striker misses chances and they are forgotten the next time he scores. Mark despaired after the game knowing that every Burnley finger would be pointing at him, some of them with hate. We all came off that field thoroughly miserable knowing that we hadn't done ourselves justice.

The result saw us slip from top to second. It was depressing and to make matters worse it was the nearest thing to a derby game that season; there was no love lost between the two sets of supporters and Blackpool were a promotion rival. There are still fans with vivid memories of standing in one area of the ground that was below pitch level with hardly any view of what was going on. Mind you, the fans who stood there will say that was a blessing. When the fifth goal went in we could hardly blame the Burnley fans who left early. They came full of confidence but you didn't need to be Einstein to work out they left thoroughly deflated.

Gillingham next and we got back to winning ways and the four goals scored could have been doubled. But I missed it because of a kick I received in a previous game. Mike Conroy was annoyed when he missed several chances and still managed to bag a hat-trick. Goalkeeper Lim, who was of Chinese ancestry and had a ponytail, quite unusual in the game in those days, made a hash of a few things. We could have scored three in the first 10 minutes but somehow Gillingham equalised thanks to some careless defending. More chances were squandered and the crowd grew restless; they remembered Blackpool. But all went well and eventually we rattled in four goals. It was important that we won after the Blackpool defeat and restored our morale. As a bonus it took us back to the top of the table. It looked good.

It was around this time that Jimmy Mullen was lucky not to end up in prison. He was found to be well over the legal limit of alcohol in his blood when he was breathalysed after he'd collided with the vehicle on front of him. His former boss at Blackpool, Owen Oyston, reportedly said he was surprised because he'd always thought Jimmy was teetotal. Footballers are merciless with their humour and fun-making. John Deary joked that perhaps Jimmy thought he could plug his car into the cats' eyes in the middle of the road and his car would drive itself home. There was the inevitable: 'Great that's another three points then.'

We used to take turns to go to the cash-and-carry to stock up on drinks for the players' lounge and bar that we used after a game. It was only a tiny, drab room under the Stand. It was our job not Jimmy's but I did an impersonation of him on a shopping trip to the cash-and-carry.

'Ooh I'll have six of those,' I said and mimed putting six bottles of whisky into the trolley. 'Ooh I'll have six of those please,' and mimed putting six bottle of vodka into the trolley. 'Do I want orange juice? No, but let's have six bottles of gin.' And so it went on and had the lads in stitches. It was crude and insensitive, but that's footballers' humour for you and maybe the gaffer was just the same when he was a player.

February was a month of late goals and exciting come-backs. We came through the month unbeaten. The 2–2 draw at Walsall was typical of the come-backs. Walsall went 2–0 up but with defeat

161

looming we came back with goals from me and Mike Conroy with just 5 minutes to go. We just never knew when we were beaten.

I have a memory of this being a game when I got the proverbial bollocking. The gaffer had a real go at me at halftime for catching their giant centre-half Colin Methven with a few late tackles. Big Colin was having an outstanding game. He was kicking and heading everything and marshalling his back four well. In the second half I accidentally caught him again late, and he had to go off. It was the only reason we got back into the game. After the match the gaffer was jubilant. I shouted over to him, 'Gaffer good job Colin got injured wasn't it?' He just looked and smiled this time, and shook his head.

The psychology of 'the bollocking' or 'the hairdryer' would probably provide enough material for a book of its own. There are countless stories of managers laying into someone. The team comes in after a bad game maybe. The manager glowers. Everyone sits there worried sick in case it's them who's going to get it in the neck. The manager starts, the spittle flies, the voice is thunderous, the eyes narrowed—and in my experience usually aiming at someone who won't answer back. The rest of the team sit back and wait for it to finish, totally relieved that someone else is the victim. Why do managers do it? I can't think it happens in any other job.

When a manager loses it, it's like nothing you can imagine. I've been in dressing rooms up and down the country, seen doors punched and kicked, cups thrown across the room, raging anger, and on one occasion a manager breaking down into tears after one 20 minute non-stop rollicking.

There was a struggle to beat Lincoln in the next home game by just 1–0. But now there were two games a week and there was no way you could play scintillating stuff every game. It was scrappy, the crowd were restless but a win is a win.

It was made up for by the next game at home to Northampton. They themselves were a good side and were unbeaten in ten games. But for us this was a game when everything went right; it was one of those great nights under the floodlights when Burnley were brilliant. The first goal was Harlem Globetrotters stuff. Mick Conroy in midfield flick headed the ball on. Yours truly instantly flicked it on with a heel to John Francis. He did the same for John Deary to run on to. John waited for the goalie to come out and just rolled it in. It was just brilliant. When you get skilled players playing with confidence, anything can happen. If I had two qualities it was speed and aggression. Speed and aggression got me the second goal when John Francis played a simple ball in front of me and on I went and unleashed a savage shot that even though it hit the goalkeeper, still went in. A pass might look simple but even the most simple pass needs skill, perception, touch and the right weight. The goals piled in and the supporters found one of them hilarious. A long clearance sailed over everyone's head with Trevor Quow miles ahead of everyone in the chase that followed. Mike Conroy gave him a 20 yard start and still beat him to the ball and walked it past the stranded keeper. It would have been no surprise if Mike hadn't looked back and waved at Quow as he tore past. To be fair Trevor was injured and had pulled a hamstring when Mick flew past him. After we scored I joked with Trevor, 'Trev you must be the slowest black man in the world'. It was just one of those games when everything comes off, down the middle, down the wings, crosses headed home, great football and when Harps scored it felt like party time as we all piled on top of him. It was fitting that John Francis got the final goal; he'd had an outstanding game. There'd been five goals and five scorers.

'What can I say?' was all that Jimmy Mullen had to say afterwards, as it all clicked into place.

Scunthorpe and two goals down with 45 minutes still to play. We were really struggling but the supporters as ever were playing their part with their songs and chants: 'No Nay Never and 'We are Burnley super Burnley'. At last we got a breakthrough. The ball broke to me inside the penalty box and one of their two giant centre-halves came through me from behind. That was the only invitation I needed to make the most of his outstretched leg. Penalty! Mick Conroy strode up to make it 2–1 and we were back in the game.

All hell broke loose when their 'keeper Chris Marples was sent off for lashing out at Mick who had certainly made the most of the situation, something that I would have been proud of. The handbags were out; there was pushing and shoving and I lifted one of the Scunthorpe players off his feet. One of their outfield players went in goal and had a blinder. We just couldn't get the equaliser until then, in the 95th minute, big Stevie Davis towered above everybody to power in the perfect equaliser from a Joe Jakub corner. We went wild; the supporters went wild. The whistle went and there was total jubilation until it all kicked off again in the tunnel. The Scunthorpe players were still incensed by the sending-off. It was mayhem and I caught a real belt on the ear from a flying fist. The verbals, the fists and punches were all over the place but we were capable lads and more than a match for them.

Jimmy Mullen brought yet another goalkeeper in. It was like he had a box of spare goalkeepers somewhere and kept dipping in to bring another one out. This one was Nicky Walker, reportedly the heir to a biscuits fortune. Funnily enough his first name was Joseph. Mullen was yet again ruthless with Chris Pearce. Chris was upset and you couldn't blame him. So often the goalkeeper carries the can. But a manager isn't there to be popular with the players; he's there to do a job and get the supporters the success they want.

Nicky certainly knew his biscuits and there was the occasion we had a long coach journey home. A couple of days before a mate of mine had bought over 50 boxes of biscuits and let me have a couple. So, I took ten packets to the next away game. On the way back, the lads were starving and the gaffer had said we were not stopping for anything to eat. I pulled out a packet of biscuits. The lads looked at them, their tongues hanging out. 'Come on Dodge,' they demanded. 'Share them out.'

'A pound a pack,' I said enjoying the usual banter and brought the rest of the packets out of my bag.

'No chance,' they replied. I said nothing but placed them in full view on the coach table until John Deary about an hour later pulled out his pound and threw it over. The rest of the lads soon followed. Ten packs of biscuits gone in quick succession. But then Nicky took hold of an empty packet and pointed out that they should all have been eaten at least three months earlier. 'You know these are all out of date, don't you lads,' he said laughing. At this point I swiftly moved to the front of the coach with the directors for the rest of the journey home, out of harm's way but I did offer a refund only if I got the goods back in one piece.

Over 18,000 turned up for the top of the table clash with rivals Blackpool. It was only a draw but I scored one of the best goals of the season. Blackpool were probably the better side and we were okay with the point. Blackpool's play was simple. Get a long ball up to big man Bamber who would flick it on. There was incessant pressure until I put a stop to it. I got the ball in midfield somewhere and with a man on either side of me headed for goal. I just shrugged them off and from some distance tried a shot. Other Blackpool players dived in to block the shot, there seemed to be a dozen of them round me. The ball came back off them and I got it again and found the gap between goalkeeper and yet another defender. It went in. It was one of those goals a player remembers, from midfield all the way on my own, just brushing off defenders.

'Eli gives Burnley vision of the past' was the title of the report in the *Daily Telegraph*. It was a nice article about the club's great tradition and how in the old days a clash between Blackpool and Burnley was a top fixture when people like Stan Matthews and Jimmy Adamson played. It was nice to be mentioned alongside such names.

> The atmosphere was no less tense than in the days when Harry Potts took Burnley into Europe and Blackpool challenged for First Division titles. Clubs with a famous history like these will continue to throw up players of talent and enable the old timers to recall the days of Matthews, Coates, Johnston and Adamson. Roger Eli is proof that Burnley folk still need their footballing heroes in this more sophisticated era and his brilliant goal, a blend of sheer determination and pure skill in the 31st minute thrilled his supporters. (Peter Keeling)

Unfortunately within a minute they went down the other end and equalised. They had a couple of decent wide players, one of them Trevor Sinclair who went on to become an international. He crossed to Bamber of all people and he headed home. They also had future Claret David Eyres. But for us Nicky Walker looked a class keeper. There were chances at either end but in all fairness the majority fell for Blackpool. It was a good point.

For supporters of any club Cardiff was never a happy or safe place to go to at the old Ninian Park. There was a time when trouble was routine down there and no supporter was ever surprised to be waylaid, or see bricks hurled at the coaches. Cardiff fans might say the same about Burnley of course which could also be an intimidating place. Cardiff were flying high at the time, about the only team that could generate support as big as Burnley's. The kick-off was delayed to get 16,000 people in. It was a tough game and looked to be heading for a 0–0 but then two late goals clinched the points. Nicky Walker stopped everything from Cardiff. It wasn't in the Cardiff script and the crowd turned ugly. Coins and stones rained down on the Burnley end. Coach windows were smashed; fans walking away to their cars were intimidated. It wasn't a day when I had a particularly good game and I remember a dog running loose on the pitch. Players and stewards tried to catch it and the dog did a better job of eluding them than I did of escaping the Cardiff defenders.

February ended with the Clarets unbeaten that month but Gillingham brought Burnley back down with a bump in the first game in March. What was worse was that it was only in January that we had beaten them so convincingly at home, 4–1. The versatile Andy Farrell was deputising for big John Pender. But no matter how versatile and talented Andy was, he was only half the size of big John. After the 3–0 defeat it was disappointing to slip to third. It was a long and dismal journey home. I've been on coaches when the manager or assistant would be straight down the aisle and would be furious with any player laughing or joking after a defeat or a poor performance.

The legend that was Barry Fry brought Barnet to Turf Moor. He was in his pomp, an absolute character. It didn't stop Barnet from being on the end of a good 3–0 win for Burnley. Barnet had scored a ton of goals but had let even more in. The third goal was one of those that infuriate an opposition goalkeeper when he sees the ball slipped though his legs and it rolls home. Top spot was nicely reclaimed without us having to work up too much of a sweat.

But on March 10th there was the most awful tragedy when Ben Lee a young apprentice climbed onto the Longside roof to retrieve a ball. Alas he fell through the roof to his death on the terracing below him. He was a teenager with everything in front of him. It was devastating. The ball had been kicked there during a schoolboy international the week before. There weren't many Health and Safety rules in the nineties and tragically Ben paid the price. That night we were due to play York and the game was rightly called off. Nothing seemed more important than promotion up until that point but this tragedy put it into perspective. Football was, and is, not the most important thing in life. Our hearts went out to his heartbroken family. Ben was a huge Manchester United fan and it was heart warming that several of their players came to the funeral.

I was with Chris Pearce at his home when I heard from him about the terrible news. Chris had been at the ground and was one of the first to see poor Ben unconscious after the fall. Chris was shocked and distraught. I'd got to know Ben quite well and our minds were on nothing else for several days. He was a lovely, well brought up young man. It was tragic.

Another win in mid-March but it was a subdued game. It was the first time that any sort of Burnley team had played since the awful accident. The game began with a moving one-minute silence. Few of us had our minds on the game in the build-up but once it started, the effort sort of kicked in. It had to. Captain Pender scored, rising high in the box to head home a free kick. The celebrations were minimal.

Nor was there anything pleasant about the next game played in a howling gale at Mansfield. Field Mill was a shabby, nondescript place. The game was scrappy, ruined by the wind. There was just one moment of skill. Mansfield never quite cleared Steve Harper's ball into the box. John Deary picked it up and played it on to Mike Conroy who stood with his back to goal. He passed to John Francis on the edge of the area. Mike ran behind John and called for the ball to be returned. John deftly flicked a backheel into his path. Mick shot as three defenders closed in. The keeper couldn't save it. I wasn't involved at all in this brilliant move and just stood and admired the interplay and skill. It was pure football, absolute class, and here we were in the Fourth Division. The win put us back above Mansfield into second place after this top of the table game.

Nicky Walker had proved to be a top keeper. But his month's loan was up. Jimmy Mullen and Frank Teasdale did all they could to keep him but Hearts were having none of it. He was courageous and energetic and the fans took to him. He was a good lad, tall, blonde and good looking; makes you sick doesn't it? The rumour was he had a Porsche 911 and lived in a castle in Scotland. But, he would never talk about his family wealth. Of the goalkeepers so far in the season fans rated him the best. Chris Pearce came back yet again. You could have forgiven him for feeling thoroughly resentful but he was a true pro and took his place again totally prepared to do his best for the team.

The 26th March was transfer deadline day and Mullen didn't quite manage to sign another goalkeeper. Surely if he had, six keepers in one season would have been a world record. There was talk of Arsenal's reserve keeper Alan Miller, then Andy Marriott again, but it came to nothing. But he did sign another striker Robbie

Painter. We were puzzled. There was already me, John Francis, Mike Conroy and Graham Lancashire and we couldn't quite see the need for additions unless Jimmy Mullen was now trying to bring his own players into the squad. We thought a fifth was unnecessary even though he was a good player. There was nothing personal in our feelings but what it did do was quietly send out a possible message that Jimmy Mullen wasn't entirely comfortable with the players he had.

The day's major news was that Aldershot finally went out of business. They were the first league club to crash out since Accrington Stanley 30 years earlier. Burnley came close in 1987 but the grapevine says that there were people who would have re-financed the club had they been relegated. As it happened even though we'd beaten Aldershot twice and had the six points expunged, Burnley benefited. The other top sides had all beaten them home and away by larger margins than Burnley. So by the time the deleted goals were taken into account Burnley actually went back to the top of the table level with Blackpool on 66 points; but above them on goal difference. First place was reclaimed courtesy of Aldershot. It was up to us to hang on to that spot.

Maybe nerves were beginning to affect us and fans for that matter. The club was edging nearer to the unthinkable — promotion. To understand the magnitude of the prospect you'd had to have been there for all the years they had floundered. I'd been there long enough, since '89, to understand at first hand just what it meant. I'd been there in the dressing room when on occasions hundreds of irate fans had demonstrated their anger at the two Franks. They were in a sense just the symbols of that period in the doldrums. Supporters had wondered after some games would this club ever succeed again. Now the end was in sight, getting close. It was a tantalising prospect. In the next home game against Maidstone it was touch and go. They took the lead and their goalkeeper Ian Hesford had one of those games when everything stuck to his hands like he had glue on them. They took a shock lead early in the second half. They time wasted at every opportunity. Chances came and went. Hesford was magnificent. I'd started on the bench and was brought on. By then we'd equalised. A run took three players out and the cross I put over was blocked when Mike Conroy shot.

But then with a few minutes left Mark Yates headed on from the edge of the box. It dropped to me, I collected it on my chest, and then I volleyed it low through the gap that Hesford had left. There were just three minutes to go. The place erupted, nearly 11,000 fans. You can't imagine the feeling when you score what you are sure will be the winner with just minutes to go. There's no feeling like it. Joy, elation, madness, a crescendo of noise all rolled into one. It's like a drug. It's why you play.

It all got a bit tetchy at the end. Maidstone got a corner; there was a huge scramble with bodies everywhere. Boots were flying all over the place. Pearcey got a boot in the midriff. Everybody piled into the melee and a fine scrap ensued. This was the way we looked after each other. It was all good fun, the spectators loved it. I wasn't involved in the fracas as I was up at the far end, but I enjoyed watching it all. It showed we cared. As the commotion subsided Chris lay on the floor grinning. We asked him if he was OK. He stood up still smiling and then held the ball up in the air for the crowd to see as if it was a trophy. They loved it and cheered. Oh and Maidstone's Henry was sent off. The newspaper had a headline for me to remember— 'ROGER HOOKS PRECIOUS POINTS'.

The PFA divisional teams were selected. Only Steve Davis was selected from Burnley. There should maybe have been more. John Deary had been outstanding; so had John Francis. There was never any chance of me being selected by my fellow professionals. I irritated the opposition too much and got under their skins. I never expected any accolade such as a PFA Award, all I was bothered about was the three points, at all cost. That was my only focus back then.

By the end of March, the finishing line was a few inches closer; injuries and suspensions were beginning to tell. Burnley 2 Hereford 0: job done and another crowd over 10,000. Burnley top, with three going up automatically and we were six points above the fourth placed team. Only our own carelessness or a huge slump could stop us. 72 points from 35 games with Blackpool behind in second on 67 points but they had played one more game. Mullen set his target.

'Get promotion, that's all that matters. That's the be all and end all, to get up there and out of this division. And if we can do that as quickly as we can in the next two or three games, then we'll have a couple of games spare, and maybe we can go on and win the Championship.' It was hard to see us not going up. It was time to believe.

You could argue that Burnley had been such an illustrious club that they had no place in the Fourth Division and that their escape would one day be inevitable. But for seven years it had looked anything but. Yet, here we were, on the brink.

But we lost the first game of April; Crewe 1 Burnley 0, just when you thought it was safe to be confident. It brought us down to earth with a bump. They were a decent team and very solid at the back. They had some good young players and this was a time when Dario Gradi had a lot of success selling his players to bigger clubs. The pitch at this time of year was hard, dry and bumpy, the sort that players hate with the ball bouncing all over the place and Crewe seemed to cope better than us. It was also the game where at half-time I came back into the dressing room to find my gold chain had been removed from the peg where I'd hung it. My dad had given it to me on my 18th birthday. The loss really sank in after the game, especially the thought that gold chains like this don't walk off by themselves.

And the next game was lost as well, although it was only the Autoglass Northern Final at home to Stockport so you might think no-one cared about such a competition. But we did and over 13,000 fans turned up. We were keen as well and put the same pride and effort into every competition; this was just two games away from Wembley. When you get that close you damned well do want to win even in a little competition. But by now injuries were taking their toll. Some of the squad players like Paul McKenzie were now going to get their chance. He'd come from the Highland League and had been a postman. He used to tell us some hilarious stories of his time as a postman. If he knew it was a tape inside the package he'd 'borrow' it, make a copy and then post the letter again. George Courtenay was referee and booked me for elbowing someone. It was the first challenge I'd made so the booking was a bit unexpected. Usually you could make a few before any booking. He talked to me as if he was a major star. When I protested he told me to shut up. I felt like a schoolboy with my tail between my legs in front of a headmaster. He was a FIFA listed referee. Maybe he saw this game and the players as beneath him.

The giant Kevin Francis played. He was about 6' 7' maybe bigger. He was a real gentle giant loping along towering above even our tallest player. You know a player like this can influence a game. He was a real handful and difficult to play against. He scored in each game. Stockport won the first leg 1–0 and then the second-leg as well 2–1. So, no trip to Wembley and we were very disappointed.

The home game against York had been postponed due to the untimely death of Ben Lee. Now the away game at Rochdale was postponed because of a waterlogged pitch. No game but it meant two games in hand. It was Scarborough at home next and we assumed it would be a win. It wasn't. April 20th and we had yet to win a point during the month.

How we didn't beat Scarborough remains a mystery. I scored after nine minutes. I charged through the middle and Mike Conroy played a fabulous ball over as I steamed in and the header went in firm and true. It was a great move at pace. We and the fans waited for the deluge of goals. It didn't come. Another chance for me, a turn and a shot but the goalkeeper saved. A goal would surely come. It did but at the wrong end. They equalised. Then another great run from me twisting and turning trying to create something. Sometimes you just feel the ball will do everything you want it to. You want to run at them all afternoon. You fly past them at will. Everything comes off except the final act of scoring. But you are convinced the goal will come. We threw everything at them but the break wouldn't come. The goalkeeper made a wonder save from big John Pender's header.

Another crowd of over 12,000 but it was only a 1–1 draw. The game was significant for two things. Chris Pearce was injured and it became his last game. I was injured and in truth the injury was very much the beginning of the end for me. It was certainly the end of things for me that season. It was my last goal for the club. It's a curious thing but we never lost a game in which I scored. There would be an operation—eventually. I would be left on the sidelines for the most of the remainder of my time at the club; another couple of years and just a handful of games. For me, though I didn't know it, the party was over.

Of course I had no idea that all this was to come. Soon, I would be no longer part of the action, and in a situation that almost makes you an outsider. No longer are you part of the dressing room spirit. You might be in there with the team, but they are in their kit, covered in mud, sweat, cuts and bruises. You are in your suit. After the game they come in, boot studs clattering, cut knees, bruises, sweat and

171

mud all mixed into one, the steam rising from the shared bath, the noise bubbling, the banter incessant, the back slaps and the congratulations. After a win the adrenalin still flows, the feeling of being on a high is incredible. There's nothing quite like it. But not for you; when you haven't played it stops; it's a horrible feeling. Even though some of the players are your best friends, you still feel like an intruder at the party.

I'd never ever been superstitious. Mind you, my wife Andrea would say I was. 'You had a haircut every Saturday morning. You would only eat steak and pasta on a Friday before a game.' 'But they were routines not superstitions,' I'd reply.

Some of the others were definitely superstitious. Brian Miller was. I had a new pair of boots and it might well have been the Scarborough game. There's an old superstition that you should never put shoes on the table. In I went and put the sparkling, new boots on Jimmy Holland's physio table in the dressing room. Brian looked aghast. 'Don't put boots on the table!' he yelled horrified. 'It's bad luck!' Funny though: that game marked my last goal for Burnley and the injury that cost me my place in the side. My troubles started from then. Maybe I should have been aware of that superstition.

You'd call it a routine rather than a superstition but we had a 'secret' habit before every game—Joe Jakub's wife was the inspiration. It can be revealed now after 20 years of secrecy. We'd come into the dressing room after the warm-up on the pitch and do our stretching exercises before a game and other simple routines. Then, at the signal, we'd drop on all fours into the doggy sex position and at the tops of our voices yell, 'IREEEEN!' Don't ask me how it started but it possibly related to Joe being the most hen-pecked husband you could ever meet—or so it seemed to us. Footballers do the daftest things. To this day I wonder if he ever told her.

April had so far yielded just one point; four games without a win but the game at home to Cardiff put us right back on track. Supporters claimed it was the best night so far of the season with a 3–1 win. Reserve David Williams was in goal. He'd had that superb game for Rochdale at Turf Moor when he saved everything thrown at him. Robbie Painter was now playing instead of me. The frustration I felt was indescribable and the anger at the knee that had let me down again. He scored after just 16 seconds just to make me feel even worse, not at Robbie but just a bit of professional jealousy.

It probably remains as the fastest ever Burnley goal. Jimmy Mullen hadn't even reached the dugout.

Thousands of fans went to Carlisle expecting the win that would mean promotion. It was a memorable day for them but at the same time disappointing. It ended as a 1–1 draw and Burnley were as good as promoted you might say. It was a day of fancy dress for hundreds of them and a party atmosphere. They'd waited for a day like this for seven years. The expectation and excitement levels were off the scale. Brunton Park had never seen anything like it; the colour, costumes, masks, banners, painted faces, Elvis masks and alien masks. Fans kept pouring in and somehow they squashed them in so that they seemed to fill the whole ground. This was carnival time.

I travelled up on my own and I watched as it began to get ugly. Yobs from both sides took the opportunity to confront each other. For a brief period chaos reigned. For most of the 8,000 fans from Burnley the game and the event was the thing. Jimmy Mullen wearing a claret and blue shirt acknowledged the importance of the day:

> I've been out there and had a look at the painted faces, the kids, the children with claret and blue cross faces and chequered faces and striped faces. That's what football should be. That's what it's all about. For me it's the best supported club I've ever been at. I've been at four or five different clubs but Burnley Football Club is the greatest in terms of passion and feeling.

But the day didn't quite work out as planned. The team started nervously; maybe the occasion had got to them a little. John Francis scored with a stunning goal from the left hand corner of the box. It was unstoppable and flew past six defenders after he had dribbled past the two defenders that were closest to him. After this there should have been more and the missed chances were regretted later when Carlisle equalised. Over came an agricultural cross to no-one in particular. The clearance was sliced; the resultant shot went in off a deflection.

It was a real dampener and the draw was against a side that was destined to finish bottom. It was not a good result. Thousands had come to see Burnley return home in triumph and glory but it didn't quite work out that way. Burnley were just about up, promoted in all but the maths. If Mansfield won their last game while Burnley lost their last three heavily, they would deny us. Fans were convinced this wouldn't happen but . . . how could they be absolutely sure? There's always a 'but' and they needed absolute certainty.

In the dressing room there was disappointment, but the players knew there were still three games to come. The next one was at York. One point would ensure promotion. All three would mean promotion as champions. Fail there and there was still Rochdale away and Wrexham at home. But all ended well. At 9.46 pm on 28th April 1992, Burnley FC became champions of the Fourth Division when they won at York.

The away game at Rochdale should have been just two days later but was postponed because of a waterlogged pitch. Rochdale meanwhile were still in there with a chance of a play-off place so it remained a meaningful game. The game was re-arranged for the following Monday.

May 2nd and 21,000 turned up at Turf Moor for the Wrexham game to celebrate promotion and the Championship. It was the highest Fourth Division crowd of the season. This was extraordinary. Fans came an hour early to get the best places. They sang, they cheered, they chanted Jimmy Mullen's name. He'd worked that season without an assistant manager. The day was filled with sun and warmth. It was incredibly hectic and there was a fantastic party atmosphere. Chris Pearce who knew he was to be released did a lap of honour dressed in his best suit and then climbed on the dugout roof to take the applause. Outwardly he played the hero. Inside he was gutted. I don't know how he had the courage to do that after the way he had been treated during the season.

There were presentations: Robbie Painter for fastest goal of the season. Young Player of the Year was Graham Lancashire. And then me; I was Burnley Football Club Endsleigh Player of the Year and in addition to that, scorer of the Goal of the Season. But I'd have swapped all the cheers, acclaim and waves from the massive crowd for a place in the team. With quarter of an hour to kick-off the Fourth Division Championship Trophy was presented to the captain John Pender and the team. They were in their kit and track suits but I wasn't. I felt strangely on the outside as if it didn't involve or include me. Football is like that. I was outside the bubble. In hindsight I should have changed into my kit and taken part in the pre-match and after-match celebrations and been included in the celebratory team pictures. It's ironic. I gave so much to that season but the end of season pictures left me out; part of it, but not part of it.

But football always has a sting in the tail. Burnley lost. The game was a let-down. Mike Conroy scored and Burnley went in at half-time leading 1–0. But then Wrexham scored twice in the second half. There was a plan for a lap of honour after the game but as the final minutes ticked away it became clear that fans were intent on a pitch invasion. They massed in their hundreds on the touchline and it actually became impossible to run the game safely. The linesmen couldn't run up and down and then things got silly when a Wrexham player was 'tackled' by a fan. The referee did the sensible thing and called a halt slightly early. The fans poured on. There was no lap of honour.

The final game of the season was at Rochdale just three days later and Rochdale needed a win to be in the play-offs and in no way wanted to lose to Burnley. There was no love lost between Rochdale and Burnley supporters and over the years in the Fourth Division Rochdale had handed out more than one humiliation to their 'big club' neighbours. Burnley won 3–1 and Barnet went into the play-offs with manager Barry Fry watching from the stand to ensure 'fair play'.

The game reminded me of an incident there during the previous season. After that game we were all in the players lounge and I went over to see a group of Rochdale players that included old pals Micky Holmes and Tony Brown, then at Rochdale. I'd known them a long time and it was good re-union. But then as I turned and walked away I overheard one of those old racist remarks that came so often at that time. 'Fucking black bastard,' said the voice. You stop and do a double take. You think to yourself did someone really just say that to me. They did. But I had better things to think about than whoever made that comment. The coach was waiting for us to take us to Manchester Airport and the trip to Bermuda. More important things had my attention than the voice that made that remark.

As we write this book racism is a hot topic involving comments from Brighton manager Gus Poyet and FIFA President Sepp Blatter about Evra and Suarez, and Terry and Ferdinand. Suarez was deemed guilty of making racist remarks to Evra and was banned for eight games. You put things to the back of your mind and in fact as good as forget them. But then along comes a nudge that brings them to the fore again. I received plenty of racist abuse during that championship season and the seasons before but I never let it bother me not the least of which was the number of opposition managers who would instruct their defenders to 'get that fucking black bastard'. Abuse usually comes from ignorant people and remarks are often quickly retracted when the shit hits the fan if they become public. If I had a pound for every time someone used the word 'nigger' in my company and then said, 'Not you Roger, you're okay', I'd be a rich man.

And that was it. Season over at Rochdale. Probably three quarters of the 8,175 crowd were from Burnley. It was another winning night at the end of a great season. With a re-shuffle of the leagues and the creation of the Premier League this was the last game of the old Fourth Division and Robbie Painter scored the last ever goal in the Fourth Division. He was there because I was injured. I should have been able to enjoy it more, savour the moment, but to do that would have meant wearing a claret shirt at Rochdale as part of a triumphant team. But I wasn't part of it. Dressing room celebrations pass you by when you're not really involved on the field. I was on the sidelines and sadly that's where I would stay.

The coach to Rochdale was laden with our cases and luggage so that straight after the game we could head for Manchester Airport and begin the journey to Bermuda. That coach and the plane was a boisterous and exuberant place to be. But not for Chris Pearce who wasn't there, released by the club. My turn would come two years later and I would truly learn then what rejection would feel like.

They say every player, no matter how many clubs he plays for, is destined to be at home somewhere and to feel as if he belongs. It's as if you are meant to play for one club and do good things there. That club for me was Burnley. Mike Conroy later said exactly the same and that Burnley was the place he should have stayed.

You could say the same about Jimmy Mullen. In just the same way that Burnley was where I had a real impact as a player, then so it was for Jimmy Mullen as a manager. It adds to the view that for every player or manager, there is a club somewhere where they will fit like a glove and have the best years of their career. If they are lucky they find that club.

11

A Test of Endurance

So I missed the last games of the promotion season, the climax and the best ones. The knee needed an operation because of bits of cartilage floating around. I must have been one of the few footballers who could leave defenders behind me even though I ran with a limp. You've to look hard to see it but there's one video clip where I fly past one defender with a knee that only had 90% bend capacity and left me with the faintest limp. Over time I had to find new ways to run to cope with it. Those coaches and managers in previous decades who said that black players had no heart were so wrong. The operation could have been done as soon as the season ended. Why wasn't it? It was left several weeks until the '92–93 pre-season after we came back from the Bermuda trip. It was a decision that looking back had severe effects on the remainder of my time at Burnley.

Brian Miller came with me to meet the surgeon in Manchester. He was the one at that time, I was told, who did all the Man United operations so we kind of assumed he would know what he was doing. So in we went and he thought I was Dion Dublin. 'Hello Dion, how are you?' he said. What chance did I have with a consultant who thought I was Dion Dublin? Brian was just aghast as we drove home and in his blunt, down to earth way with his rich local accent, shook his head in amazement and commented on the bloke's mistake. He eventually got the job done but only months later I would meet him again for operations on the other knee. If only I'd known then of how much of a mess that would become.

Two weeks at Lilleshall for recuperation followed. Meeting up with players from all four divisions was a great leveller. Steve McManaman was there along with Ronnie Whelan, real superstars at the time, along with big John Gayle. Status didn't matter when we all had one thing in common. We were all crocked, as the saying goes. There I met goalkeeper Paul Gerrard from Everton. 'Ah I had this surgeon as well,' he said. 'We called him the butcher.'

Despite the operation, my knee remained a problem. It was what I now call the Blackburn knee dating back to that reserve game years earlier when I was at Leeds United. Paul Gerrard got an infection in his and was really struggling. Mine too wasn't much better. The surgeon shall remain nameless, but the word 'bodge' comes to mind yet again when the top man thinks you're someone else. I've always assumed he did okay for Dion Dublin.

You'd think a club would want to get its players fit and if an operation was needed would want to get it done quickly. But the ill-thought timing of the delayed operation meant I played catch-up in training and fitness. If it wasn't the knee it would be something else. Nothing went right. It took until October '93 in the new season to get back and I was only on the bench. And then when I got back into the swing of things there was a niggling groin strain.

Burnley had signed Adrian Heath during the time I was out injured to form a partnership with Mike Conroy. Inchy had been a top player with Stoke City and Everton and would eventually go on to manage Burnley. A game that I remember well when I got back into action was against Bolton Wanderers. The knee was healed. I was raring to go, and on a beautiful, sunny afternoon the Burnley fans had done their best to take over the ground. In the first half John Clayton was taken off and on I came.

I had a great game, hit the woodwork, was everywhere and then brought down for a penalty. Although Steve Davis missed it, and by the end of the game we'd lost 4–0, on a personal level I'd had a storming game. It was one of those performances when everything came off and I seemed able to take players on at will and skim past them. That game sticks in the memory because it was like I'd been given a pair of wings. Adrian Heath had probably never heard of me before but in this game we clicked.

After the match of course we were disappointed with the result but I was delighted to be back in the thick of things especially as I was awarded Man of the Match. Jimmy Mullen was all over me, heaping praise and telling me how good it was to have me back on top form.

I thought, 'This is it. I'm back. He's not going to say these things and then dump me again.' I was sure that after this performance I would be in the next team. I wasn't. It was one of those key watershed moments when you ask yourself, 'Just what do I have to do?'

There were just a handful of games when I actually stepped onto the field as sub but January 23rd 1993 was the final first-team appearance. Mike Conroy was sold but I was pretty much the forgotten man, fed up of seeing the local newspaper headlines 'Mullen Needs Hit Man'. From that point on it was downhill all the way until I left in '94, released at the end of a season where I played no first-team game.

What made me the forgotten man was the four months I spent early in '93 at the hands of surgeons again. It was the knee injured on January 27th. It was four months on the sidelines with the notes I found in my box in the loft outlining the whole sorry mess. It was a turning point in my opinion of Jimmy Mullen. Until this point I had thought that I had been good for him and he had been good for me and whilst there might have been the usual dressing room gripes and grumbles, on the whole you could not take away the fact that he had galvanised the team and achieved promotion.

After injuring the left knee in a reserve game the events that took place over the next year were soul-destroying. I was taken down the tunnel on a stretcher that was the oldest I had ever seen. It was like a hospital trolley on wheels and not only did I have a knee to worry about but also wondered if I would fall off this ancient contraption. Then I was placed in the care of the physio Mr Jimmy Holland. At this stage the knee was incredibly painful and swollen and I couldn't lock it out straight. It was treated with ice and then placed in a knee stabiliser overnight.

A week later I was taken to see the local surgeon, Mr Dennison. He examined the knee and came to the conclusion that it was a cartilage tear. I had two choices; one to have Mr Dennison do the operation using the old method of a straight cut, or two, go to Manchester to the same consultant I had seen before. To my regret I chose the latter. I should have remembered he'd done the other knee and thought I was Dion Dublin.

I was duly booked in to see him for a consultation and went with the physio and Brian Miller. He examined the knee and was willing to operate the following week. I was to go back to Manchester for the operation. I arrived at the specified time of 1.30 to see him. Half an hour went by and then eventually one and a half hours late he came to see me. Bear in mind by this time I should have been in preparation for the operating theatre. For some unknown reason he looked harassed and wanted to examine the knee again. So he looked and decided he would not be able to operate because there were some very minor scratches. I almost pleaded with him to perform the operation as planned but he kept going on about infection. So, I was to go back home and return in another ten days. This meant that over two weeks would have gone by since my first seeing him and all the while I was on crutches and in pain.

In my opinion he could have performed the operation on the planned day. The fact that he was one and half hours late, looked extremely harassed and was still in an operating gown suggested he'd perhaps had enough that day.

The journey to Manchester again on crutches was a struggle. But at last I got there. It was now almost three weeks since the injury but I told myself that with luck I could be back playing in another three weeks. Such thoughts give you resolve, determination and spirit. Other players had been back playing in what seemed like no time. The thought remained though; precious days had been wasted.

Sickle cell anaemia: the highest frequency of this genetic blood disorder is found in Africa but also in the Caribbean, India and the Mediterranean as a result of the movement of people in the days of slavery and migration. I had this trait although it has no effects at all. I was thankful I didn't have it in its most severe form where it is extremely serious. The surgeon decided that in his and other consultants' opinions, he would not be able to perform the operation with a tourniquet. This meant he would not be able to put strappings above and below the affected area to stop the blood flowing into the injured part. This would make his job very difficult. Well, I thought, he's the consultant, he should know, and at least he had performed the operation on my other knee only eight months earlier.

When I was taken to the theatre I felt quite confident and looking forward to getting back on the mend. Two hours later I was awake and in excruciating pain and this was not normal for a routine cartilage operation. Every time I moved, my leg tightened up. The pain was like a nightmare and I must have called the nurse half a dozen times that night for pain killers. All I could do was grit my teeth and try to tell myself that I'd be back playing soon. I'd had the operation, that was the main thing and the consultant was due to do his rounds at about 8.30 the next morning to tell me that everything had gone smoothly. Or so I thought.

He came into the room and explained how difficult the operation had been for him. He said that without the tourniquet, 'It was like fishing in tomato soup.' He went on to say that yes it was the cartilage but then to my horror informed me that he had dropped part of it back into the knee and was unable to retrieve it. He must have seen the look on my face as my head went down and quickly added that it should dissolve and shouldn't cause me any further problems. I remember thinking how can it not cause me problems; exactly what has this man done to me? What if this piece of rogue cartilage does cause me problems? I would be back to square one. My head was in disarray. How could he drop a piece back into the knee? How was it possible that he couldn't find it again?

I left the hospital the next day still in great pain and still in turmoil over the news of the lost cartilage fragment. Substitute the word shrapnel for fragment and it gives a better idea of the effect it had in my head. But I had his word that it would dissolve and cause no further problems. My gut feelings and instincts told me otherwise.

Back at the ground I started with the usual build-up processes for the knee. Days then weeks passed. It remained swollen but I thought in time the swelling would subside. I looked at it, twice its normal size, and felt like sticking a knitting needle in it to release the fluid. I started trying to run. It was near impossible. I knew with each failed attempt that I would end up back in the operating theatre. I knew it wasn't right. At times like this you suspect others think you're just a moaner. I must have looked like Long John Silver sometimes the way I limped round that training field.

The usual process began all over again. There was another consultation with him. He looked at the knee and decided to open it up again. I don't know if I felt relief or anger at that point. A couple of days later I checked in again at the hospital. He told me he had consulted with other surgeons this time and had decided to use a tourniquet for the second attempt. I was astonished. Why the hell couldn't he have done this the first time? Inwardly I seethed. In a matter of a few weeks he had changed his opinions. If a tourniquet had been used the first time the 'tomato soup' scenario would never have happened. Without saying so it was an admission that during the first operation he hadn't been able to see properly what he was doing.

Back down to the operating theatre and I convinced myself

that this time the job would be done and he would find the loose debris that was floating round and causing the continual swelling. Afterwards when I came round I waited to get the all-clear from him and the good news that it had all gone satisfactorily. In he came and switched off the TV. He began by telling me that everything this time had gone far better. Without the 'tomato soup' it was so much easier. But then came the bombshell.

He said he hadn't found the loose cartilage but what he had found was a tear of the cruciate ligament. My mouth dropped. This was utterly unexpected. I'm not sure I said anything. The words sank in. The reactions followed. It was a massive shock. I could have wept. There was cruciate ligament damage and as far as I knew bits of cartilage floating round for good measure. At that point I saw my career in football and chances of playing again finished.

I felt total and utter panic. I had been out of the operating theatre less than four hours expecting to be told that all had gone well and this time it was a success. I had been told the opposite. Where had cruciate ligament damage come from? When had I done that? Why hadn't he seen it the first time? Oh of course; he hadn't used the tourniquet the first time. Had he any real idea what he was doing as he poked about in the tomato soup? Now he was telling me that the permanent swelling was due to the cruciate damage not the debris that he couldn't find. It was bollocks. Later notes I made record that he said the cartilage bits must have dissolved.

Today I sit and leaf through the pages of notes I made. They only partly represent the mental torment, the stress and the deep anxiety I went through wondering if I would ever play again. I read them today and all the old angst and suffering comes back.

The nine pages of hand-written notes I have are in two bundles. The second bundle was written a little later. These are a shorter version of the first but with the dates added and more importantly outlining the conclusion to this sorry story.

There was no recovery. All attempts to train, run, kick a ball told me emphatically that it was clear it was another failure. It was then that the club physio made a suggestion that I should see someone else. By now Jimmy Holland had gone and new physio Mark Leather decided we should visit another consultant. Life is all about ifs and buts. If Jimmy Holland had not retired, if Mark Leather had not replaced him I would never have been sent to a new consultant by

Mark Leather. This time it was Steve McLaughlin at Blackpool Fylde Coast Hospital, immediately recommended by Mark, who would look at the knee.

Jimmy Holland and Brian Miller had intensely disliked the arrogant attitude of the Manchester surgeon. Mark was aghast at the treatment I had received so far. He, in fact, immediately ripped out some of the old equipment that Jimmy had used including the wax bath that helped keep joints warm. Some of the players were disappointed when the wax went. They'd used it to make model penises and erotic sculptures. Footballers' humour again.

Mark knew Steve McLaughlin and the first job was to put me through a series of examinations and tests to identify any problems that could be eliminated. To my astonishment, I had tests for Syphilis and Gonorrhoea. These are things that can affect the joints. The test involved a hospital visit where I was told to lie down and remove my trousers. Fair enough so far but then there was the insertion of the 'umbrella' into the penis. I lay there, aghast, with my eyes watering thinking, 'What am I doing here?' The 'umbrella' was in fact a needle that then opened up inside the penis like a mini umbrella and was then withdrawn. Just thinking about it now brings tears to my eyes.

Then there was the arthroscopy with the new man, Mr McLaughlin. Beforehand he'd scanned the knee and there on the scan were the bits of cartilage—the bits the Manchester consultant had said must have dissolved when he couldn't find them. You can't imagine how I felt; the anger, the rage, the feelings that the first consultant had been useless, but no doubt he would argue otherwise. Mr McLaughlin operated not with a tourniquet but a 'local'. He took several 'bodies' out of the knee and the whole thing was filmed. I watched him do it and was awake as I watched on screen as he plucked out the bits with his forceps. Even more astonishingly there was no mention of any cruciate ligament tear. Steve McLaughlin did the final operation efficiently and successfully and I was simply raring to go and to get back to full strength and fitness again. In my foolishness I supposed that I was still part of Jimmy Mullen's plans.

Within weeks I was back in full training. At a later date I began the process of suing the Manchester consultant. It barely got off the ground. But in my opinion he had made a real mess of things. Mr McLaughlin found the cartilage bits that the Manchester man hadn't. Mr McLaughlin found no evidence of the cruciate ligament tear that the Manchester surgeon had allegedly seen. The suffering that man caused me was extreme.

It doesn't take long to read through those old notes about this dreadful period. It all comes back every time I look at them. Four months of anguish pared down to a few scribbled pages. It was four months that felt like four years. I'd guess any pro footballer who has struggled to come back to fitness from injury will identify with what's in those pages. For supporters they're an insight into how things can go wrong in a footballer's life and how your career at such times is in the hands of others. Hindsight is easy but I sit here now and think if only I'd let the local surgeon Mr Dennison do the job immediately. There's no telling if he'd have been successful — but he might have been. The choices we make, choices that shape the course of our lives and careers, is a recurring theme of this book.

What might have been? Decisions I made, crossroads I met, directions I took. Surgeons, consultants and physios all played such a part in those hours, days and weeks of hospital visits, and the ensuing blood, sweat and tears.

When you are out for a lengthy spell you feel like a non-person. It's almost as if you're irrelevant, an embarrassing nuisance, an irritant. You are of no use to a manager when you are injured and if you are on the fringe of things you might as well be invisible. As if the surgeon who made such a mess of things wasn't continually on my mind, so were the primitive recovery facilities at Burnley. You start to think how long this will go on as operations are a failure and then there's a relapse. In my case there were times when I had faced slipshod medical practices, and hit and miss surgery. And yet, in effect, I was a valuable asset presumably worth money to the club. A racehorse might have been better treated.

All the while there was the feeling of being outside things and everyone else, all fit and well, were on the inside. And then there were all the platitudes I put up with. 'How's it going Roger? You'll soon be back Roger. Stay cheerful Roger. Keep at it Roger.' There were a lot of massive, dark days. But, I worked and trained hard on the assumption that I'd be selected again or at least would have an equal chance. How wrong could I have been?

What did Paul Lake at Manchester City say? 'I felt like a stranger in my own backyard . . . it's as if they're not interested in getting me back.' My four months was nothing in comparison to what

Paul Lake went through but nevertheless they were horrendous enough. You fret and worry, you ache with frustration and anger, you wonder if someone up above has it in for you. When you're in another person's hands, especially a surgeon in whom eventually you have no confidence, in fact you come to think he's useless; you despair of making a recovery and getting the knee right. But in the macho football world you mask your emotions; you're supposed to stay bright and cheerful, respond to banter, sign autographs with a smile. And all these were on days when I felt like an unwanted failure and seethed with anger. I wondered and worried if I would play again.

What support did I get from the management? In a word none; for 12 months I was a fully paid up member of the leper colony. They should have given me a bell.

In the coming months nothing I did would convince the manager I was fit again and still as good a striker as anyone he had. They even had me playing and training with the apprentices. There's another old clipping I have that paints the exact picture of what was happening:

> Roger Eli is back in business—now he just wants everyone to know it. The Burnley striker has had to watch his side fight their way into the Division Two promotion reckoning from the sidelines because of knee trouble. Now he is hoping to regain the interest shown in him by the likes of Hearts and Sunderland before his injury—but he knows he may have to do that without the shop window of first-team football.
>
> He says: 'I've scored eight goals in five reserve matches. I was worried my injury might take away a bit of my pace, but that has not been the case. I worked really hard on building up my leg muscles and it has done the trick. Pace is one of my greatest assets and it hasn't diminished. I scored 17 goals in Burnley's last promotion campaign and my recent record for the reserves shows I haven't forgotten where the goal is. It would be great to show the fans that in the first team. But I really don't see where a chance will come from. Manager Jimmy Mullen has just paid out for another striker, Tony Philliskirk, and he will obviously play him before me. My future is in the balance at the moment, but I know I can do a job at any level. Now I just want the chance to prove that.'

Even after all these years when I read that, the sense of exasperation comes flooding back and all the constant disappointments of being overlooked. Eight goals in five reserve games! What more did I have to do? The cutting was a plaintive cry for another chance; a chance that would never come.

I left after Burnley went up again via the play-offs in '94 with me on the outside looking in as they faced Stockport County at Wembley. That was nigh on a season and a half in the reserves or not playing at all. That final season was purgatory. It was like watching someone switching off your career. It was as if Jimmy Mullen just pulled the plug. I watched the first teamers inching their way to the Wembley play-off and felt as if I just wasn't there. Players like Adrian Heath, Ted McMinn and Gary Parkinson came in. Yet still I worked hard once I was back to fitness and in training showed I could play alongside each of these new lads as they came in, particularly Adrian Heath. The knee was as good as okay now but it was clear I was wasting my time.

There were occasions of near humiliation like the time on the training ground when I had been put through my paces by physio Mark Leather. I walked round the pitch in an absolute lather and the walk took me past Mullen, Peter Reid and Sam Ellis watching a youth game against Bury. The ball ended up in the river when one of the players really booted it over the fence. As I walked past we acknowledged each other with a nod and a wink. Out of the corner of my eye I could see Reid asking Mullen who is that? I carried on walking, maybe 50 yards away from him, and then heard Jimmy shout something.

'Roger go and get that ball,' he yelled. I ignored him. I was a 28-year old senior player at the club and had done every type of job at every club willingly from being an apprentice back at Leeds all those years ago. I certainly wasn't about to climb over a bloody fence to fetch a ball out of a river. He bellowed again as loud as he could. 'Roger get that fucking ball you've done nothing for the last six months.' There he was, the boss of Burnley Football Club trying to show how he was in charge and how in control he was. It was also a measure of how far I had fallen. Frustration and anger rose. It didn't get more humiliating than this. Using his own language I told him: 'Fuck off.' It was an expression of all the emotion I had felt for weeks. Everyone heard. You could feel the tension. I prided myself on keeping my dignity but this was him trying his hardest, it seemed, to humiliate me in front of his pals.

He marched over to me. I expected a real scene and was ready for him but instead of balling me out he went all polite and nice and asked how training had gone, how I was feeling. We talked for a minute or so and then he jogged back to his pals. There was no further insistence I went for the ball. I'd imagine Reid and Ellis thought he was giving me a real bollocking. I'd guess that was the object of the exercise. But no he wasn't. I certainly didn't go and get the ball.

To me it seemed he and Harry Wilson played mind games with me. I'd ask Wilson why he was doing this or that. He'd say it was Jimmy Mullen's decision. I'd go and ask Mullen why he'd done this or that. He'd say it was Harry Wilson.

Sometime in the spring of '94 I got a call from Mark Leather the physio. Apparently Jimmy Mullen had told him to get me fit. At the time I was in agony with a hand broken in two places. Still, in I went because I was led to believe there was a chance to return to the squad. I trained and would have had no hesitation in playing with a broken hand. It's what you did then, like the time I played against Huddersfield Town with a fractured cheekbone where centre-half big Peter Jackson was waiting to inflict more damage There was no return to the squad. More mind games perhaps? It was as if I was being punished for being injured. I'd be called for extra afternoon fitness work. It often consisted of me and any other injured players working at the ground on the terraces. If we could run up and down the terraces that's where we went. If we were unable to run because of leg or knee injuries we'd find somewhere to do pull-ups or press-ups. It was belittling. We felt like second class people at the club, like a performing seal. If the manager said jump, we jumped. I can't imagine John Barnes ever being treated like this.

The play-off Final at Wembley would see John Francis badly injured and that would end his career too. While I wondered what the hell to do next and where to go, sponsors Endsleigh treated the squad to a trip to Mauritius. I was only 27 when I left Burnley and it was a depressing and miserable time. The icing on the cake was remembering Harry Wilson telling me I had no heart. All that was left was to try and salvage a career.

The club had this phone-call thing where players recorded a message and an interview that fans could listen to. I did one. Club

Secretary back then was Mark Blackbourne who had the interview removed. I said a few things they didn't like. I hadn't lied, just told the truth. I'm told he said I was a bitter man and didn't know what I was saying.

One of the old newspapers I have has the back page from the July 3rd *Lancashire Evening Telegraph*. There's a feature about the released players. There's my picture along with four other players. Lower down the page is a brief mention.

> Long-serving forward Roger Eli has been given a free transfer. Jimmy Mullen paid tribute to Eli. 'I feel really sorry for Roger. He has had a horrendous couple of years with injuries and that meant we had to bring new men in.' Eli, 28 joined Burnley on a free transfer from Bury in 1989. He wasn't an immediate success but became a cult hero when he was switched to the forward line. Along with Mick Conroy he was the spearhead of the frontline in the Division Four championship side two years ago but a series of knee injuries have kept him on the sidelines since then.

So that was it. My five years at Burnley in just six lines. Two nights later on July 5th in the *Lancashire Evening Telegraph* there's a near half page picture of the squad departing for Mauritius. I remember John Francis coming round before they left all full of bounce and excitement. The cutting gives an impression of a player, me, who was not fit enough to be picked. It was totally wrong. I got back to fitness in the final season I was there and I was fit and well enough to play. I suspected then, and still do, that it was not my fitness that was the problem but the fact that my face just didn't fit any more.

12

Have Adidas Bag Will Travel

You could say I've led a nomadic existence wandering from Bradford to Leeds to Wolverhampton to Cambridge to Crewe to York to Bury to Northwich to Burnley to China to Scunthorpe to Scotland; and finally back to Bradford (oh and Cyprus). Everywhere I went, until Bermuda, I had this enormous, old, worn, travel-weary Adidas sports bag. But inside it everything was pristine and immaculate. I loved to keep everything freshly washed. At Wolves they used to tell me that I spent more time in the laundrette than anywhere else.

Travelling makes for a huge percentage of a footballer's life and you lose count of the number of hotels you stay in. Some are splendid and some horrendous. The one we stayed in during the Stavropol Russian trip was not so good. When Mark Monington slammed a door shut, half the wall fell down. But if you put up to 20 or so boisterous, testosterone filled lads in a hotel for a weekend, you can be sure that some of them will let their hair down and the beer flows freely no matter what the hotel is like.

We lost count of the hundreds of miles spent driving up and down motorways. Hughie Jones was our driver at Burnley and we called him Barabbas because of his biblical beard. I usually sat at the back near the card school although I didn't join in. The only game I ever knew was a West Indian game called La Guab which I tried to teach the lads at Crewe. The first thing I'd always do was look under my seat. This same coach was always used by Manchester United on alternate Saturdays and quite often someone would have left something under the seat out of sight. Sure enough one day there was a lovely pair of trainers left there, hardly worn. They had the name 'Brucie' inside. I didn't mind they were a size too big; thanks to Steve Bruce I was now the proud owner of an expensive pair of trainers. This was the nearest I ever got to following in his footsteps.

If we were treated well at Leeds and then at Burnley, it was certainly make do and mend at a hard-up place like Crewe. At Crewe there would never be any overnight stays and you'd travel on the same day as the game no matter how far it was. The pre-match meal would be in a motorway car-park and even on some occasions in a lay-by somewhere. There'd be soup and a roll, the soup carried in an enormous plastic flask when you could taste the plastic in your soup. For afters it would be a Mars Bar and a milky coffee. The memory of them still makes me feel ill. Dario might have been a great coach but on this evidence his knowledge of nutrition was zero.

Don't think football is all glamour. Travelling is 50% boredom unless you are suddenly woken out of it when a brick comes through the window as it did at Cardiff. But there are perks—as a youth I went to Italy, Denmark, Yugoslavia and Switzerland. I sampled Bermuda and southern Russia. For most of the time during my short stays here and there I lived out of that Adidas bag, whether it was Bermuda or Bury, Yugoslavia or Yeovil. At Cambridge I'm not sure I actually unpacked it fully.

There was a month in Scotland too, but that was a last desperate attempt to stay in the game. By then I'd progressed to a suitcase but only because my brother Rohan borrowed the sports bag and then broke the zip. Our Kid, by the way, must be the only black person I know who had a six week sun-tanning course to get ready for a holiday. That bag had seen me through from early days at Leeds to the trip to Bermuda in the summer of '92. You could say I'd lived my life out of it and it was so big I'm not sure if I put the bag in the car or the car in the bag. It had the remains of over 10 years of my life inside when I finally passed it on. If there was a Roger Eli museum it would take pride of place.

After the disappointment of the Torquay play-off games, the pre-season for 1991–92 was marked by a trip to Russia and Stavropol. The players were agog. Russia! Surely this was where only the wealthy big boys went. Little Burnley of the Fourth Division! It was almost sensational news.

But where was the money coming from? These trips didn't come cheap. A supporter called Harry Brooks, then a Burnley councillor, was critical. He was a longstanding supporter and as angry as anybody at the years spent in the humiliating Fourth Division. His letters peppered the local paper, usually critical of the Burnley Board. I'd guess there was no love lost between him and Frank Teasdale. Frank thought the trip was a 'great honour'. Harry Brooks thought the money would have been better spent on a top striker like John Pearson from Leeds. He might have had a point but I was quite happy to have a free trip to Russia.

We presumed that one of the directors must have had connections there. A Russian side, Dinamo Brest, had already been to Turf Moor the season before. I knew Chris Kiwomya. He was a Bradford lad who'd had a good career at Ipswich and then got a big money move to Arsenal. We'd kept in touch. 'The food there is terrible,' he said, 'take plenty of your own.' Ironically, the year we went, the old Russia of the USSR was replaced by the new one, with democracy and votes and a new President, Boris Yeltsin. They'd just had the elections in June before we went. It was big news. But it was still a place where travel was difficult. Communication was difficult. Everything was difficult. Red tape filled the place. A phone call home was difficult. Phone calls had to be booked a couple of days in advance and that was when you could actually find a phone. Some of the lads managed it. Secret police really were everywhere. The lads swore you could hear the heavy breathing down the phone.

I shared the food information with all the lads, especially Ian Bray my new roommate. I shopped with my girlfriend Andrea for supplies. I loaded up as much as I could carry into a bag that was big enough to fit a small Tesco. Anybody rooming with me would need their own extra food supply. I wasn't sharing. They weren't going to be dipping into my bag. And it's true, the food was awful. I lived on noodles and biscuits from my private supply. If I was desperate I had some of the hotel 'soup' which seemed no more than a few bits of cabbage floating in hot water.

Other information came from Chairman Frank Teasdale. From him we had serious advice about wooing Russian ladies. We'd need to shower them with gifts, he said, stockings and perfume would be particularly welcome. Frank was good fun outside the boardroom; we affectionately called him Benny Hill. Armed with Frank's good advice several of the lads, led by John Francis, went on shopping expeditions for lingerie.

At first we'd no idea where Stavropol was. We discovered it's actually thousands of miles from Moscow. This place was down in the southwest of Russia near the Black Sea. So this gaggle of excited footballers left from Manchester Airport for flight number one to Moscow. That was the okay bit but at Moscow we had to change planes for the second leg of the journey. We looked in horror at the battered old Aeroflot thing that stood on the runway. It looked like a relic from World War Two. We expected to find Biggles at the controls.

'Dear God it's got bloody propellers,' said scouser John Deary in his strong Liverpool twang. 'I bet Buddy Holly's still in it.' Our luggage and bits and pieces went at the back of the plane behind a moth-eaten curtain. We looked at the pile of cases and bags as it grew higher and higher until it almost touched the cabin ceiling and we thought the plane might tip up. I began to worry that if the load had to be lightened the first thing they'd look at would be the Adidas bag and my food supplies. Those of us who weren't good fliers at the best of times were now feeling really scared. We joked about the drinks trolley. Would there be one? Would it just have vodka? The state we were in, anything would do.

Things might not have been so bad if what we thought was smoke hadn't begun to come up from under some of the seats. Actually it was a fine mist but it sure looked like smoke to us. Mike Conroy led the panic. Someone was shouting *Dad's Army* style, 'Don't panic, don't panic; the plane's on fire'. By now this mist was billowing all around the cabin. In fractured English a stewardess told us not to panic any more. Somehow she managed to convince us that it was only condensation. It was the same stewardess who earlier had said we didn't need to put safety belts on at take-off. We'd been a bit surprised at that but then we saw why. Half of them were missing.

Some hours later we landed. All of us sprinted off before the old thing could set on fire. The thought of returning in it back to Moscow was horrendous but we put it to the back of our minds. We had 10 days to look forward to in, what turned out to be, an attractive city and beautiful warm weather. This was a place with very hot summers that was actually nearer Turkey than Moscow.

The political regime might have changed. The KGB, however, were still alive and well. Everywhere we went two spooks followed us. If we turned round, there they were. If we thought we'd lost them, no we hadn't. They were behind us. Oh no they're not. Oh yes they are. They camped in the hotel with us, lurked in the shadows, behind the potted plants and never left us alone. We joked they were under the beds when we went to sleep.

I was struggling with an Achilles tendon injury so didn't play.

Injuries—the story of my career. To our surprise there was terrific local interest in the games. A crowd of 16,000 watched the first game (we were the first English team to play there) and 8,000 watched the second. Both were 1–1 draws, but in the second game I have a vague memory of the Russians scoring the equaliser right at the end. The travel was draining but it was a great ten days. As a bonding exercise it was a terrific visit despite some of the lads losing weight because of the food situation and others being semi-comatose on vodka much of the time. The second game against Asmerol took place in a city called Kislovodsk. It sounds like a place in the middle of nowhere but really was a beautiful spa town on the edge of a mountain area. We came across some really good players but in those days getting any of them across to the UK to play for a UK league club was impossible.

Some of the lads did indeed strike it lucky with the Russian ladies and the lingerie was a good investment. Don't think that Russian women back then all drove tractors and did weightlifting. Some of them were stunning.

In Bermuda after the York win in '92 we (and the Adidas bag of course) stayed at the Sonesta Beach Hotel for 10 days. Endsleigh the club sponsors footed the bill for this trip, our reward for winning promotion. It was a freebie of swimming, fishing, scuba diving, boating and golf; all that plus the inevitable lazing around and eating. As a general rule the routine was swim . . . drink . . . swim . . . drink.

Frank Teasdale was there of course. He'd had the torture of that last day game in '87 against Orient and all the aggro and abuse hurled at him towards the end of Frank Casper's reign, especially at Scarborough. Now he had 10 days of enjoyment in Sonesta Bay. Who could blame him?

John Francis had family over there so he tended to disappear to spend time with his Uncle Steadman I think. Maybe the two lads who enjoyed it most were Adie Randall and Paul McKenzie who pretty much sank into the local lifestyle as if they'd been born there. Talk about laid back the pair of them. For them it was a chance to disappear and absorb the local culture which consisted of lots of chillin', and then a bit more chillin'. How does that reggae song go— no worries no cares? They acted blacker than me over there. I think they'd have stayed there forever if they'd had the chance.

Adie Randall was a great character. At Burnley in training there was the occasion that we were doing a really hard running session. At Aldershot Adie got away with doing as little as possible in training. At Burnley he had to knuckle down and work hard like the rest of us. Suddenly he stopped running and just walked away towards the changing rooms.

'Where are you going?' yelled Jimmy Mullen, furious.

'I've 'ad enough mate,' he yelled back as he disappeared.

The two Endsleigh bosses were there, Mike Naylor and Mike Alcock. Endsleigh was, and still is, a thriving insurance firm and the two Mikes weren't going to miss out on this one. I suppose they'd argue it was work. Mike Naylor sadly passed away as a result of a car crash. The two of them were so much a part of Burnley Football Club and the 1992 shirts had the Endsleigh logo on the front. I always felt that if these two had been on the Board at Burnley things would have moved on at the club so much quicker. It was a club that seemed stuck in its ways like an old train chugging along in need of a new engine. One of the directors even had a stopwatch and he used to time every journey to away matches we made on the coach. In contrast Endsleigh and the two Mikes seemed so dynamic and go-ahead. We liked the way they treated us and their staff. They even had their own works football team kitted out as if they were internationals and had their own bus to ferry them around. I'm not saying that we had nothing at Burnley; far from it. We had more than many other clubs in the division but we were certainly made to feel that we should be grateful for it. But Endsleigh made such an impression on us that we used to talk a lot about how good it would be if they had bought the club. They had their corporate headquarters and residential centre at Cheltenham where we would often stay. Believe me it was party time whenever we stayed there with members of their staff designated to look after us. Let's just say the drink flowed freely and there were some wild times.

After a Saturday game in that part of the country we'd stay over on the Saturday night. The drink, be it champagne or vodka, flowed copiously. The following morning those who could manage it indulged in a huge breakfast. Then we'd play the Endsleigh team. Some of the players could hardly stand up. It's hard to imagine that happening today.

But what a time we had in Bermuda. We took to going out with another group we met there on the motor bikes they'd hired. I don't think any of these bikes ever went more than 20 mph. For one trip out I had to nip up to my room to get some money. Up in the lift I went still wearing a black helmet with the visor pulled down. Going out on motorbikes was a strict no-no for a footballer back then. It was in the contract if I remember right and a sackable offence. The lift stopped at the fourth floor and my heart stood still when Frank Teasdale got in. Bloody hell I thought what if he knows who I am? I kept quiet, turned my head away with the visor still down, and let Mike Conroy who was also in the lift do the talking. He won't know who I am with this helmet on I convinced myself. Up it went to my floor. I never said a word. Out I got confident he'd no idea it was me. 'Bloody hell, I've got away with it', I thought.

'Be careful on that bike Roger,' said Frank, with a grin, just as I was leaving. If it was a film it would be one of those sublime comedy moments.

He was an entertaining chap when he was relaxed. But I found out how stubborn he could be in the boardroom one summer when I was in a contract dispute that involved the PFA. There were definitely two Frank Teasdales; the hard-faced one who sat behind the desk, and the smiley-faced one in social settings when there was a bit of a laugh to be had.

Some of the lads met up with the girls on holiday out there. Out in the bay was a wooden raft we'd swim out to and sunbathe. Many times we'd just sit and chat. Needless to say it was also a great place for one of our lads to take a girl for a bit of you-know-what late in the day. Trouble is there was also a lot of tar on this raft that did tend to get quite sticky by the end of the day in the heat. Out swam our Burnley hero with his girl and there's no need to say what they got up to. The tar came back with them. It was all over them. It was everywhere. It took him a day to get it all off himself and the bath, carpets and the bedsheets.

China was almost a sort of casual throw of the dice. In the summer of '94 I was finished at Burnley. With my head in a real mess filled with a mixture of anger and feeling let-down, when the China idea came up I thought why not? I think, in effect, I was running away from reality. At the end of a season your name goes on the PFA list of 'free' players if you are released. An agent called Mr Yu spotted my name. Out of the blue he got in touch. Cue the usual jokes.

'Hello is that Yu?'

'Mr Eli, I have a Mr Yu on the line for you . . . pardon, Yu who?'

Truth is I was ready to finish. The last year with Mullen and Wilson had drained me. I felt they were messing me about so much I tried everything to stay focused. There was the occasion of my brother's wedding. It coincided with a period of me doing really well in training and I got the vibes and believed that I'd possibly be in the squad for the weekend game coming up, on the bench if not in the team. So I attended the wedding in the morning but then rushed over to Burnley and missed the reception. Now this was my brother for God's sake who I loved. Missing the rest of the wedding day was a big sacrifice. So I got to the ground but wasn't required. I was absolutely livid but kept quiet and bit my lip.

I even paid £40 a session to see a hypnotist several times. I can't say I got anything out of it. I know she put me under but what she did while I was under I'd no idea. Well you wouldn't would you if you were in a trance? For all I know she might have nipped out the room and done the ironing. It was as much to do with counselling and positive thinking and I wanted to do anything to restore some self-esteem and sense of achievement. Both were slowly being destroyed. Bloody hell, I'd been Player of the Year not that long ago, physically and mentally strong, sound of mind and limb and back to fitness. But mentally I was down in the doldrums, sunk, self-esteem drained and with no-one else to talk to. There was Mullen, Wilson, Middlemass and not one of them showed any interest in me or my career. None of them were 'arm round the shoulder' kind of people you could relate to. Andrea must have been in despair at the moods I was in. I wasn't a problem to Mullen. I didn't undermine him, I wasn't a thorn in his side; I wasn't the classic dressing room lawyer and agitator. I still worked hard, trained hard but I might as well have battered my head against a wall. I was in Harry Wilson's reserve side and I had no time for him. It was futile. So the hypnotist seemed a good idea.

Anyway Mr Yu: what the hell I thought. I talked it through with Andrea and sent Sammy Yu a video I put together. It was a chance to earn some serious money as well, more than doubling the Burnley wage. Nearly £1,000 a week in 1994 was not to be sneezed at. Mr Yu is still around in the game, believe it or not, part of the Hong Kong businessman Carson Yeung's group that took over Birmingham

City.

Can you imagine it? My head was in a mess, I'd as good as lost interest in football; I'd even tried a hypnotist and I decided to fly off to China on the other side of the world where I didn't know a soul and not one word of the language other than 'Chow Mein' and 'Crispy Duck with Pancakes'. Only five years earlier there'd been the riots in Tiananmen Square so there was the worry that this was still a volatile and uncertain place. It was a country where you could be dragged off the street by the police never to surface again. Anyway: Mr Sammy Yu wanted a striker for Foshaan, a city of 1,000,000+ in southern China in the Guangdong Province not too far from Hong Kong. I'd always wondered about playing in Hong Kong where there was decent money so this seemed the nearest thing. Surely it would be a bit of a doddle as well. Surely even blindfolded I could run rings round a Chinese footballer? Surely they couldn't be any good? I imagined them to be gentle and little, and would even politely bow before they tackled you. How wrong could I be?

To my surprise, technically they were excellent, tough, skilful and incredibly quick. And they knew a few tricks as well including how to interfere with a long throw I'd developed, good but not quite Rory Delap. Four times this player stood right in my face as I ran to take a throw. The fifth time I thought, right, you're gonna get it pal. So I followed right through with my arms and laid him out. The crowd of 20,000 went wild. Shortly after, he got his revenge and took his turn to lay me out. He tackled me with everything he had, followed right through and nearly crippled me. The melee and mass brawl that followed was as good as anything you'd see on a bad day between Burnley and Blackburn. I lay on the floor and let them get on with it and they were still at it as I was taken off on a stretcher. The opponent was sent off. No sir: any ideas that it was going to be a doddle were soon out of the window. I was quite happy to disappear on the stretcher. His teammates were lining up to have another go at me. The dressing room was the safest place to be.

Amazing how things happen sometimes and life works in funny ways. The day before I was due to travel and everything was sorted, Walsall got in touch. Did I fancy joining them along with Graham Lancashire to form their new strike-team for the coming season? It was too late then to think about it. I'd have probably turned it down anyway; I'd had enough of English football. On the other hand maybe I would have said to myself, yes, go to Walsall and show Jimmy Mullen I wasn't finished.

I sat on that plane for thousands of miles in between a Chinese couple who each looked at least a hundred years old. The old lady kept on trumping and smiling; boy did she have a problem. Then the old man would lean over and jabber away sounding like he was giving her a real telling off. I swear she must have farted once for every year of her life. I sat there in a sort of trance, dazed and knocked for six by the events of the last few weeks plus the old woman's flatulence. I was half asleep when I got on the plane. I was half asleep when I got off. In this half-alive state suffering from jet lag, leg lag, brain lag and every other kind of lag you could think of I still couldn't believe what I'd done. Suddenly Walsall seemed a very attractive place. The hours of travelling weren't over. From Hong Kong airport it was a three-hour train journey to Foshaan.

Sammy met me at Hong Kong airport. I was drained and exhausted. I resisted the temptation to ask him 'Sammy is that Yu?' If he'd announced 'Hello Roger I'm Yu' I'd have cracked up. Silly really I know. For all I know the word Eli might have meant something rude in Chinese. The manager was called Mr Wong. Cue more jokes . . . hello I'm Wong . . . the manager's decision is always Wong . . . two Wongs don't make a wight . . . sorry Wong number. He had nicknames for us. He called the full-back Chow Pan which meant Fat Guy. The centre half was Da Tow which meant Big Head. He had these names for all of us and he'd use them in meetings and training. He called me Ha Tai. I looked it up. It meant Black Boy. 'You pillock' I thought, but to him it wasn't racist, or offensive, just what I looked like and to be sure there weren't many of us in China in 1994.

During the three hour train journey to Foshaan Mr Yu talked. The train was filled to the rafters with passengers. I sat watching miles of paddy fields pass by tended by farmers in straw hats shading them from the sun. I'd seen the same scenes in *The Deer Hunter*. After two hours Sammy was also getting a little boring as he told me endlessly all about what a good footballer he was and had been captain of a Hong Kong XI and what a football hero he was. After two hours of this he'd convinced me he was the Chinese Pele. By then I was sitting there thinking and wondering about how the hell I'd ended up there.

But, in Foshaan we checked into the most magnificent hotel which would be my home for the next four months. All the staff recognised Sammy and smiled at him and wanted to shake his hand. Maybe he was the Chinese Pele. My room was superb, the staff were great, though I couldn't understand a word they said and I could see they were a little puzzled by the colour of my skin.

We had a couple of nights in the hotel before another plane journey to Beijing, hundreds of miles up in the north, to organise paperwork and take fitness tests. It gave me a chance to see the stadium and prepare for the fitness tests to come. I saw a lot of China; trouble was it was from 30,000 feet up and 400 miles an hour. Up north they spoke Mandarin. Then it was all the way back again. In the south they spoke Cantonese. It made no difference to me. I understood neither. The intensive tests were gruelling but I passed them, not without problems however. Test one was to run eight laps of a 400m running track in under 12 minutes. Then there was a series of intensive shuttle runs each run of 25 metres. I tore into them too fast so that by the final couple I was exhausted. I failed.

'Take your time, take your time, pace yourself,' two Koreans encouraged me as they watched and knew full well I'd gone at them like a bull in a china shop. Meanwhile a TV station was filming all this. I had a chance the next day to do them again—and did them without a problem. What did hit me though was the humidity. This was almost a subtropical climate. On a bad day it was draining.

Foshan, or Foshaan, or as it was once called on old maps 'Fatshan', was a modern, industrial city that had been around and grown over many centuries, 5,000 years said one guide. It had its share of modern glitzy buildings and four-star hotels but never far away were the fantastic temples, pagodas, amazing statues, beautiful gardens, the museums and all the relics of an older age. The city was situated in the northern end of the Pearl River Delta so no-one was ever short of fish or rice.

There I learned to appreciate the food; Foshaan Manggong Cake, Pricked Hoof, Daliang Pheasant Roll, Fried Milk, Double Leather Cheese, Xiaofeng Biscuit, Nanhai Fish, Jiujiang Fried Biscuit, and Sanshui Gouzi Duck. If you thought a cuppa tea was important in the UK, in Foshaan a cuppa cha was a way of life and a bit of a ritual. It took a little while to get used to everything coming in little bite-sized portions. A slap up Full English with fried bread seemed a million miles away. There was an old proverb out there that said that anything that walks, swims, crawls or flies with its back to heaven is edible. At first I drew the line at braised snake or stir fried shredded snake meat. On the other hand twin pigeons in rose wine sounded okay. But then I started to eat everything or at least try it. Team meals were at a long table sitting altogether and the food was cooked in front of us in the middle of the table. The Chinese lads laughed at our attempts to use chopsticks and then laughed at me eating Chinese food with a knife and fork. Sometimes they'd get their chopsticks and attempt to force-feed me with the things that I'd try to avoid. There was a bewildering variety of ways to cook—steaming, boiling, stir-frying, double boiling, braising and deep frying. The common dishes were based on fish, pork and duck nearly always served with freshly steamed rice. Everything had to be fresh. That's why the markets, especially the farmers' markets, were such amazing, noisy places filled with cages of live ducks, chickens, piglets and tanks of fish and lobster. The restaurants had tanks outside the front windows filled with fish. The live fish or lobster would be brought to your table to prove its freshness. Then there were the wonderful soups boiled in clay pots for hours. Every dish was supposed to be good for something or some illness—even raw egg. For example watercress was supposed to be good for sore throats. I never found a dish to fix my knee though.

Getting to grips with the place was an experience. There were masses of people everywhere, bikes, cars, rickshaws and buses. It was teeming. Imagine being in London's Oxford Street at Christmas when you can hardly move. That was Foshaan all the time. Sammy had succumbed to a stomach illness on one of the stops to the training camp. It was another endless train journey. He'd eaten some raw meat and tried to convince me to take a taste as if it was some kind of delicacy. I declined.

I met up with the lads somewhere in deepest China. They all came to greet me at the entrance. The looks on their faces yet again revealed the Chinese curiosity about a man being my colour.

The distances we travelled were enormous. We flew to games or went by train. Train journeys were an education and they often meant travelling overnight. I'd spend long stretches just watching the countryside passing by as we rolled through farmland, country villages and yet more paddy fields. We were the lucky ones with sleeper compartments where we could shut ourselves off from the manic, crowded carriages and corridors. Every inch was crammed with people and luggage, sometimes even tied-up piglets and cardboard boxes filled with chickens. They weren't quite as bad as trains in India where they hang out of windows, ride the buffers and sit on the roof but they were filled like tins of sardines with a vast range of people of all ages and sizes and class. I don't think I ever slept a wink. The whole experience was a culture-shock especially using the loo in a Chinese train. It was a hole in the floor in the squatty loo compartment. You squatted and performed and it fell through the hole on to the track below. British Rail this was not. The worst sight was the rats hopping onto the train at the station stops. They'd scamper round the corridors and under the seats mopping up the bits of food. When the whistle went for the train to depart, en masse these bloody things would scuttle off the train. I wouldn't have believed it possible.

There were two Scotsmen in the team, Steve McMahon, 6' 5", ex Swansea and John Marr ex Clydebank. We had an interpreter the club used, a lovely man who was a professor. Trouble is his English wasn't too good, something that caused a few problems. There was a great example during a running session on the track that went round the pitch. The three of us were in the lead and running strong. Our interpreter, Mr Su, yelled at us. 'Manager say you boys MUST go faster, MUST go faster.' I should have asked him if his wife was called Peggy.

We were already a hundred metres in the lead but okay we went faster. He yelled at us again. 'Manager say you boys MUST go faster MUST go faster.'

Bloody hell we thought, we can't go any faster, if we go faster we'll take off and by now we were knackered and dripping with sweat and groaning with effort. When he yelled this out a third time we stopped absolutely exhausted. Mr Su and Mr Wong came over to us as we lay in agony groaning and panting. Mr Wong though was beaming. Mr Su was beaming. They were well pleased about something. It turned out that what Mr Su should have said was: 'Manager say wow you boys sure go fast.' He was actually delighted with us.

After a while we got to know the Chinese boys in the team. They were desperate to learn a few words of English. Imagine trying to learn English from a Scotsman. They wanted to learn simple words like hello and goodbye. We told them the English for hello was, 'Fuck you'. We taught them that to say goodbye you said, 'Bugger off'. This we thought was highly amusing. Footballers humour again eh, there's nothing quite like it.

This was funny until a few of them came to our hotel one day. There were lots of people from various countries including England of course. In come the boys and see us talking to a group of English people. They smile and come over. 'Fuck you, fuck you,' they called out smiling and waving to our great embarrassment. They felt well pleased with themselves and very excited. It didn't go down too well with the hotel management or the English people. After that we taught them how to speak English properly.

I did manage a couple of trips home but on the return journey on the second trip only pure luck got me back to Foshaan. Landing in Hong Kong as usual I'd booked a boat back. When I got to the dock there were two boats waiting. But there were no signs in English, no one to speak to in English, and only by guessing and by pure good fortune I got on the right boat. Good job, the other one was heading to Shanghai.

Eventually real homesickness took over as I hadn't seen Andrea for months. There I was in a city of a million people and comfortable and eventually confident enough to get out and about. I'd enjoyed my football playing a holding, midfield role, and we'd come third in the table. Nevertheless it was a fairly lonely time out there even though the hotel was quite westernised with a lot of Europeans staying there. With a dictionary I bought I did actually manage to learn a few basic words. The Scots lads were good company even if they were head cases and were always out clubbing whenever the chance arose. But I was desperate for home. Bradford beckoned once again.

While I had been out there I'd had to pay for very few things. Nearly everything had been paid for. I managed to save some decent money. If I arrived in China in a state of utter confusion, I left it at least with a better bank balance and some experiences that I wouldn't have swapped for anything.

13

The *Final* Journey

So Scunthorpe was next even though I knew in my head that it was pretty much over. But it's hard for a footballer and I couldn't let go. I couldn't resist the offer of a trial. I'd come back from China and wrote to a few clubs. I'd had good games in the past against Scunthorpe; maybe they'd remember me and think, 'Oh yeah Roger Eli he always scored against us.' So they wrote back and said come on trial. I got a couple of games and who was there but a very young Graham Alexander. I did wonder what sort of a reception I'd get. There'd been a Scunthorpe–Burnley game when trouble had kicked off and I was in the middle of it.

My heart wasn't in it though. With such a negative mindset, the legs didn't move as fast, and recovery seemed to take longer. And the sad thing was that I wasn't even 30. Legs that once took me past players didn't do it anymore. The head won't quite acknowledge that the finishing line has appeared, but there's a little corner of it that still says your day isn't done just yet; maybe you can get one more last club. It's a poignant moment that comes to all footballers. The body has just had enough. On cold wet days the bed is warm and cosy and you don't want to bother with training. There's no spring in the step anymore. There's a great line in a boxing book somewhere about Sonny Liston and when he couldn't do it anymore it says he'd just got to the falling off place at the end of the track. It was where I was at, the end of the line — almost. But there's still that little voice in the head that says you can still do it. After a couple of months at Scunthorpe there was however, one last throw of the dice. I suppose you could call it the last journey. Against all common sense, like a boxer always thinks he can manage one more fight, the footballer always thinks he can cope and have one last shot in the game.

It's funny how life takes its course and matters can turn full circle. A Scotsman had sent me packing from Leeds years earlier and here

I was about to look to other Scotsmen to prolong my football life. The head said let go of football you know you've had enough. But the heart couldn't. It was that notion of letting go of an old girlfriend that you once loved or the reluctance to throw away an old pair of shoes or slippers that once fitted like a glove but were now worn out. The suitcase came out again when there was one last attempt to continue an ailing career. In the old days, the golden age of travel they used to call it, travellers plastered their cases with those old sticky labels of all their exotic destinations. If I'd done that my case would have been barely visible, although you'd hardly describe Crewe, Northwich, Bury or Scunthorpe as exotic; and an old Adidas Bag would never have been seen in the golden age of travel.

An agent by the name of Ray Sparks had set up an opportunity for me to join Partick Thistle in the SPL. With a name like that you'd have thought he'd have made a good comedian. It was a chance to join them on a non-contract basis with a view to a permanent deal. When I look back on it now I have two regrets, one, that a similar chance hadn't presented itself when I was younger; and two, that I wasn't really in the right frame of mind or in peak physical shape to have been able to take what would have been a great last opportunity. I was never one of those from south of Hadrian's Wall who belittled the Scottish game and I would have loved to play there. If points were awarded for passion and love of the game up there the Scots would probably win hands down.

Believe it or not I'd never set foot in Scotland before. It meant taking out the road atlas from the car and sitting down to figure out how to get to Glasgow. I can remember sitting at the kitchen table and looking at the atlas pages and I actually had butterflies in my stomach, more so than going to China. Going to China was a great experience. I hadn't had butterflies since those long-ago formative years at Leeds United. Now they were back, giving a sort of nagging discomfort. Why were they there? Maybe because I knew that if this didn't work out, then football was done with me.

As a teenager I was always used to a bit of nervousness. My dad always said it was a good thing, made you careful; stopped you taking things for granted. In my twenties I'd been more confident despite the knocks. But now the butterflies were back. If I fluffed this—then what was next? And yet at the same time there was the feeling that I'd had enough of football anyway. I'd had enough but still couldn't let go. It was all I'd known since the age of 16. It was like an old affair when you knew it was over and should be ended, but you still hung on because you were so used to it and it was such a part of your life.

It was difficult to concentrate. Should I take this route or that, which motorway, head across to the M62 to the M6; or, head east to the A1 and go up via Edinburgh and then cut across to Glasgow? Andrea knew I was nervous about the thing. She knew that if it didn't work out we had to sit down and decide what to do with our lives. Maybe only a footballer can understand the enormity of it. When you leave football, you're on your own. It's back to that bubble thing again. Suddenly you're outside it. There's no-one there to make decisions for you. As a footballer much of your life is organised by others. All that stops in an instant.

As I sat with the atlas working out the route; and even as I drove up there, there were nagging doubts and one worry was how I would be greeted by the locals. Kenny Burns was a Glaswegian. If he was anything to go by, then the prospect of living up there was worrying. Glasgow had this reputation then of being a tough, hard city. The idea of it being a 'City of Culture' was years away. Funny the things that come into your head on a long drive though. Kenny Burns liked the greyhounds and for some reason I knew that Glasgow had a Dog Track at Shawfield because Clyde FC shared the stadium and people were raving then about a player called Pat Nevin.

It was the M6 I chose and the drive triggered a train of thought and a sort of replay of people and places. The Wigan turn-off made me think of Danny Sonner who I thought was a really gifted player. It was his strong Wigan voice that made me smile. You could have bottled it. It was something else. At the time he was re-discovering his form with Ipswich Town before going on to Sheffield Wednesday and the Premiership. He was a terrifically bubbly character and it was great to see his career flourish after he was shown the door at Turf Moor by Jimmy Mullen. He vanished somewhere to the backwaters of eastern Germany some time after the Berlin Wall was destroyed but worked his way back into the Prem. He was a classic case of rebuilding a career after others have shown little faith; you can take the man out of Wigan but not Wigan out of the man. Other discarded young pros could well take a leaf out of Danny's book about how to resurrect a life in the game and prove other people wrong. He went on to play for Northern Ireland 13 times.

He was a continental style player but with a rich north-west accent, strolling around Hoddle-style, pinging the ball with great accuracy—on a good day. He also had the most appalling dress sense and his demand for a pay rise at Port Vale met with a classic reply from the chairman who told him if he thought he was working for next to nothing he should try work in the Potteries for 40 hours a week.

As I passed Junction 32, which is the M55 turn-off to Blackpool, one of Scotland's greatest ever players came to mind and the evening when in Blackpool there had been a game with Burnley in the Autoglass Trophy. It was the night each one of us kidded ourselves that King Kenny had come to watch us. Earlier at our Gawthorpe training ground the word on the Lancashire football grapevine was that Mr Dalglish was attending the game. John Deary was adamant it was true. As an ex Blackpool player he had been told by a mate who worked in the Bloomfield Road office that he had been there when a fax came through with Kenny's application for a Director's Box ticket.

It got the lads talking big-style and it was even a distraction at the team meeting when we discussed tactics and set plays. Jimmy Mullen must have wondered why no-one was listening to him and might even have been suspicious that some of us had been out on the town the night before, so pre-occupied we were. Eventually a huge debate began as to which of us King Kenny might be looking at. Then it switched to a discussion about if any of us would ever dare join him at Ewood Park and Blackburn Rovers of all places such was the bitterness between the two sets of supporters. Dalglish had just taken over there and had been given a bottomless fund of cash by Jack Walker to develop a team capable of winning the title.

John Deary brought the talk down to earth in his characteristic West Lancashire tone and blurted: 'Well he isn't gonna be signing me for fucks sake'.

We were intrigued. Who on earth could he be interested in? No way would he be attending an Autoglass game for the sake of a fun night out. Realistically only Steve Davis was a player who had the capacity to play at that level and had already played a handful of games for Southampton in the top flight. It still amazes me that no big club ever took a chance on him. The fact that he was voted into the Burnley legends group alongside people like Jimmy McIlroy and players from the 1960 title team and other great individuals from the seventies tells the story of how good he was.

Meanwhile: Adrian Randall had God given talent and Mike Conroy was hammering goals in for fun. Maybe it was them I pondered, but could it possibly be me now that I was producing some decent and consistent form? I think it was at that point I sat back and reality took a grip. And anyway how could I leave the love affair with the Burnley Longside and move to their hated rivals who were out to buy a title? As it turned out, it was Blackpool's little full-back Alan Wright he was after.

Ironically in front of Kenny I had a storming game and scored twice in a 3–1 win. Jimmy Mullen, as usual, was in his agitated state before any Blackpool game. The goals were crackers. One of them I think was one of the best I ever scored. When the ball came, I controlled it on the edge of the box, swivelled and rifled it home. The other was a perfect volley.

I almost laughed out loud whilst driving, thinking about the incidents in the same game involving Blackpool's Gary Briggs. In his Oxford days alongside Malcolm Shotton they were known as Briggs and Mortar. Briggs was as tough and ruthless as they come and his trademark was to head the back of an opponent's head as he did with mine twice as we went up for challenges. He had no hesitation in chopping you down in an age when it was as good as legal. After 15 minutes I'd had enough of him and politely asked him to refrain from anything else that was beyond legal. My polite request fell on deaf ears and he blanked me yet again. Out-psyching an opponent was part of the game. I'd made up my mind that if he came at me from behind again, that was it, and I wouldn't stay on my feet. Yet again he came in at me with a lunge, I side-stepped but made it look like my fall was a bad foul. Bingo, out came the yellow card. But it didn't calm him down, it made him even more determined to maim me. The process was repeated. Out came a second yellow and off he went. The Blackpool fans booed me for the rest of the game and the aftermath spilled over into the players' lounge. As per usual John Francis was first to the bar and had got the drinks in. Normally after a game all bad feeling is forgotten and even the hardest players in the game like Terry Hurlock or Billy Whitehurst are thoroughly chatty afterwards.

On this occasion a group of us in our stylish claret and blue shell suits were happily chatting when over in the corner there stood Briggsie. We made brief eye contact and then ignored each other. His mate, however, who must have been seven feet tall, did not ignore me. Over he came with a face like thunder, his wagging finger an inch from my face, and then began to hurl expletives at me about his mate being sent off. Immediately half the Burnley squad gathered round me, bristling, ready for action, camaraderie fully evident, and the verbals and tension increased. The bloke went away. Mayhem had been just inches away. The incident showed, even though nothing really happened, just how close that group of players at Burnley was. It doesn't happen all the time, in fact far from it, but we, in this particular team, were loyal to each other.

I passed the signs for Carlisle. It reminded me of the title season in '92. It reminded me of the good days and all those fans dressed up and the supporter on a lilo pretending to swim on the pitch. It reminded me too of Mullen in the last year, the one who switched me off at Burnley. From being a bloke who once asked me my opinions on things he changed to the man who seemed to ignore me.

When I arrived at Firhill Park in Maryhill to sign for a month, there was a small group of reporters and photographers already waiting. It was hardly Paul Gascoigne rolling up at Ibrox, or Paolo di Canio marching into Celtic Park. But it still generated a level of interest that showed the intensity of football in Glasgow. It's one of the greatest football cities in the world. On the way up I'd stopped for a break at Johnstonebridge on the A74 and bought a couple of Scottish newspapers, the *Scottish Sun* and the *Daily Record* I think they were. I was staggered to see the number of pages devoted to football.

I was only in Scotland for a month. I should never have gone really. There's that great film *This Sporting Life* by David Storey. It's about rugby not football and the story of a battling bruiser who finds his moments of triumph. But then as age and weariness take over, opponents whom he would once have flattened or skipped past, now dish it out to him and he's the one who comes off the field black and blue aching from head to foot and mentally worn out. In Scotland that was pretty much me. It was physical up there and I wasn't fit. The edge had gone. I was caught too often. But above all, my heart wasn't in it, my mind not focused. The spark had been extinguished.

There were two players there I vaguely knew, Rod McDonald and Chic Charnley. Rod was mixed-race, born in London but with a Scouse accent. I knew that he'd spent some of his younger life in the notorious district of Liverpool's Toxteth so he probably felt quite at home in the infamous Glasgow district of Castlehill. The thing that I remembered was that he had once aimed some abuse at me that was totally uncalled for during a game. He was trying to make his way in the game and was playing for Tranmere reserves and I was playing for Crewe reserves. The ball was running towards the dead ball line by the corner flag. In defensive mode I ran over and guarded it so it would roll out for a dead ball but Rod being the competitor he was showed real determination to keep it in play. Rod was frustrated and deliberately bumped into me with a force insufficient to attract the referee but enough to show me he was aggravated. And then he bellowed: 'You Uncle Tom.'

It's a racist insult that derives from the cotton fields of the old Deep South when some of the slaves worked their way into the master's house and were accused of betraying their colour. I was the only black guy in the Crewe team. But he was likewise the only black person in the Tranmere team. It was an odd thing to call me. It was the only time I'd been racially abused by someone with the same skin as me.

I got to know him well at Partick and we shared a few car rides home together. I never asked him about the Uncle Tom incident. It was all such a long while ago. We never discussed that incident or his religion though he was a religious man. If a player crosses himself when he runs on the pitch 99 times out of 100 no-one thinks anything of it. Rod used to do this but on the occasion he did it at Rangers he blessed himself leaving the pitch at half time. He'd done the same thing hundreds of times but this match official spotted it, thought it was provocative, and promptly marched into the dressing room and booked him. In the second half he was late into a challenge and found himself on the end of a second yellow and was sent off. The crowd were bemused because they had no idea about the first card.

Over the border and into Scotland and the A74 takes you to Ecclefechan. I remembered that one of Partick's famous sons was Alan Hansen, another player who was wary of Billy Whitehurst. Ecclefechan is famous for its tarts—the sort you eat. Nearer Glasgow the name Chic Charnley came into my head along with a degree of apprehension. When the good Lord made Billy Whitehurst out of the same mould came Charnley. He was a legend in the city. He'd been tipped for greatness at an early stage of his career but what probably held him back was the small matter of 17 red cards during his career. He was ferocious in the tackle, knew how to look after himself and his idea of nutrition was to add more orange juice to his vodka. He must be the only footballer ever to have been attacked by two fans waving samurai swords during a training session. One punch, so the story goes (and a cut hand), laid one of the fans out and the other ran off. He ended up having played for something like 20 clubs. As I drove on up the motorway, I wondered just how to approach someone like this, and whether or not he would take to me.

I needn't have worried. He was friendly and welcoming. He used to light up the dressing room as soon as he walked in with his stories and anecdotes about the game. He was a great example of the way Glaswegians extend a welcome to strangers. Like other players there he went out of his way to help me feel at ease, and that's something you can't say about every group of players. His ferocious tackling and accurate passing impressed me. I never saw the famous temper in action while I was there, though I could see it existed.

There was another thing to consider as well when I'd studied the map deciding which route to take. It occurred to me I'd be back in digs again. Not for me The Hilton or The Marriott where the wealthy clubs put their players who had just arrived. For me it was someone's house in the Bishop Briggs area. Memories of those appalling digs in Wolverhampton came back. Anything similar and I'd be back home before you could say Jock Stein. On top of that Andrea and I had just set up a house together. But, alas, non-contract players with the job of proving themselves didn't get luxury treatment at hard-up Partick. The digs turned out to be fine with some good people.

When I actually arrived in Glasgow I had to ask no end of people how to find Firhill Park. But they were patient and friendly and as a stranger I felt welcomed. The problem was that even though there was no end of warmth, I continued to feel like a stranger. Even with the China trip I still couldn't get the good times at Burnley out of my head. I was struggling to draw a line under those days and it shouldn't have been like that. Glasgow and the SPL could have provided a fabulous stage for me to regain my appetite and enthusiasm. It wasn't as if I was too old but for the life of me I couldn't get into the right frame of mind or dig deep enough to rekindle the flame. The joy of the game had vanished. I just hadn't got the ammunition or the verve to convince the Partick fans and management that I was worth signing. The *Sun*, on April 14th, had a feature about my arrival with a big colour picture.

'LUCKY CHARM ELI' it was headed:

Partick boss John Lambie has ordered up his tastiest ever Chinese carry-out. And hitman Roger Eli, whose last club was Foshaan in China, reckons he's brought a touch of Oriental good fortune to Firhill. The 29-year old has made just two substitute appearances but Jags have been unbeaten since he arrived last month.

Eli's sure there's no way Partick will be relegated now and grinned: 'We're definitely staying up. I've brought them some Chinese luck so it's the Year of the Thistle.'

Lambie hadn't even seen him play before handing him a one-month deal. Now, the wandering striker looking for his first start against Hearts tomorrow is desperate to put down his roots in the Premier League.

He added: 'I've already seen enough to know I want to play in the Premier League against the likes of Celtic and Rangers next season. Our players are really confident of staying up and reckon another six points will do it.'

Yorkshireman Eli headed for the Far East when he was released by Burnley after a year out with a cartilage injury. But he got a real culture shock after signing for Foshaan.

Eli recalled: 'It took us a month of upset stomachs before we got used to the food. We once had a 20-hour journey by train and when I woke up in my sleeper in the middle of the night there were rats scurrying all over the place, which the Chinese didn't seem bothered about. I thought I'd have a reasonably easy time over there but the standard was much higher than I expected. Their technique and skills are fantastic but they lack discipline and they're also a bit short in the physical department, which is why they're keen to have British players. But our teammates didn't take kindly to us because we were earning a lot more than they were. There's plenty of poverty in China and the only ones who seemed to have any money were policemen, government officials and footballers. We did reasonably well though. We were favourites to win the B Division but ended up missing out by just two points.

'At Firhill there is at least one thing in common with my time in China. I couldn't understand what the guys in the dressing room were saying either'.

It was a feature that certainly built me up although it wasn't accurate about being out for a year with a cartilage injury. I'd recovered from that and was fit and well. I was out for those 12 months because of managerial decisions.

Truth is though, at Partick, I was only going through the motions and was back in Bradford at every opportunity. Racial abuse reared its head again during one visit home. Andrea and I were on the bus on one occasion and someone began making monkey noises. We ignored it but it went on until an old lady complained to the bus driver and told him he should eject this nuisance. He did. But unfortunately he ejected him at the same stop where we got off. It was kind of funny in a way as he carried on abusing us as we walked down the street.

I was playing from memory. Training was a chore. Whereas once I'd leapt out of bed to get stuck into the training I loved, now it seemed a better idea to stay in bed. There'll be dozens of old pros out there who'll know the feeling. The rain seemed wetter, the mud seemed thicker. The jokes and banter weren't funny anymore. From playing in front of 18,000 at Burnley or over 20,000 in China to a couple of hundred people at a Scottish reserve game. How has it come to this I asked? The periods of boredom were longer. Disinterest grew. It was as if I'd been kicked down to the bottom of the pile again. The penny dropped. All I was doing was trying to recreate what I once was. The game was up. It was time to put the suitcase away. If I'd still had it, it would have been the Adidas bag.

There was a reserve game against Celtic and I scored the goal in a 1–0 win. Then there was the game against Hearts when I didn't start but came off the subs bench for just 12 minutes. It was the last game for me. Manager John Lambie wanted to see me one more time in real competitive action to be able to make a decision but I knew deep down even before he told me to warm up on the touchline what the likely outcome was going to be. In fairness I didn't do myself any favours by driving home as often as I did and then returning at the crack of dawn the next day for training. The fact was that Partick might well have been the right club at the wrong time. Had I been there in my late teens or early twenties who knows how well I might have done instead of being shunted round to Wolves and Crewe and York and all the rest until arriving at Burnley? If I'd gone up there straight from Leeds I'm certain to this day I'd have been a hit.

So a final 12 minute appearance brought it all to an end. I doubt I touched the ball half a dozen times. Did I have a shot on goal? Did I make a tackle? Was I just waiting for the whistle to go so that I could walk away? There's that film again, it would be in sepia, in slow motion, with no sound track. The laughing faces of the winning team; cut to the departing figure, head bowed looking at the floor, close-up on the expressionless face and the blank eyes of the departing hero.

After the game with Hearts, the assistant manager, Gerry Collins, pulled me to one side. He was a top bloke and a straight talker. He asked me to be honest and tell him if I thought I had done myself justice over the last few weeks. I gave him a frank and honest answer that no I hadn't and that he and the other staff had not seen the best of me. We agreed there and then it was best if we went our separate ways. John Lambie came in and rubber stamped the agreement we had made. We shook hands and that was that. I went into the players' lounge and said goodbye to Chic Charnley, Rod McDonald and a couple of the other lads. I'd had sinking, churning feelings in my stomach several times in my career but nothing like this. The falling off place at the end of the track—I'd reached it.

I knew then that it was all over after 12 years in the game. I was saying goodbye to a career. I'd started out as that young idealistic kid at my favourite club, Leeds, with teenage visions of playing for England and being an Elland Road first-team regular who'd go on to play hundreds of games. But that only happens for the chosen select few. So what had I got to show for it; over 12 years and not much more than a couple of hundred league and Cup games and more from the subs bench?

But, there was a Fourth Division winners' medal and a Player of the Year, and Goal of the Season trophy at the place where I found a home. More than half of those appearances were at Burnley. There's just something about that club, the town and the people that will always be a part of me.

How can I grumble? The buoyancy and positivity in me tells me I was lucky to play the games I did and it was great while it lasted, although looking back it all seems so brief and that it was over far too soon. But I got a foot on the ladder and made my mark. Some lads don't even manage that. They don't even step on the train. I suppose considering the state of the knees I did well to last that long. But then I always get to thinking that even with that handicap, I had a couple more years at Burnley denied to me. There were times in the final 12 months there I knew that I could have played comfortably.

Don't ask me to talk about that final drive home from Glasgow. On the way up my head had been filled with memories and reminiscences nudged by road signs and the names of towns as I drove along. Whereas then my mind had been racing, now it was doing the opposite. It was in a kind of neutral. It was as if there was nothing in it other than a grey blankness. I wasn't even aware that the petrol gauge was going lower and lower until the warning light began to show. The car made it to the edge of a service station and free-wheeled the last 20 yards or so to the pumps. I'd never done that before, or since, but it showed the empty, numbed state I was in. For a footballer who has loved the game, when the time comes to call it a day, it is a quite horrible, hugely emotional moment, not to mention the massive anxiety of wondering what on earth you'll do next. That particular drive was two journeys. It was me driving home and it was also me driving away from the game.

I was still in a haze when I reached West Yorkshire and missed the turn-off I needed so I had to go on to the next junction and double back. It was days, if not weeks, before my head was adjusted to the notion that I was finished with professional football and that it was time to become acquainted with the outside world. I was no longer inside the bubble. Reality had arrived.

14

Lucky Dip

People are different aren't they? It takes all sorts to make a world. I sometimes think people are like a box of Liquorice Allsorts. Some you pick first out of the box because you like them, some are okay so you choose them next. And some you just leave in the box untouched because you can't stand them. The people you meet in football are much the same. We meet such a huge range of people in our careers, all so different; some you'd run through brick walls for, others you're glad to see the back of. Some make you feel like a million dollars; others make you feel so small. You have to put up with it and learn to live with it. It's like a lucky, or unlucky, dip. Some young footballers can cope but others can't and drop out. Football is filled with stories of young lads or even established players who have had their confidence shattered by heartless coaches and managers. Others are lucky enough to work with a manager who can make them feel ten feet tall. A footballer thrives on confidence and the feeling of being wanted, but all the time managers and coaches are coming and going, in and out of a player's life, affecting him and the way he plays. They can build but also destroy. A change of manager can turn someone's life inside out. A change of manager means you start all over again.

Eddie Gray made me feel confident and a good career at Leeds was possible. On one of the official pre-season squad picture there I am, a very young excited lad on the back row, full of hopes and dreams. There was all to play for and ahead I was sure there would be a long career at Elland Road. I think if Eddie hadn't been sacked I might have fulfilled my aspirations with him. But it wasn't to be. I learned about the pitfalls and effects of a managerial change very early in my life. It changed the course of my career. The togetherness amongst the players with Eddie was second to none.

He never really got enough credit at Leeds for what he did. What could he do other than move out the high earners and phase in the

215

younger lads that he had nurtured? Out of the three Leeds managers I had, Eddie, Allan Clarke and Billy Bremner, Eddie was the one who suffered the biggest financial constraints. His spell as manager coincided with the club being £2million in debt and directors having to dig into their pockets. At one point the Inland Revenue came to the ground to recoup some of the tax that was owed by taking away the club cars. But the players were cushioned from all this. The team still travelled in style and were short of nothing.

It seemed to me Eddie was one of football's thoughtful and generous people. Albert Johanneson used to visit Elland Road when Eddie was manager and tell him he wanted to start training again and get fit. But, he couldn't afford any boots. Eddie used to give him all the stuff he asked for even though he knew he would sell it and then spend the money on drink. Eddie was being kind, but in effect was doing Albert no favours. But that's the kind of bloke Eddie was.

He had benefited himself from Don Revie's faith in youth and had been given a first team place at an early age. So it seemed perfectly logical to him to do the same and if the kids were good enough he put them in the team. In went John Sheridan one of the most gifted players I'd seen, Tommy Wright, Scott Sellars and Terry Phelan. I was about to get my chance too but injury prevented that. It was the knee that I twisted in the Blackburn reserves game.

Eddie was about to give me a debut playing at full-back. 'I can't believe your luck,' said Eddie. 'You'd have had a debut against Derby County on Saturday.' Looking back, that simple act of standing up badly cost me so much.

By the time I was fit again Peter Lorimer had come in, signed for his experience and the guidance he could give to the young lads on the field. The pitfalls of football: the chance to emerge alongside the group of lads that I was such a part of, had gone.

Not that Eddie Gray was right in every decision he made. One player he let go was David Seaman.

But Billy Bremner let go all of the young lads that Eddie Gray introduced. In my opinion it set the club back several years and then he suddenly left to return to the less pressured demands of Doncaster again. The Gray biography is maybe overly kind to Billy Bremner. More than a few of us just wondered if the deal to bring Bremner to Leeds and replace Gray was started six months before he actually arrived or if Bremner himself had instigated it behind the scenes. He replaced the young lads with older more seasoned pros and he had a bit of money as well from player sales. Eddie Gray says he talked to Bremner some years later about why he had released all the young lads. Bremner said it was because he felt the lads were all too attached to Eddie and that he would have found it difficult to get them to respond to him as they did to Eddie. The bottom line perhaps is that every manager wants to build his own team with his own players and that's exactly what he did.

Fans and players were both upset and angry when Gray was sacked. The fans demonstrated in the West Stand car park and Peter Lorimer made an openly public statement criticising the decision. But it was all too late. Me, Dennis Irwin and so many of the other lads were on our way. Whether Bremner had taken a personal dislike to me I'll never really know but there was one incident for which I can think of no logical reason or cause. On Billy's third day back at the club he singled me and Dennis out for one of the most gruelling and punishing running sessions that could have been inflicted. There was nobody else and it went on and on until we could no longer physically move because of the shuttle runs and 100 metre sprints we'd had to do. For a long time I could think of no sane reason why he would want to have done that. It was quite bizarre. We had given him no cause.

Then, years later I came across Peter Lorimer's book. It was clear that whilst Lorimer rated Billy as a player, as a person he rated him less. Nor was Billy the most popular person in the dressing room. Some years earlier when Revie moved on, the way was clear and ready for Johnny Giles to become manager. Bremner was not best pleased and went to see the chairman and more or less said that he too wanted to become manager. The chairman was in a quandary. It ended with Giles saying forget it. Leeds' troubles began that day. Johnny Giles would have had players who respected him, money in the bank and would have held the place together. Bremner ruined that. Lorimer describes him as ruthless and self-centred and he too mentioned the running punishment routine. Whenever he felt that someone or one of his signings was not working out, he would keep him back late and subject him to endless running round the pitch with the object of sickening him so much that he would want to move.

'I could never fault him as a player,' said Lorimer. 'But some of the things he did to people on a personal basis were baffling.' Funny, how all these years later I came across that in his book. I was one of those who had fallen victim to this.

Despite that punitive running session I still didn't want to leave. The beneficiary of Bremner's inability to see how good the kids were that one by one he got rid of, was Joe Royle at Oldham who snapped up Dennis Irwin, Tommy Wright and Andy Linighan, plus later on Andy Ritchie. John Sheridan was another who went, in his case to Sheffield Wednesday. In addition to all these, a number of other lesser known young players who might well have gone on to have good careers were released.

In some ways I wasn't old enough at the time to really understand what was going on. I didn't have the first team experience and wasn't mentally mature enough to be able to sit tight and ride things out until Bremner himself left. But reading what Lorimer has to say about him puts things in some kind of perspective all these years later. And the irony is that Bremner didn't last all that long there. If I were to say these critical things about Billy Bremner, after just two games for Leeds who would listen? They'd say it was sour grapes because he let me go. But when a legend like Peter Lorimer says them people take notice.

Bremner and Gray were opposites. Whilst the perception of Eddie Gray might have been of a gentle, kindly man, nevertheless he could be hard and critical when he needed to be. But Bremner was visibly rough and abrasive. He smoked incessantly. Whilst Gray had faith in youth, clearly Bremner had none. There was a hard side to Bremner and clearly from the running incident, he had a streak of callousness in him. Whilst Gray was open and honest, you were unsure of Bremner. That's not to suggest he was dishonest, but whilst you could approach Eddie, you were wary of doing so with Bremner. There was just this feeling that he wasn't really interested in you. And don't forget, we were just young lads in awe of everything about these legends, trying to do everything that was asked of us. Billy was only really interested in surrounding himself with his own men. There was an endless stream of Doncaster Rovers players coming to see him at the ground which really annoyed the senior players at the club.

He didn't speak to me too often and wasn't like Eddie offering advice, but there was one occasion just before I left. It was the last game I played when the reserves beat an experienced Aston Villa 5–2. We all played so well. The passing was superb; we turned it on and I was having a great game. We were stringing together 15 to 20 passes in a row just like the old Leeds of which he had been a member. At half-time he was waiting in the tunnel. 'Don't get cocky son,' he said. 'Just play the game.' This was from a man who had played in a team that could put moves together of 20 and 30 passes just for the fun of it that enjoyed ridiculing and embarrassing the opposition with their keepball. As a young lad I'd tried to emulate him and play with his flair, spirit and fire. I found his comment in that tunnel strange.

But he lived and breathed Leeds United and thought it was the greatest thing in the world when he became manager. It was his spiritual home as far as he was concerned.

Why did Kenny Burns at Leeds leave such an impression on me? Even now all these years later he's still large as life in my head. He was hard as nails, not everyone's cup of tea as a bloke and if you had any sense you never crossed him. He had not been born with any proverbial football silver spoon and so what reputation he had achieved he proudly guarded. He never went round looking for any trouble, but he did expect to be treated with the degree of respect due to his standing in the game. His reputation was based on two European Cup medals won with Nottingham Forest, not to mention his Championship and League Cup honours that sat nicely along his collection of 20 International caps for Scotland in an era when Scottish players had exceptional talent.

Don't forget he called me 'Harvey' which being young and naïve I thought he meant as a term of endearment. It was in the canteen one day that the penny dropped when he yelled out 'Hey Harvey Moon' and it dawned on me what it rhymed with. There was no chance of me pointing out to him that this was out of order even when the other players would cringe and shake their heads. But, it was never personal with him. He had nicknames for other players and used to call Kevin Hird 'Worzel'. I thought it was a reference to Jon Pertwee's TV character and Worzel Gummidge but then Kevin would walk into the dressing room and Kenny would start to sing 'I've got a brand new combine harvester' and 'I'm a cider drinker'. He mimicked the worst West Country accent that you could imagine after the fashion of that awful seventies' group The Wurzels, who had those two dreadful hits. Kevin, a model, placid and talented professional used to blank him completely and get on with his business.

None of the senior players messed with Kenny. The only person who ever got away with it was Brian Clough who used to make some sort of reference to Kenny's supposed liking for dog tracks. But Kenny was just Kenny and I never thought of him as racist nor do I now. And on the pitch you were glad to be alongside him because he looked out for you like a brother. I remember in a reserve team game one afternoon we were the centre back pairing. I was the kid and he was the Scottish International. The opposing striker was becoming increasingly nasty with me, both physically and verbally. Kenny soon put a stop to it all. When the referee had his back turned he strode up to the defender, went right up to his face and growled menacingly: 'Anymore and you're done for.' The aggressor stopped immediately. The one warning was enough. The term: 'That's not a threat it's a promise,' was made for him.

I witnessed him really losing his rag one day. Leeds had a talented young winger called Mark Gavin who went on to play for Hearts, Bristol City and Rochdale. He had real pace and trickery. In the corridor, before training, a large group of us with all the senior professionals would often practice one-touch, passing skills, by playing piggy-in-the-middle. One of the objects of the game was to nutmeg the player in the middle. Mark nutmegged Kenny.

'Ye dinnae dee that tae me,' snarled Kenny in his distinctive patter, clearly angered. 'There willnae be a next time.'

Like a kid not heeding a parental warning near bedtime, Mark ignored the advice. The older pros watched with interest. A couple of them cheered sarcastically. During dressing room banter Kenny escaped a lot of the verbal flack because no-one wanted to incur his wrath or retribution. As a result they now rather enjoyed seeing his discomfort.

Again Mark got the ball and again nutmegged Kenny. He couldn't resist. The sarcastic cheers were now roars of laughter. Kenny was visibly agitated. He did not appreciate being made to look like a mug by a kid.

This time a finger wagged and Kenny uttered quietly but threateningly: 'Another one and yer hids down the loo son.'

Astonishingly Mark did it a third time and had all the lads

cheering. It was a morning when he could do no wrong. But this time Kenny's head just went. He tackled him in a style reminiscent of Murrayfield, yanked him up by the scruff of the neck and marched him towards the toilets. The rest of the players followed, keen to see the consequences, most of them laughing out loud.

Poor Mark. Kenny jammed him into the cubicles and selected one that had not properly flushed. He rammed his head down into it, allowed him to savour the aroma and then flushed. 'Dinnae mess with me son,' Kenny admonished him as his head rose up drenched. 'Dinnae mess with me.'

Kenny stomped back out to the corridor. Mark cleaned himself up, his hair now a sodden mess and his face as white as a sheet, went back out and got on with things. There were no more nutmegs. Would such a thing happen today? The nutmegs maybe yes. The toilet treatment, probably would not. Back then such things were part and parcel of a young lad's education if he stepped out of line at a football club. It was the unwritten rule that you wholeheartedly respected the older professionals.

There was the time when, as an apprentice, it was my job to run the water for the bath ready for the players after a game. I left the hot tap running but forgot to close the door that separated the bath area from the changing room. The steam billowed out in clouds and eventually filled the changing area as well. The players' clothes became damper and damper. It was Gary Hamson who gave me the biggest balling out imaginable describing all manner of things he would do to me if his suit was ruined. I stood there shaking until he grinned, ruffled my hair and said; 'Only joking son.'

If Kenny had earned respect, so had Billy Whitehurst; the name still sends shivers down peoples' spines 20 years later. A game at Doncaster was certainly memorable, the one Burnley won 4–1. Probably every player who played against him has a story to tell. For a start he was born in South Yorkshire, a sort of training ground for hard cases. It was always a joke at Leeds that's where all the hooligan supporters came from. Including loans, non-league clubs and abroad, he'd been to at least 23 clubs. It's no exaggeration to say that centre-halves would always look to see if his name was on the opposing teamsheet. If it was, they said a silent prayer. Even Vinnie Jones and Neil 'Razor' Ruddock considered him the hardest player they ever played against. Colin Hendry once had to play against him four times in a month.

The stories grew: at Oxford it was rumoured he supplemented his football earnings with bare knuckle fights against the local gypsies. Billy says he once played with 30 stitches in the back of his head. He'd gone into a boozer, he said, and had a fight with a kid whose friend then pulled a cosh and smashed him over the nose with it. Someone else hit him on the back of the head. So there he was with 30 stitches, a hole in his cheek, his nose smashed up and there was a game in 10 days. He played. During the game his nose was smashed again by the goalkeeper. The doctor came on, saw the mess, and thought 'what the hell do I do with this?' His answer was to rip out the stitches and staple him up. In those days there was none of this 'Come off when there's blood', and there was blood everywhere. Billy says he looked like Frankenstein but just carried on playing.

There was the game where I made the mistake of calling him a 'useless fat bastard', after he had embarrassingly mistimed a jump and the ball had sailed out of play. I don't know to this day what possessed me to do that. I might have been fearless but abuse like that wasn't normally something I did. I'd probably apologise to him if I met him again one day. He looked at me coldly with glassy eyes and then sidled up next to me. 'Thart finished pal,' he said in his South Yorkshire dialect. Just three words and I got the message. It was the only time in football that I was genuinely scared. This was the man of whom Vinnie Jones once said he had the best right hook he had ever seen. I spent the game trying to keep out of his way. Just the once he managed to catch me with an elbow to the ribs. God, did it hurt but I shrugged it off whilst inwardly screaming in silent agony.

'That's only for starters,' he said. 'Thart not goin' 'ome in wun piece today.' Ian Measham had cottoned on to the spot I was in and afterwards he must have told kit man George Bray.

George was in and out the dressing room but then he came in and announced: 'That Billy Whitehurst is hanging around by our door, I can't think why, does he want to see one of you?' My mouth dropped wide open and my heart rate doubled. Once I was dressed I peeped out and saw no-one there and then fled to the coach faster than Carl Lewis could do a hundred metres, even missing having a drink in the players' bar. John Francis was mystified and came to ask what I was doing on the coach so early. It was some weeks later that

Meash told me that it was all a wind-up by George Bray.

Years later Billy was in China more or less at the same time as me except, fortunately for me, he was in Hong Kong with South China FC. Allegedly he left after he had lamped someone who fancied himself as a hard man. They're skilled in the martial arts out there and maybe even Billy Whitehurst thought that discretion was the better part of valour.

He'd probably never given me a second thought but then we did actually meet again. We were both at a Bury versus Lincoln game after I'd come back from China. Bury had allowed me to train there to keep up some fitness and I'd gone with the reserve team to give some support. I don't know if Billy had a Lincoln connection then but I felt this knee in the back of my leg. It was Billy and that was his greeting. We talked for a long time about the game and life in general.

* * * * *

Frank Casper brought me out of obscurity. I'll be forever grateful. You could say he changed my life. Leaving Northwich and coming to Burnley put my career back on a path that brought some success. I was actually on loan at Northwich from Bury. But Frank was manager at Burnley at a time when supporters were so desperate to get out of the Fourth Division. Up until Torquay they'd had six years of it and so it was no wonder he took the flak that he did and some of it was beyond acceptable. They took their anger out on him and Frank Teasdale. When you think back you have to admire his determination and fortitude. He put his head above the parapet and took all the aggravation that came his way. At the end of '90–91 the local papers were filled with letters from fans who were angry and disillusioned. Frank was the target in most of them. It must have been hell to read them but he came back for more in the following season. He was sure he had a bunch of players that could succeed. At Torquay we didn't play well. But it was the manager who carried the can. At the end of that awful game at Scarborough after which Frank decided he'd had had enough, fans stood absolutely right next to him screaming in his ear, 'Fuck off Casper'. How can anyone endure that?

Frank had got the job at Burnley in the late eighties when Brian

223

Miller simply got fed up of the pressure and wanted a normal life. Having been sacked by John Jackson some years earlier, Brian was then later brought back again by the next chairman Frank Teasdale. Frank Casper remembers Brian taking hold of him one day and asked if he fancied the job. Remember Frank had already once done the job on a temporary basis when Brian had been sacked. Frank who had never got on with Chairman John Jackson had then been replaced by John Bond and all Burnley fans know what a mess that season was. Anyway, the board knew that Brian was weary of it all so they asked him to sound Frank out. Frank remembers they talked about it in the gents' urinals and Brian said he'd had enough and did Frank fancy it. So there they were discussing something as big as the Burnley management job in the gents' urinals. Then Brian had to go back and tell the board. So that's how Frank took the job on—after an off-the-record chat in the gents' toilets.

At Burnley, while he was there, I roomed with Ron Futcher and by then he'd done the rounds. He used to share his stories of life in America with me where he had played for a number of clubs. He'd played with and against some of the greats like Pele, George Best and Rodney Marsh. Some of the stories of the after-match parties they went to had me wide-eyed. He didn't give a damn about what he said or who he said it to. He loved playing for Burnley and would lay into anyone there who wasn't pulling their weight either in a game or in training. He was from Chester but seemed to have a touch of that cheeky Scouser about him. Stan Ternent's book has the story of how he gave Ron a good seeing to at Bradford when he was either coach or manager there because Ron had annoyed him in training. Ron, long before Stan wrote his book, told it to me differently—it was Stan who got the good hiding with a smart head butt.

Ron could moan for England. Nothing was ever right but most of it was tongue in cheek. His one-liners were hilarious with Joe Jakub often the target. Theirs was a love-hate relationship and Ron would certainly wind him up. He always had me on that Frank Casper told him that he had bought him to score goals, but Frank added that he wouldn't need to run around a lot, because he had found him a new pair of legs called Roger Eli. To be honest he wasn't far wrong. You wouldn't find Futch running in the channels, or down the wings. He always used to shout: 'Feet, fucking feet!' Meaning that's where he wanted the ball. If you didn't you got a terrible tongue-lashing. He was a typical English striker who knew how to put it about a bit. But ask anyone who played with him and they will tell you his touch on the ball and finishing ability were second to none. In a career of over 600 games he played far too few at the top level and wasn't that far short of a goal every two games.

Futch was hard on and off the field and taught me a lot. He was the experienced pro and there was I learning the striker's role from him. Off the field he didn't mind a verbal confrontation with anybody. There were several times I had to lead him away from a situation. He had been brought up with the right coaching and playing values at Manchester City and would spend hours talking with me about the game. He showed me the art of finishing and having the necessary attitudes in a striker's role. I was grateful as he was the first strike partner I ever had in a partnership that often worked like a dream. On the pitch we would look out for each other and get into many a scrap with opposing defenders. We'd take it in turns to leave an elbow in whilst challenging for a ball. If I took one in the face he'd shout: 'You okay Dodge?' and then collect yet another yellow card for giving out his own little bit of justice. It's just possible that if Frank Casper had paired us earlier we'd have hit it off and scored the goals to have ensured more points and automatic promotion in the season that ended so poorly against Torquay. I was bitterly disappointed when Futch left in the summer of '91.

I met more than my share of managers during my nomadic wanderings including Stan Ternent who sometimes appeared at Bury to help when I was there. I liked him and wouldn't have minded playing for him. I have a hunch I'd have been his kind of player because I always gave 100% and never shirked any challenge. I'll always remember how some managers had a book that seemed to be their bible. It might have been the *Rothman's Football Year Book*. Whatever: it was always a huge, thick thing that had pages of players' appearances and clubs. The lower down the leagues you go the more desperate managers were to get players on the cheap and sometimes they'd take a player on for a trial after thumbing through this book, finding the player's name, and then muttering, 'Oh yeah. So and so, he's played a fair few games, he must be okay, he might do a job.' I was with a manager in his office when he got a call from an agent who was touting his player round. The manager had never even heard of him but immediately got his 'bible' off the desk, and looked him up. 'Yeah send him along we'll take a look.' The greater the number of games the more chance the player had. It wouldn't surprise me if this was the book that Jimmy Mullen maybe used when he was desperate to find a striker during the relegation season. He brought so many in it was a joke with the supporters.

There's a similar kind of book for used cars, or used to be, that salesmen fish out of their pocket when they're trying to give you as little as possible for your old car. Old footballers and used cars—you could say there are some strong similarities.

It's a funny thing this player attitude to managers: Johnny Giles wrote about it in his book. He talked about something John McGovern said about Brian Clough. 'I'd swim an ocean for him, but I wouldn't be going out for a drink with him afterwards.'

A player who shall remain nameless said of his manager: 'He was the biggest c**t I ever met in my life; great manager though.'

Maybe the sentiments I felt towards Jimmy Mullen were something along those lines; that whilst on the pitch some might have run through a brick wall for him, off the pitch, you were less impressed with him. Once upon a time I'd have walked over hot coals for Brian Clough and was in awe of the man. But Jimmy Mullen, if he put you down, you'd turn away muttering the word 'tosser' under your breathe. That's something I'd never have muttered after a conversation with Frank Casper. On the pitch, you climb mountains for your teammates, maybe more for them than for the manager. Teammates are everything. If one of them was kicked I would have my eye on the culprit. My inspirations were my teammates and the supporters, not the manager.

If you ask Frank Casper today what makes a good manager he'll simply say: 'Good players.' But players will say there's more to it than that. Of course we'll talk about people we've played for and there are always things that players like to see in a manager. We know they have to be ruthless and hard sometimes, but they also need to be fair and respect their players. A player wants to feel appreciated. Sarcastic put-downs are disliked. Communication is all part of the knack of good management. Some managers are aloof and distant. You never know what they're thinking. That leaves you uncertain and unsure. You have to feel that you will get a fair crack of the whip and that if you are good enough your chance will come. Good managers display confidence and optimism; they're able to get you to bounce back after a poor defeat somewhere. Success comes from feeling part of the whole picture. It's what used to be called the 'family' atmosphere at a club. Maybe it still is at some places. It's the feeling of belonging. If you're on the outside, excluded, it produces resentment, bitterness and criticism. The club spirit becomes broken. The best managers will always fight for a player or protect him from unjust criticism especially in the Press. He has principles and clear views and sticks to them. And if on top of all that they come in every morning with a smile on their face, filled with enthusiasm and energy, it rubs off on players. There's the feeling that training is a good place to be, that it's enjoyment not work, and quite simply football is the best job in the world. And the best of them, with their positive thinking, will convince you that a 5–1 defeat was just a blip. Positive thinking can make an average player good, and a good player, very good. You begin to believe in yourself and self-confidence grows.

Jimmy Mullen's coaching and tactics were simple, never to over complicate things. But with Frank Casper it was more instructive. He'd stop a practice game and tell you how to do things, where to go, how to make a run, make suggestions as to how you might do something better. You knew he'd been such a good player. You listened.

But why did things work out so well for Jimmy Mullen? I happen to think that the biggest factor was that the enormous pressure felt by Frank at the hands of success-starved fans towards his final days, was lifted not just off him when he resigned, but off us as well. We heard the screams and abuse that were hurled at him and it got to us just as much. Burnley fans are a hard and demanding lot. The pressure on us to win for him, because we certainly wanted to, increased in direct proportion to the pressure placed on him. We truly felt for him. He was a good man and we respected him. The jeers hurt us as much as they must have hurt him. He still lives in Burnley and football wasn't exactly kind to him by the end. He'll tell you about the Norman Hunter tackle that injured him so badly. He'll maybe tell you never to become a football manager.

Then suddenly the jeers and howls stopped and it was like being released from a straightjacket. We happened to win the first game for Mullen. There was nothing magic about it, and then we happened to win another by an astonishing 6–2. Of course confidence grew and if there is one word in any footballer's dictionary it is that magic word 'confidence'. It's nothing you can touch or feel. It's this invisible attitude that's inside your head. And it began to grow. Then before you know it you go on that field thinking you can't lose. Confidence is such a fragile quality and football is a mental thing just as much as physically kicking a ball.

Jimmy Mullen—should I mention again the occasion at a dinner at Turf Moor in 2011 when he came over to me and apologised? Why was he apologising? He actually said to me he'd never treated a footballer as badly as he treated me. I was quite taken aback. Can you imagine that? It's a hell of an admission but it was no consolation. It didn't really help. I think the way he treated me affected any chance of me seriously prolonging my career and to this day I can only guess at the reasons. It feels like a painting that's unfinished or a book that's only half written. Maybe he felt I needed taking down a notch or two; but if so, why? Maybe it was because I was a 'Casper' man. Maybe it was because I was lucky enough to be a 'popular' player. Maybe he just decided to write me off after the four-month lay-off. I could never understand the attitude he developed towards me from roughly midway through the season after promotion. I trained hard and prided myself on being a model professional. No matter what team I was selected for I worked hard and gave 100%. The basic standards drilled into me at Leeds United stayed with me throughout football. Was that in itself the reason for his treatment? He brought in a lot of players; none I could see that were any better than me in my position. He froze me out and even had me in the 'A' Team with the youths one time at The Cliff against Man Utd. He played me wide so that I was up against a young kid called Phil Neville. I gave Phil a bit of a hard time which was expected as he was just coming into the game. But Coach Harry Wilson told Mullen that Neville had run rings round me. I was astonished but not surprised. If one good thing came from this it was the chance to play against the bunch of brilliant youngsters coming through of whom, for me, Nicky Butt was the outstanding player along with Frank Casper's son Chris, both of Chris and Frank's careers ended by bad tackles.

He demoted me to sub for the reserves. It was as hurtful for Andrea, who was still attending even the reserve games, as it was for me. I can remember a game against Bradford City and as the reserve team was read out to us and my name came up as number 12, I sat there wondering just why they were doing this. This is the way you treat the outcasts. Day after day I went home dejected and baffled.

This idea that some managers will deliberately set out to 'break' a player is not fantasy. Bremner used to do it when he had victims endlessly and needlessly running round the pitch. To my last day I'll wonder if it was what Mullen was trying to do to me at Burnley. But if it was a form of constructive dismissal it didn't work. Brian Little used to tell us how Ron Saunders tried it with him. There was a hill that Saunders used to have them running up and down. Brian was ordered not just to run up it but carry someone on his back. Brian refused.

You could write a book about all the footballers who have had their spirits crushed, or managers who have tried to crush them. Jimmy Adamson when he was at Leeds tried it with Peter Lorimer. He knew Lorimer was declared unfit to play but he still ordered him to travel with the reserves to Manchester. Peter turned it to his advantage and spent the afternoon in the boardroom drinking whisky, eating sandwiches and watching the horses. Then he came back and on Monday in front of Adamson in the treatment room said to Paul Madeley what a great time he'd had. Adamson fumed and stormed out.

What right have managers to do this? In what other industry does one man wield such power and have such a hold over someone's life and career?

The trouble is, now, you could come across as being bitter. But, it's not the word I'd use. I'd use the word 'angry'. Today there's a bunch of us who will rarely talk of Jimmy Mullen, despite his record of two promotions, with much affection. I was just 27, put out to grass, and perplexed. I'd eventually got the knee back in shape and was fit to play. I knew I could do as good a job as the players he brought in. And yet, I was yesterday's man for no apparent reason that I could identify.

Funny the things you think about doing. Jimmy Mullen had been banned for drink driving. Terry Pashley would drive him in from Blackpool. Terry became a youth coach, and is still at Burnley, but we'd joke it was just a way of paying him for being Mullen's driver. Sometimes I'd see Mullen's car keys and I'd think about taking them and his car and driving up through Padiham at high speed through the cameras to get him deeper in trouble. Sad you might say, but that's how it got to me. But I got more and more bloody minded and determined to see it through. He actually said to me one time: 'I would never give you a free transfer.' What was I—Mullen's slave? Today players can engineer moves almost at will with their agents. Contracts are meaningless. Managers back then were still damned powerful.

With Andrea I drove down to Wembley for the 1994 Play-Off Final. We weren't part of the official party. How's that for a thank you for helping get them promotion in '92? We felt like real outsiders. The official termination letter didn't come until June 1st but weeks before that I'd guessed my contract would not be renewed. Jimmy Mullen said not one word to my face about it. But sussing it out wasn't exactly rocket science. We parked and walked down Wembley Way mixing in with all the fans. It seemed like all of them wanted to speak to us. They had no idea what was going on in the background but I knew I was on my way out. It felt like I was saying goodbye to them all. Driving home I felt gutted not to be part of the official party or the after-match celebrations. I was good enough to have been out there. But here I was; the outcast, outside the bubble. The last 12 months had been dreadful and Andrea knew what all this had done to me. She hated it. During the promotion season she'd come to the games and enjoyed being in the Stand. Slowly all that changed so that she resented going. She could see what was going on. I owe her a lot for propping me up. How many footballers owe their wives a huge debt? Probably hundreds of us I'd bet. Part of the hurt came from feeling at home with Burnley so much and loving the supporters. I adored Burnley and wanted to stay. After Wembley they went to Mauritius. But not me, I went home to Bradford. Chris Pearce was discarded in '92. There was no Bermuda for him. Now it was my turn.

The new problem was that because I'd played no first team games at all for something like 18 months, other managers assumed that Roger Eli was finished. The offers didn't exactly come flooding in. It seemed I was forgotten. If used footballers could be put on shelves, I guess I'd have been on the very bottom, or even left in the storeroom out the back.

I was just 27, with no club, and on the scrapheap like an old used car. It was soul-destroying, hurtful and utterly puzzling. There was no need for it and no logic in it. And it was a disgrace seeing some players come in for the money, and who saw the chance of a few nights on the booze enjoying themselves. There was a hotel up in Nelson called The Hawthorns where players stayed. For some of them it was just a knocking shop. Down below in the basement there was a night club. It was known for its wild nights and some of the Burnley players made full use of it.

At Burnley I spent hours with the physio, Jimmy Holland. He was a smashing, but annoying, person which sounds a bit of a contradiction and he'd been at the club for years when I got there. He zealously guarded all the stock of tapes, plasters, creams, Vaseline and clearly thought you were a nuisance if you ever wanted some and usually asked why you wanted it. If he used the ultrasound on an injury he'd sometimes get engrossed in a conversation and forget to keep moving the 'wand' and boy did that hurt. Some lucky players hardly ever need to see the physio. I was on the treatment table in his little room, far too often. After 25 years of blood, sweat and jockstraps he could have written a best-seller. He knew all the secrets. Footballers will talk to a sympathetic physio in a way they will rarely open up to anyone else.

Jimmy was in his early sixties when I knew him, and had started as a physio in 1954 at a Burnley hospital. He'd done 10 years in the army including a stint in Korea. He'd seen the injuries that ended the careers of Frank Casper, Mick Docherty and Brian Miller. A good physio is there to provide mental support as much as physical assistance and Jimmy was good at that. Immediately after an injury a physio has to convince you that you'll be back. As an injury heals he has to get you back on the field. It's a mental thing when you have to put in the first tackle or make a hard shot when you've been on the treatment table for a long spell. I never got tired of hearing his football stories that went back to the mid sixties. He was one of those blokes that footballers like to play pranks on but he never grumbled. Truth is though he didn't like it and having been in the army didn't think much of the fourth form antics of footballers. I sometimes thought he actually disliked footballers. Who could blame him? Mick Docherty remembered once when they balanced a bucket of water on the top of a door that was just slightly open ready for when Jimmy walked in. On long coach trips he snoozed much of the time. On one occasion while he was asleep they covered his head and face in shaving cream.

But Jimmy's favourite prank, one that did make him laugh at the memory, was the time the club had an end of season trip to Majorca and he played in a game against a local side (he called it) though we think it was just a team of waiters. He broke his arm. On the same trip he was whacked in the face by a tree branch. So on the way back home, going through the airport, he had no idea of the label that had been fastened to his back as they went through the airport. He had a patch over his eye and his arm in a sling, and a bag of duty free in his free hand. The customs men began to laugh, he told us, and he thought they were just laughing at the sling and the patch. But after he had gone through customs he discovered the card stuck on his back. 'This man is a smuggler,' it said in large letters.

I spent more time with him than I care to remember. He told me tales of old chairman Bob Lord and various players. We always knew when he was in a good mood after a game because he would treat us to some foam and bubble for the communal bath in the dressing room. If there wasn't any you were careful not to pee in the bath — or something worse. If anyone did it was always usually obvious who the guilty one was and he would be battered. The trouble was though, if Jimmy had put some foam in you didn't know what you were sitting in.

On coach journeys Jimmy Holland always sat with the kit man George Bray. George was one of those amazing football people who had spent decades in the game. He'd joined the club in 1937 and was a member of the Cup Final side of 1947; he never got tired of telling us. He used to tell us his first pay packet was £3 a week. 'Ee them were the days,' we'd pull his leg. 'And you could get a pie and a pint for a penny.' He was one of the thousands of footballers who had to serve in World War Two. The club took him onto the coaching staff in the fifties and carried on right until he retired in 1974, although he then came back later as kit man. He and Jimmy argued and swapped stories and jokes from one end of a journey to another with Jimmy moaning that George was always right. They were like two sparring partners. He had the habit of always calling in at his Catholic Church on the way to a game to say a little prayer and ask for a bit of luck. It certainly worked before the York City game when we won the title. It was fun to sit behind them and listen.

Much as I liked Jimmy, the new physio Mark Leather, did more for me. Although Jimmy was up to speed with a lot of developments he was from the old days when trainers ran on with a bucket of water and a sponge. Mark's knowledge was far deeper. In fact in the summer he lectured other physios at Lilleshall. He had a great sense of humour whether it was making fun of himself and his total absence of any suntan, or the time he took the field during a Preston game with a shirt that said Judas on the front with dollar signs underneath it. That was because he once worked at Preston and he was taunted by their fans as a 'Judas'. Funnily enough when he eventually moved on to Liverpool, the players there called him Judas and that was because he'd worked for Burnley. He got into football by accident. He worked just two minutes away from Port Vale's ground. They were so hard up they used the local hospital physios but then John Rudge took over, called in to see him and asked him to cover their games. At Burnley his real work began at quarter to five after a game had finished. He then had to decide if any injured players needed to be in on a Sunday. Sometimes he was in the club seven days a week and that was in addition to being on call during a game, and for reserve games. His wife was a physiotherapist and when things were really busy she'd be in there as well helping out. You could say then that Burnley had the first woman physio.

I used to enjoy talking to George Bray and then there was Violet the laundry lady. Footballers have a soft spot for laundry ladies wherever they play. They've no agenda and you usually get a smile, a cup of tea, and a bit of sympathy. Maybe we footballers all miss our mums a bit too and that's who they remind us of. Parents don't call their kids Violet any more do they? It was a name belonging to the era in which she was born. Her husband was Jim Thompson who also worked at the club doing all sorts of odd jobs. He's still there today in the ticket office and in charge of turnstiles on matchdays. He won a national football award in 2011 for being one of those unsung, long-serving, behind the scenes employees that still work in football. He's been at Burnley since something like 1947.

I never met John Bond but he was manager of the Shrewsbury team we played in the FA Cup in December '92. For some strange reason he was wearing a steward's jacket and a flat cap and standing at the back of the stand. And if you've ever seen pictures of how superbly he usually dressed, a steward's jacket would be the last thing you'd expect to see him in. It all happened because we'd been drawn to play Shrewsbury in the FA Cup at Turf Moor. That game was a draw and then there was the replay. I played in both games. I've a vague memory of getting their centre-half sent off in the first game. When the first game was announced John Bond said he wasn't coming to Turf Moor. We wondered why. We were told that it was all to do with his spell as Burnley manager for just one season a few years earlier when he had apparently become a figure of scorn, derision and even hatred for the mess he had made of things. So, the minute the tie was announced he was the target of hate mail and threats and abuse and took the decision not to attend the game. Anyway, it caused a bit of talk and a few jokes in the dressing room especially as he'd once been a top manager with a huge high profile. The first game at Turf Moor was a draw and fans brought an anti-Bond banner that must have been 100 feet long.

He must have been rubbing his hands at the thought of winning the replay but two goals in the last three minutes won it for us. Big John Pender dived in for a spectacular equalising goal after a flick from me. And then Mike Conroy got the winner with seconds to go. The fans went wild. Until then they'd given Bond a dreadful time but when the whistle went their shouts were for us and Jimmy Mullen. If you were at the Burnley v Bolton Carling Cup game when Burnley beat Owen Coyle who had left them for Bolton, you'll have some idea of the reception the fans gave us and Jimmy at Shrewsbury for beating John Bond.

The people I've met along the years have given me memories both happy and sad. There isn't the space to write about them all. Overall the good outweigh the bad. I'm thankful for that. But I won't forget the words Jimmy Mullen said to me at the dinner we both attended in 2011. 'I never treated any player as badly as I did you. I've learned that now.'

15

Outside the Bubble

I remember the day I got my first wage slip as an apprentice. I thought it was so terrific to be paid for doing something so enjoyable. My school mates were training to be electricians or plumbers. Some had nothing to go to. But I was at Leeds United and had so much to look forward to; I never gave a thought to being anywhere else or doing anything else. As it turned out, by the time I finished I'd had so much bad luck with so many injuries, my mum should have called me Jonah.

I look back now and remember those truly happy early days. My first wage slip: I couldn't believe it and looked at it for several minutes before it sank in. There was a basic £25 a week and then an additional £25 living expenses. Most of the lads were in digs and that's where their £25 went. But I lived at home so the club paid the living allowance direct to my mum but she didn't really want it so paid it straight into a savings account for me. I was always a good saver but did have a weakness for clothes so that's where much of my money went. Not all my wardrobe looked like it had come from the Grattan's Catalogue.

It's more or less 50 years since the football maximum wage was abolished in 1961. It was then £20 a week no matter how much of a football genius you were or how many times you'd played for your country. Today the top players need a wheelbarrow to carry their wages home. The argument is that the Premier League generates so much money, it's only right that the top players share in the wealth. In just the same way back in '92 at Burnley, it seemed reasonable to think that because Burnley had just done so well, then the players should have a bigger share of the money that they had generated at the turnstiles in the promotion season. Not that we were ever greedy at Burnley. During that pre-season when some of us stuck out for a little more than was on offer it did not seem unreasonable. Yet we were labelled 'the five rebels'. The way it came across painted us as the bad guys, five greedy footballers. But we certainly weren't. I was never asking for big money, just the recommended PFA wage for the level that I was at.

Today the vast sums of money in the game seem to have produced a gap between top players and fans. When I played I thought I had a duty to talk and be sociable with supporters. I never minded going to their meetings or being in the club shop on Friday mornings to sign things. The fans paid my wages and I was grateful. It was the crowd that provided my inspiration during every game.

Of the players involved in that promotion season and the wonderful night at York, none of us had ever, or would ever make any great fortune out of the game. In money terms we were football's working class, the blue collar workers, at the lower-league end. Yet we loved our life if we were first-teamers, despite all the ups and downs, and for some the frequent hardships. We were never at the glamour end of the business. Today even an average player can earn a fortune and I wonder what the great players of the past really think.

In my day I was just an ordinary, approachable person. I was part of that great majority of players who never got to be famous. I never saw myself as a star. I was never a prima donna. I never had any strops or tantrums. I was never a player who made a manager's life a nightmare so that he had to tread carefully and say, 'Hey I'd better be careful with Roger'. Perhaps if I'd been more like that I might have got more respect from the management at Burnley in those last awful 12 months.

And yet having said that about being 'ordinary', in some ways the football world I lived in was like living in a bubble. That's something that Johnny Giles said in his book and I can't think it can be said any better. He said it was like living in some sort of parallel world, the football world that we lived in where everything was done for us, and then the actual world and all its demands outside that. I used to scribble down a few raw thoughts. This was about the starkness of leaving the game:

The curtain closes. The show is over. Reality hits you straight in the face. You are alone. The banter is long gone. Friends, pals, teammates are now only former colleagues. Once you battled hard together, took the knocks together, laughed together; cried together. Now you walk alone, no club owns you. You don't belong. Had enough of carting boots around the footballing world, mentally shot, low ebb

. . . confidence absent. Move on again . . . getting found out, tank
empty.

Doing things for yourself . . . no overworked club secretaries,
Pauline, Gill, Maureen or Keith to fix this, arrange that. Carry your
own passport now, register with a new doctor, so many things taken
for granted . . . now it's do it yourself.

Drive by a pub . . . now I can have a few drinks . . . maybe have a
smoke . . . eat a full English breakfast . . . and do it again tomorrow .
. . and tomorrow . . . and the tomorrow after that . . . making up for
lost time . . . waking up but there's no training, no match, no focus,
no team to belong to. Like being on a desert island and seeing the
ship sailing away until it's gone. Fitness, professionalism slips away.

Autograph hunters are gone and no more fan mail. In your head
you're worthless. Football on TV, watch the games . . . not part of it
any more . . . stare at the pictures . . . your own skills fading . . . no
more need to practise . . . no more need to be perfect . . .

In the back of your mind, as a player, eventually comes the point
when you realise that a football career is short, or that you are
approaching the end of it. Look at me. I was as good as finished at 27,
not so much because I was unable to get fit again, but because of the
way I was just left on the sidelines. The club wouldn't even pay an
insurance policy premium which I vaguely remember being about
£200 a month. It would have given some security. But how could I
possibly afford to pay that on what I was earning? I can't remember
any footballer I knew at our level at that time who insured himself.

Footballers' wives are so important and are unsung heroes.
They're not all WAGS. For every Posh Beckham or Colleen Rooney,
there are scores of wives, and always have been, who lead ordinary
humdrum lives and run the home while their husbands are away so
much. They look after the kids, do the shopping, pay the bills, keep
the house going, supervise moves, put up with moods and injuries
and generally try to keep their man happy, often by tiptoeing round
the house the night before a game or on a Saturday morning. Even
the night after a game they are at risk when husbands in their sleep
re-live a game and kick and thrash around in bed. Footballers, for
sure, are not the easiest people to live with. It's only the tiniest
percentage of wives that make the headlines and parade themselves
on TV or in *Hello* magazine.

I met Andrea at Shipley swimming baths in 1989. She was a
lifeguard. I remember wondering 'Should I pretend to struggle?'

Maybe she'd jump in and give me the kiss of life. No she wasn't in a costume she was in a track suit but looked stunning. Funny how things happen by chance and you meet people. You can't really swap telephone numbers when all you have on is a pair of swimming shorts so we arranged to meet at a club we both knew. I wondered if she'd turn up. She did.

The mixed partnership and eventual marriage after several years has never been a problem. Both sets of parents were fine. There was nothing awkward for me and Andrea. In fact the funniest thing was the first time I picked her up in the car from her home. Her brother had no idea who she was going out with and saw me waiting in the car outside the house. He thought the cab had arrived.

'Your taxi driver's here,' he yelled to Andrea. Her mother, a good Catholic, gave him a clip round the ear. 'I'll have you know that's a good Catholic boy out there,' she told him knowing full well who I was.

Andrea shared my ups and downs, good times and bad times, joy and dejection. She was a rock when I needed one. That last depressing year I had at Burnley almost sapped the life out of me. Whatever I tried or however hard I tried, a wall had been put up in that final 12 months. Of course I changed and sometimes became irritable and ratty. It wasn't the real me. Andrea shared all that and was the rock. She shared my good feelings about Burnley the town and the club, and the bad feelings about how the manager treated me. At Burnley I'd had such great beliefs and self-image until then. They were the same beliefs that I'd had in the early days at Leeds but had then vanished during the years I'd drifted around. People's respect for you is so important. That feeling of being respected had been shattered when I left Turf Moor.

It gave neither of us any satisfaction to see Burnley immediately relegated after the promotion in the summer of '94. But neither of us had any sympathy when Jimmy Mullen eventually left the club midway through season '95–96. Whereas once it was Teasdale and Casper who took the flak and abuse, now it was Teasdale and Mullen. I felt no joy at Teasdale's discomfort but for Mullen the chickens had come home to roost. What goes round comes round, as the old saying goes. Players who felt he had treated them badly had little sympathy for him. Some might have described him as jovial, enthusiastic, passionate and emotional. Others might have described him rather differently.

With Andrea I watched it all happening and it was all so sad to watch from a distance. There was a period of three years when she hated Saturdays. Where Saturdays were once a joy; now they were hell as I moped around. In the garage was the hi-fi that I'd won when I was Man of the Match in the Derby County game. How's that for irony? More notes here that I scribbled down not long after those lean years.

Tinkering in the garage . . . a bit of gardening I can do . . . kicking my heels and wasting time. The radio might be on but it's like being in a kind of daze . . . the sound comes out but you don't listen . . . don't hear it . . . hearing a commentary but it doesn't sink in . . . a part of the brain that's still football . . . it still flickers and says I could still be playing . . . a grey, grey period and one that many footballers will recognise . . . 101 Ways to Waste a Saturday afternoon. Looking out of the window . . . thinking and mulling things over . . . wondering if I'd done this or that, would I still have been playing . . . if I'd ducked out of that challenge would I have avoided the next injury . . . why didn't I stay at Leeds . . . what did I do to become the player who was eventually just ignored at Burnley . . . did I really deserve all the injuries?

Thoughts drift in and out of my head as if I was in some sort of hazy daydream. Saturday afternoon . . . should be the best afternoon of the week and all you can think about is how you'd missed out on the big-time . . . the European Champions . . . wanting your signature, almost camped out in my Mum and Dad's front room . . . making you feel so special . . . being tracked by Leeds United home of all your heroes . . . fading images of signing for them . . . training with some of the biggest stars in the country . . . at 16 playing with and against lads who had represented their countries in international tournaments.

More memories that come back . . . the broken leg . . . Leeds United . . . Sir Bobby Robson of all people and I was getting back to fitness . . . Eddie asking me to play in a Northeast team that would play against a Hartlepools side . . . driving up there with Andy Linighan and Peter Lorimer with the headlights of Andy's car on even though it was broad daylight. Strange the things you remember . . . Sir Bobby managed the team . . . playing alongside big names like Peter Beardsley and Gary Pallister. Gazza was supposed to play but didn't . . . 75 minutes and I came off . . . into the dugout and squash next to him all of us snuggled closely. 'Well played son,' he says and pats me on the knee, giving me all kinds of advice. What a lovely man. What you saw was what you got. How many managers are like that?

Suddenly the garage feels cold and lonely.

Sitting moping: One of Eddie's boys . . . like the petals of a flower . . . but one by one the petals fell . . . the flower never allowed to reach full bloom . . . never reaching full glory . . . Eddie's seeds . . . never allowed to flourish.

Burnley images . . . images of me preparing, training, building up hopes. But what you can't prepare for is rejection . . . cast aside, placed in isolation away from colleagues, the people you have played with, and enjoyed success and failure . . . having to train with the kids just starting out in the game . . . all the same hopes and dreams that I'd once had . . . confused to see me there . . . feelings of degradation, hurt, the first team over there on that pitch, me on another . . . the manager sucks you in . . . then spits you out. 'Report Saturday morning to play with the apprentices.'

Coaching staff walk straight by you . . . trying to humiliate you . . . break you. Once the darling of the terraces at Turf Moor . . . now a walking corpse, trance-like, the smile just a fake and confidence shattered . . . confidence, that amazing thing without which a footballer is nothing.

Dogged by all these recurring thoughts . . . what would have happened if I'd said yes to one of those Italian clubs after that youth tournament so long ago—where would I have been by now? Why did Mullen keep me at the club when he could have said: 'Roger, get yourself fit and we'll help fix you up with a club.' Why wasn't I strong enough then to confront him? You can be fit again but if the mental engine shuts down it's worse than a physical injury.

A gust of wind . . . the garage door slams . . . the reverie is interrupted. The moping and thinking does no good. Fame is fleeting for most footballers. Then almost overnight they can be nothing when the game has finished with them. That first year, maybe longer, I spent out of the game was dreadful. The whole experience taught me never to take anything for granted, that things can be taken away quickly. Shortly before he died Gary Speed, in an interview, said, 'Football breaks your heart all the time'. It nearly broke mine. But Andrea stuck through it with me. She knows to this day how bad it was. A chance meeting at Shipley Baths, fate works in many ways.

While I was out in China and then up in Scotland trying to salvage something from the fragments of a disappearing career, Burnley were trying to find their feet at the new level of what is now the Championship. They stuttered and started, and spluttered. John

Francis was still there and we'd meet up sometimes after I got back from China and he'd let me know what was going on. It was the usual story of players coming and going with such frequency that a revolving door would have been more than useful.

It was not a happy season. You can only wonder at the devotion of fans who follow their team through thick and thin and when they go straight back down after a promotion. They were the same fans who the year before would see me in the streets in and around Burnley and stop and ask, 'Are you playing Roger?' It became embarrassing and monotonous saying that no I wasn't. Professionalism stopped me from saying, 'No I'm not but I could do as good a job as anyone if I was picked'.

It wasn't until the end of October (I was in China) that there was a first home win. But the word was that the next home match was a game of poor football, poor performances and a game where an accurate 5-yard pass was an occasion to celebrate. Only Steve Davis was spared criticism.

Yet somehow there was an unbeaten run of several games, although mostly draws, and at the end of November there was a cracking 4–2 win over Sheffield United at Turf Moor. Burnley by now had big John Gayle on loan. He was 6' 4' and built like a tank, one of Mullen's increasingly frequent forays into the market to find answers to his problems. Fondly known as Big Bad John, he scored. By now, of course, part of me had had enough of trying to resurrect a career in football, but another part of me longed to be back in proper action playing alongside David Eyres, Kevin Russell or Adrian Heath. The old question re-surfaced; just why did Mullen throw me on one side? Okay I'd had injuries but the knee was fine. But I never got another game with him. The Sheffield game was live on the box but I was in China. There was no-one there at the club now that I had any affinity with other than John Francis who now was mainly on the bench.

But into December and I was back home again; I noticed that the defeats began again and more strikers were brought in to try to solve the problems. Yet there was me now almost finished with football, the one left on the side.

It was into January '95, and the dreadful run of defeats was underway. Fans grumbled that there was no-one there who could score goals. By now Jimmy Mullen was being abused at the end of games. Fans decided that his attempts to find a good striker was a bit like finding snow in June, just possible but unlikely—or the lottery, always possible but very unlikely.

Into February and me in Scotland at Partick; Jimmy Mullen was venting his spleen at the local newspaper, a sure sign of pressure. Fans had decided that the team looked more clueless with every passing game, managed by a man who had no answers. They berated him in the pubs and clubs and letters to the Press with accusations that he had no tactical nous at this level, his side was unmotivated and he was unable to sign a goalscorer of any real calibre. Many wanted him out. It was sad to see them second bottom. The club had been my home for nearly five years. For the majority of his reign at the club Jimmy Mullen had been the toast of the town.

Halfway through February and boos that were yelled at him at halftime in the Grimsby game were loud and clear. As they left the field at full time, they changed to chants of: 'Mullen out.'

Burnley were thrashed 4–1 at Tranmere. He'd just spent half a million on Kurt Nogan and Steve Thompson from Leicester. It was a defeat that put Burnley to the very bottom of the division. Believe it or not I still felt a connection and had no wish to see what I'd helped achieve a couple of years earlier, end up in relegation. A few players were still there that I respected very much.

The hopeful signing of yet another striker resulted in Paul Stewart arriving at Turf Moor. In his prime he had been a top player but to this day Burnley fans refer to him as being one of, if not the worst ever, Burnley signings. As I attempted to get on with my own life I could only shake my head. In four appearances he had been booked three times and was then sent off in yet another defeat.

Ironically one of Burnley's best strikers had been sold—Mick Conroy, still a class act when he left.

In April Burnley managed a rare win. Alas in the very next game they were thumped 4–0 at Derby. Three wins in the next four games raised hopes. By now yet another striker had arrived, Paul Shaw. Home form was not bad. Away form was miserable. A home defeat to Portsmouth assured Burnley of relegation. It gave me no pleasure whatsoever. I wondered though what would happen to Jimmy Mullen. The chants of 'MULLEN OUT' at the end of the game were the loudest and lengthiest of the season. Before that as the game neared its end the chants of 'WE'RE GOING DOWN 'COS

OF MULLEN' were loud and clear reaching across to the dugout and the directors' box. I didn't wish relegation on the football club.

During the season Mullen had decided that the battling and totally committed John Deary was not needed. Fans were aghast when he was sold. He was tough, cheeky, cheerful, inspirational, strong, mobile, a fantastic box to box player and was able to score important goals. Was it just that his face didn't fit any more?

Jimmy Mullen was retained as manager. By January '96, I was out of football altogether, and things were going so wrong again at Burnley. Hundreds of unhappy supporters demonstrated and not since the days of Casper and Teasdale after the Scarborough defeat years earlier had the jeers and abuse been so vicious. Mullen brought in yet another striker, Ian Helliwell, for £25,000 from Stockport. He made just three starts. Another defeat at home to Crewe on 10th February and fans at a pre-arranged time during the game turned their backs on the pitch. It was well planned and the media were there to see it. They called it the 3:33 campaign because that's the time they all stood backs to the game. I couldn't believe it. Those fans had been great to me and I would have run through brick walls for them. I felt desperately saddened by the whole thing. Even today they still talk about it. 48 hours later Mullen was put out of his misery and he was dismissed. The treatment dished out to him and his family had been appalling. The abuse they and he received was cruel.

But, on a personal note I will say that the way he had treated me in the final 12 months I spent at the club was utterly mystifying. And, as I then watched striker after striker brought in unsuccessfully to save the day I felt a deep resentment that I had been continuously overlooked. I was still not yet 30.

I certainly thought of the fans. They had been tremendous with me and to this day they still are. For some away games even in this terrible relegation season, up to 2,500 of them would travel and support the team. Their passion was unrivalled. But home attendances had dwindled. Who could blame them? They saw some players in the team that they thought should never have been there. If they took to you they were immensely supportive. If they did not; if they saw players who put minimal effort into a game, they could be savagely cruel. A player could be the most skilful in the world but if he was lazy he would be given short shrift. It was clear what the fans appreciated, skill yes, but it had to be allied with heart, effort and dedication. Players like John Francis and John Deary personified that ideal player, and I hope me too. We never ducked a challenge; we ran till we dropped, we went in where it hurt. That was the thing about the team of '91–92. We were pretty much all like that. With a team spirit like we had, you could climb mountains.

By now Leeds United were in the Premiership under Howard Wilkinson and yes I did continue to think about what might have been. When we won promotion at the end of '91–92, Leeds had won the old Division Two title. The old Division One they joined then became the Premiership. All the lads I'd started out with at Leeds, Scott Sellars, John Sheridan, Dennis Irwin, Tommy Wright and Terry Phelan were still in the game, well established at their clubs, and went on to play for many years more. Was I the unlucky one of that group or was I never good enough? I constantly tell myself of course I was good enough but at key stages of my early career new managers came in to affect things. Billy Bremner was now retired from football. Eddie Gray eventually returned to the club as youth team coach and continued an on-off relationship until 2004, including spells as reserve team manager, assistant manager and then acting-manager.

In a way Mullen's dismissal brought closure to my feelings. It was as if I could now get on with my life. I wasn't a lad who'd left school with a string of 'A' levels although I had some very good qualifications. I used to say to my sister Rhona that I wished I was clever like her. She'd tell me off for that. Some of the most successful people in the world left school at 16. I was buoyant, gregarious and energetic, with a mind that buzzed with ideas and common sense. I wasn't shy with people and even as a footballer had been a bit of an entrepreneur on the side. By the time of Mullen's dismissal I was well out of the game. Partick Thistle had been my swansong. When that ended it was time to really plan out what to do with the rest of my life and I was sound-headed enough to be practical, sensible and realistic.

What other footballers do when they finish always intrigues me. The vast majority were like me, just ordinary lads and football was all they knew. The day comes to finish and where do they go next unless they stay in management or coaching?

Long before I finished playing I enjoyed using my spare time selling. Most players at the club would enjoy a game of golf or snooker (and drinking of course). The rage was Desert Strike on Sega Megadrives. At least six of the players had consoles and games, me included. We used to take them to the hotels to relieve the boredom. But most of all I enjoyed trying to make money.

I used to travel up to a warehouse in Leechmere, an area of Sunderland, with Andrea and spend hours browsing through all the different kinds of sportswear wondering about which were the best lines to sell. This was the time when shell suits were in fashion, personified by Harry Enfield and his 'calm down, calm down' Liverpool characters. These suits were our best sellers, not only to the lads at the club but also the good people of Bradford who I helped turn into multi-coloured, polyester, fashion victims. The streets of Bradford owe a lot to me. I had always had this strong sense that I had to prepare for life outside football.

But don't think I was just a Del Boy. There was structure and planning to what I did and Ben Lee the poor lad who had the dreadful accident helped me out. He was a really good and intelligent lad and I still think about him. He sold some of the gear in Northwich that I brought. There was an award named after him, at the club, given to students who had taken community scheme coaching courses. He was a lovely, sociable lad whose character stood out. I have not forgotten him.

Andrea, who could sell sand to an Arab, used to sell the sportswear at her workplace. There were over 200 staff there and we had a network of people selling on a commission basis for us. It worked well.

The boys at the club couldn't get enough of the gear so that I was selling it as fast as I got hold of it. On one occasion the warehouse gave us a fantastic deal on a silver-blue and green Adidas number. It was the worst colour combination that I'd ever seen. I sold five at Turf Moor and when four of the lads who'd bought them turned up on the same day in them, it looked like astronaut Buzz Aldrin and his space crew had just walked in. I am not a swearing man as a rule but some of the stuff I sold the lads was so garish I could only stand, stare, grin and mutter as they walked away, 'Bloody hell! If only you knew what you looked like'.

It was goalkeeper Mervyn Day at Leeds who first introduced me to the fun of selling. As a 16 year old I'd noticed he always had a boot full of sports gear that he sold. A lot of footballers used to do it; there was probably one at every football club, some of them I'm sure with contacts in the fallen-off-the-back-of-a-lorry trade. Sports gear and shirts were the most frequent items on offer but you could also find TVs and radios if you knew who to ask.

Mick Rathbone who played for Birmingham and Blackburn Rovers used to visit the Burnley training ground after he finished playing. But where I had gaudy shell-suits, the latest in tastelessness, he had what looked like real designer gear and Armani suits. He says now they were the just the end-of-season stuff his mate couldn't even sell in the sales. The Burnley lads were so pleased with what they bought from him it meant they were easily satisfied or it really was Armani. There he was on my patch. But I always used to have the last laugh. I could always make sure I got paid and I knew who were the good payers and those who you had to chase and even those you avoided altogether. But Mick allowed credit and I still wonder if he ever got paid by Adie Randall.

It was Ron Futcher who once arrived at training with a large selection of branded perfumery. Well, the bottles were branded; I'm not sure about what was inside. The lads crowded round and were hooked on buying perfumes for their wives and girlfriends at knock-down prices. They snapped up the lot and Ron made a killing. Everybody was delighted — except the wives and girlfriends, most of whom came out in a facial rash.

I had a good friend called Ken Shackleton who was a fabric designer. We'd met in the oddest way. There had been a game away at Rochdale and I'd made my own way there. I parked next to a family who got out of their car and of course they saw me and started chatting. It was Ken, 20 years older than me, and he lived in Bingley not far from where I lived. That chance meeting led to a friendship and eventual business collaboration.

In China I'd made a few contacts in the clothes trade. I was always a snappy dresser, loved clothes, was interested in design. I found how easy it was over in Foshaan and how cheap to have suits made up to your own specifications. I had some made up with my own touches added to them. My head buzzed with ideas of setting up an import business, not just suits but ceramics as well because Foshaan was a great ceramics manufacturing centre. Another idea was that Ken would design and manufacture materials and I'd sell them. Failing all that, the police force was always an option. I'd have had no hesitation in applying. Inspector Eli of the Yard had a nice ring to it. But business was the thing and I was always interested in other footballers like Franny Lee who after the game had become successful businessmen. I was aware too of how many ex-footballers invested money in businesses with no real idea of what they were doing and failed miserably, usually ending up bankrupt. Then there were the footballers who went into business with a partner only to find the partner would end up fleecing them.

I got my head down and enrolled at Huddersfield Polytechnic to do an 'A' level textile design course. I needed to understand about fabric structure and have all the technical knowledge to enable me to talk to customers about basic things like shrinkage and creasing. I only completed the first year but I learnt a lot; the need to earn some money then became more of a priority. It was only the first year I needed to obtain sufficient knowledge to know what I was talking about.

At college I'd learnt about design; from Ken I learnt about business, weaving, manufacturing, colour processing, exporting and importing. I studied and read up on the art of selling. Several times I sold and learnt by the seat of my pants, buying cloth from Ken and then putting on my pin-stripe suit and going down to London, from Kensington to Savile Row, wandering up and down with my case of samples. I got better and began to export to America and Singapore. I was good and had a way with customers. I learnt about taxation, letters of credit, finance and all the details of buying and selling outside the EU. From talking about life in general you got on to the cloth side of the meeting. I seemed to do well with the Arabs. One customer just used to take the case, root through the sample swatches, throw everything on the floor one by one until he found a piece and yell: 'I'll have that.' I didn't mind as long as he bought.

Starting out working from home, I began to need an office. Simultaneously I used the contacts I had made in China to import a few items like cameras and various gadgets. I missed the chance to set up a tile importing business because I lost the contact number I'd been given. But the Chinese I dealt with were excellent to work with. Everything was done on trust. Honour was paramount. I paid up front and I was never let down once. The problem was cash flow. I paid in advance and then waited for the goods. They always came but the time lapse was difficult between paying for them and then selling them in the UK. They could take six weeks to arrive.

The textile business eased into the stationery business I now run. The textile business worked well for me but then came a need to get out of this industry because of changes to the Chinese economy and market. I'd seen too many competitors lose a lot of money for me to go the same way. Andrea and me are now working together again with two other very good business partners and our sales team at Ventura Office Supplies. Life after football has been good to me; sure there have been a few difficult times but I've worked damned hard for everything I have achieved. The PFA have all kinds of statistics about footballers when they leave the game. Those who hit the bottle, gamble, lose investments, go bankrupt; even get involved in crime. The divorce rate for a start is something like 20%. Football is a profession from which you can't just walk into any other job. What else are you trained for? Football is a life of 'highs' and almost overnight they are all gone. From insider to outsider, from fame to anonymity, the list goes on. The PFA does more now for ex-players than it did when I finished.

I think it took me three years to recover fully from that final footballing period, from the sense of loss, the sense of what might have been, and the hurt it brought. Thankfully I had Andrea, some good business skills and a determination to succeed. Nothing beats the thrill and excitement of scoring a goal in front of 20,000 people, whether it's a 25 yarder, a flashing header, or a lucky rebound. But, I tell you what, when you enjoy selling, then the clinching of a sale, or the culmination of a successful business deal, can come very, very close.

16

Catching the Right Train

In the Gwyneth Paltrow film *Sliding Doors*, there are two storylines. In one we see what happens when the main character misses her train. In the alternative story we see what happens when she catches it. It's about how fate can change a life. In my story when Eddie Gray is sacked by Leeds I miss the train and there's an ensuing journey that takes me all over the place. In my alternative script Eddie Gray is not sacked and the great bunch of lads he has stick together, get on the train and take Leeds to glory. I'm one of those lads, the kid from the council estate in Bradford, the lad whose ancestors were once slaves in the West Indies, the battler, the bruiser, the one who took the knocks. It's the storyline that didn't happen . . . if only . . .

I'm blessed. I have two young sons. How will I help them or other young lads if they want to be footballers, if they have the same dreams that I had? What will I tell them about the traps and pitfalls they'll meet all along the way? I'm in a good position to offer advice to anyone about football's hurdles and how never to take things for granted. I'll say what I would say to anyone or any other parent; that it's not just about hard work and effort and having all the skills needed; but it's also about luck, fate and the decisions that others around you make. One man, the manager of any team he plays for, can make or break a young player.

A boy might well be the best player in his class, then the best lad at his school; but then as he gets older and further up the ladder he'll meet boys just as good as him, if not better. That's when he really has to become accustomed to fighting tooth and nail for a start or a place at a club. It happened to me. Until I was 16 I met no-one who was better than me. Until then you believe, and others might have you believe, that you have already made it into the big time and that along will come a top club and snap you up. There I was at the youth tournament in Italy and two Italian clubs wanted my signature. I had such aspirations, such dreams.

Thinking of it as an obstacle course is the best way I suppose, for any aspiring player, and that's before you've even mentioned the bad days and injuries and the need for luck. For every Jack Wilshire, only 20% of 16-year olds make the grade. Any boy can have all the aspirations, hopes and dreams in the world but does he know of the pitfalls ahead of him? He could learn from me.

You can churn out the words that sum up the temperament that is needed in a player—commitment, passion, desire, character, determination; competitiveness, willingness to learn, to listen and to heed advice. And maybe above all else he needs a degree of single-minded ruthlessness so that when he goes into a game, a tackle, a header; he believes that the ball is his and no-one else's. He might well have all the silky skills of a Fabregas or a Messi, but he needs to know that the game is littered with the failed dreams of scores of players who had the skills but not the attitudes, or players who were victims of injuries.

There are parents who might want their boy to be a footballer but do they know he needs to be prepared for everything that he will come up against? For that, only mental toughness will get him through. And one more thing he'll need; a thick skin to withstand the taunts, and all the abuse and criticism.

I managed to make it, just. I thought I was destined for a long life at Leeds United, but then I took the wrong train and left when I really should have stayed. The story of my career was that of one injury after another. But despite that, I did have enjoyable times, loved it all, made my mark and I wouldn't have traded it for anything. I loved every minute especially the great times at Turf Moor until of course it was decided I was of no further use. And that's something else any hopeful boy needs to prepare for, that the day will come when the game will have chewed him up and then discarded him. He might have more good years than I ever had, but it all ends one day. If he's like me he'll know when that time has come.

Would I want anyone to face what I went through, the catalogue of injuries and operations, cortisone injections, ice-packs and taking painkillers like sweets for years? Given the time again there's one surgeon I'd sue for the mess he made of my knee.

It's a game that's full of sorrow as well as joy. Every now and then I think of Ray Deakin. He was my first Burnley captain but our paths first crossed when he was at Bolton. When he finished his career he seemed to slip off the radar and the word was he was somewhat disillusioned with football. He set up some sort of business but most of us thought he would have a full time driving job, or even set up his own coach firm. He had an HGV licence and even used to drive the team bus on occasions to get some practice. To me he was a really dedicated pro who was never really appreciated by the fans. They had this habit of shouting a loud, long whooooooosh every time he played a long ball down the line. But there was far more to his game than that. His was a real what-might-have-been story.

Eric Harrison the coach who developed the Beckham, Scholes, Neville, Butt group at Manchester United talked of Ray Deakin in the same breath. Not long ago I met Eric at a function and he talked of Ray passionately as being one of the best kids he ever met, and that included all the United greats. Eric and Ray were together at Everton and he maintained he had never met anyone with as much talent and skill. And then as so often happens a serious injury in his late teens took the edge from Ray's game and that magic extra he possessed was gone. Had the same surgery been available then that exists today Ray would no doubt have recovered fully. But it wasn't to be. He went on to have a long career in the game but maybe his thoughts of what might have been took away his love for the game after he finished. He was not 50 when he died from cancer. A group of us went to see him in a North Yorkshire hospital and it was a heart-rending experience to see someone who was once so inspirational in such a helpless state. It makes me think sometimes that a football club is so inconsistent in its appreciation of its former players who pass away. There are times when there is a huge outpouring of grief and others when there is little, especially when the passing goes almost unnoticed. His family weren't interested in fuss or publicity, but in the football world his death just seemed to pass by without a ripple. Let's not forget how he held his nerve in that final game against the Orient in 1987 when Burnley clung by their finger nails to their Football League place. He was a hero that day.

I have no bitterness about the game, and no bitterness remains about the manager who eventually ignored me, so much so that 20 years later he felt obliged to apologise. In the final 12 months at Turf Moor when I wasn't playing, I stopped sitting in the stands so as to avoid the questions the supporters asked: 'Are you playing Roger . . . why not?'

I'd stand in the players' tunnel to watch and think: 'Why . . . why am I not out there?' There were Saturdays when I was fit to play but wasn't picked. It hurt. But I was the free transfer and football politics don't change whatever club you're at. If the manager has paid money for someone, poor though he might be, and the manager is answerable for the money he has spent, he will pick the player he has paid for.

What a great start I had in football as a raw lad at Leeds. All of us, first teamers as well, would sit together and eat fish and chips on Fridays. It was a time when I saw myself as an 'A' list footballer, and thought I was part of something special. I still remember Jack, the old boy who used to come in with the pools coupons that people did in those days. For some reason he'd make a beeline for the table I was on. I'd look at the coupons and the names of the teams, names like Crewe, York, Cambridge and Bury way down in the lower leagues. I never thought at that moment that one day I'd be playing there. I can tell any young player or parent that dreams don't always come true.

I'll tell my lads a few things and one man I'll certainly tell them about is Brian Clough. How privileged I was to have known him even for just such a short time. I'll tell them about the trip to Italy and the praise I got from Cloughie. The image of him sitting on that coach and saying 'well done' is as fresh now as it was then all those years ago. You could do the most fantastic things in training or even in a game and not get a word from him, like this young lad Eddie Mighton, a kid who never made it in the game even though he had God-given ability. In a free-kick practice session Eddie whipped in a wonderful strike from 30 yards. Cloughie was watching with his arms folded. It was the perfect strike as he made it bend round a five-man wall. It was an unbelievable goal.

Cloughie bellowed: 'Son, I'd like to see you do that again.' Eddie didn't appear fazed or flustered at all. He never even glanced at the boss but just put the ball down and repeated the same perfect goal. We all looked at Cloughie and waited for a word of approval. But he just stood there, facial expression unaltered and then walked away. It makes my 'well done Chalkie' all the more precious. If my son meets anyone in football just half as charismatic as Brian Clough, he'll be a very lucky boy. I can still mimic Cloughie and smile at the memory of the man.

Cloughie let me go. Eddie Mighton despite his wonderful ability never really made it. But this is the world of football and in truth there are no hard feelings, just lingering regrets that surface from time to time. If only . . . how often have I said those words?

But, fleeting though the good years were, I'm still remembered. I'll walk through Burnley or visit Turf Moor and there'll always be someone who calls out and smiles and mentions a goal I've scored. I can be at a dinner and they'll chant: 'Eli . . . Eli . . . Eli.' That's a wonderful thing. I'm happy with that and I'll tell the boys that as well.

Back in the sixties and seventies my father certainly encountered racism. I hope my boys won't. I remember him telling me that he sometimes had to reprimand some of the men who worked under him on the building site. He was certainly called a coon several times. Once was when one of the men came in smelling of alcohol. The idea of a black man telling a white person off in those days, or telling them how to do their job, was not exactly welcomed. He used to tell us too of how they'd sometimes call for a pint in a pub after work on the way home. He met the usual colour bar more than once but his workmates who had learnt to respect his skills used to ask the landlord to make an exception in his case. My father is a man of great dignity, persuasiveness and articulacy. 'Leave the landlord to me,' he once told the men. On that occasion the landlord barred the lot of them. He laughs at that to this day.

There's another lovely story about my own father I can tell the boys; of how he could charm the birds off the trees and talk his way into any situation. We were playing Rochdale and he'd decided to watch the game. As the coach pulled up outside the ground John Francis shouted out, 'Hey Roger your old man is standing in the main entrance.'

He hadn't told me he was coming, he'd just got into his car on the spur of the moment, and as the lads got off the bus he started filming them with his old video camera. I wasn't at all embarrassed by him being there filming; the biggest problem was whether to act cool and walk on by as normal, or act the fool and wave at the camera. I acted cool, went into the dressing room and Frank Casper closed the door. I thought I'd be able to spot Dad in the crowd when I went out for the pre-match warm up, he'd stand out all right.

Instead of being in the crowd, I saw him immediately as I came out of the tunnel. There he was on the pitch with his eye in the view finder. First he'd blagged his way past reception and the commissionaire into the boardroom and enjoyed himself on their delicious plate pies and then he'd somehow got permission to spend the game on the touchline filming.

'How does he do it?' I wondered in admiration. There he sat on the perimeter wall and at one point he even passed the ball to Joey Jakub when it went out for a throw. He walked around like he'd filmed games all his life. At the end of the game I went over to him. He'd had a wonderful afternoon and I've a feeling that film is still around somewhere if he could ever find it.

I doubt my boys will sing the songs at school that I used to sing—and enjoy. There was one that was about an old negro who played the banjo. I used to love the song and never thought twice about it being called 'Old Zip Coon'. I'd bounce round the classroom pretending to play the banjo. The teacher was in hysterics. Then I learned the old banjo player was a black man, a coon. I stopped dancing round the classroom.

I used to watch the Tarzan episodes on TV. It never occurred to me to wonder why the black natives were portrayed to be so stupid and spoke in grunts whilst Tarzan was the clever one and had been taught to speak by apes. Then there was the *Black and White Minstrel Show*. My boys will have no idea that this was a music show where the singers blacked their faces and wore white gloves singing about Mamee.

The train that I missed along with Dennis Irwin, John Sheridan, Terry Phelan and Scott Sellars might have brought me fame and glory at Elland Road. The stopping, branchline train that I did catch wasn't particularly the one I wanted and yet it brought me to where I am today so even with all the knocks, how can I be ungrateful? Life has been good to me if what I have today is anything to go by. Today I'm even an international karate silver-medallist. I've been to places, seen things, done things, and met good people that I still know today. I had the best and worst of times and sure there are memories I'd like to erase. But then there are the ones that I treasure. Above all I'm still remembered.

Somewhere there's a quote: 'We all end up where we're meant to be.' Maybe for me real fame was never meant to happen. What happens if my boys want to be footballers or have the talent? I'll tell my boys, and any other boys for that matter, if that's what they want, the effort is worth it. Go for it, I'll say. One day when you look back on things, you don't want to say 'if only'. But be warned, it's not all glamour. The disappointments can be heartbreaking.

I began this story with the curt, dismissal letter from Burnley Football Club. Its impersonal abruptness still irritates me after all these years when I read it. But as we neared the end of this book someone who saw me play got in touch. It was Harry Brooks, Burnley supporter, shareholder and former town councillor, someone I never actually met. He wrote to me when he heard what I was doing. It was a totally different, appreciative, warm kind of letter that made me smile. If I read it again 20 years from now, it will still make me smile and feel good. The mere fact that he hadn't forgotten me was heartwarming enough for is it not true that countless footballers when they depart the game, are soon forgotten?

'If Roger wasn't one of Frank Teasdale's favourite players he certainly should have been,' it began and then went on to explain that just before the Annual General Meeting in December 1989, the front page of the *Burnley Express* had headlined Harry's offer to put £100,000 into the club if the six directors also put money in. With things at the club not going that well he was desperately fed up. His £100,000 would have bought a couple of decent players. If £1million was raised, it would transform the club. It was his intention to stir things up and do his best to make sure that the Board would be soundly criticised at the AGM, if not even toppled. He then continued:

After my offer was given such prominence in the *Burnley Express* (not averse in those days to twisting the club's tail) Burnley played a second Cup replay at home against Scunthorpe United on Monday 18th December. We went into the match in the bottom half of the bottom division, having just three points from the last 18, without a win in six league games, including losses to Southend (where a brilliant central defensive prospect, 19-year old Mark Monington, picked up a horrendous knee injury that ruined his career), Scunthorpe and Lincoln.

The club, then in a fifth successive season in Division Four, could scarcely have been in greater need of a morale boost and the beleaguered Board must have offered up a silent collective prayer for a good Cup result before the AGM.

Cometh the hour cometh the man: The inspirational Eli delivered not a good result, but a brilliant result, with two goals in a 5–0 win and a display of class and flair that made you man of the match by many a mile.

I wouldn't say that your rescue act scuppered my million pound proposal, since the directors at that time seemed distinctly unwilling to invest further in the club, but it is certain that the sparkle you brought to a wet and dark Turf Moor evening a few days earlier helped make the AGM less vehemently critical than it would have been.

I'm not surprised that you have gone on to do well in business in which presentation is important. You were just about the only Burnley player of that time who knew how to dress.

Regards Harry Brooks

What a priceless letter: a letter to enjoy, the wicked suggestion being (and one that I take with a pinch of salt) that those Cup goals saved Frank Teasdale's skin as chairman. But that last line is the best: 'He was just about the only Burnley player who knew how to dress.'

The letter is now in the box of mementoes and memorabilia that I looked through when I went up into the loft, along with a few more pictures and clippings that I'd accumulated as the book progressed. For sure I'd like to have achieved more. But then I remind myself. Maybe I did get on the wrong train. But some young lads never even get to the station.

1991–92 Fourth Division Champion's medal, Player of the Year, and Goal of the Season. Thanks for the memories.